ABOUT MEN

REFLECTIONS ON THE MALE EXPERIENCE

ABOUT MEN

REFLECTIONS ON THE MALE EXPERIENCE

Edited and with an Introduction by
EDWARD KLEIN and **DON ERICKSON**
Foreword by
RUSSELL BAKER

POCKET BOOKS

New York   London   Toronto   Sydney   Tokyo

Grateful acknowledgment is made to the following for permission to reprint previously published material:
Viking Penguin, Inc.: excerpt from "Partial Comfort" from *The Portable Dorothy Parker*. Copyright 1928
by Dorothy Parker, copyright renewed 1956 by Dorothy Parker. Reprinted by permission of Viking Penguin,
Inc., for the United States, its dependencies and possessions and the Philippine Republic; reprinted from
The Collected Dorothy Parker by permission of Gerald Duckworth & Co. Ltd. for the British Common-
wealth of Nations, the Republics of South Africa and Ireland, Burma, Iraq and Jordan.

Random House, Inc.: excerpts from "Fear and Trembling" from *Rumor Verified: Poems 1979—1980*
by Robert Penn Warren. Copyright © 1981 by Robert Penn Warren. Reprinted by permission of Random
House, Inc.

Warner Bros. Music: excerpts from lyrics to "A Nightingale Sang in Berkeley Square" by Manning Sherwin
and Eric Maschwitz. Copyright 1940 Colgems-EMI Music, Inc., copyright renewed 1968 Colgems-EMI
Music, Inc. All Rights Reserved. Used by permission.

Music Sales Corporation: excerpt from lyrics to "Sunday, Monday, or Always," words and music by Johnny
Burke and Jimmy Van Heusen. Copyright 1943 by Dorsey Bros. Music and Bourne Company, copyright
renewed 1971 by Dorsey Bros. Music and Bourne Company. International Copyright Secured. All Rights
Reserved. Used by permission.

Macmillan Publishing Company: excerpt from "Next Day" from *The Lost World* by Randall Jarrell.
Copyright © 1963 by Randall Jarrell. Originally appeared in *The New Yorker*. Repeated by permission of
Macmillan Publishing Company.

POCKET BOOKS, a division of Simon & Schuster, Inc.,
1230 Avenue of the Americas, New York, N.Y. 10020

ISBN: 0-671-61109-7

First Pocket Books trade paperback printing April, 1988

10 9 8 7 6 5 4 3 2 1

POCKET and colophon are trademarks
of Simon & Schuster, Inc.

Printed in the U.S.A.

CONTENTS

5

Contents

MEN AT WAR

THE MEANING OF MANHOOD

AS A MAN GROWS OLDER

FOREWORD

I am only a second-rate man. I am grown-up enough now to be honest about it. I have always felt like an inferior specimen of the sex and have often had to pretend to pleasures I did not really feel in this or that manly pastime.

Maybe all men secretly feel inadequate. It wouldn't be surprising. If born male in my time, which was located between Calvin Coolidge and the Battle of Midway, you were exhorted from the cradle to "be a man," to "act like a man," to "take it like a man." Before you were old enough to think for yourself, they were preparing you for a lifetime of feeling like a disgrace to your sex. What was this "man" you were supposed to take it like, to act like, to be? To this day, here on the edge of dotage, I have only the most nonsensical idea, much of it gleaned from the foolishness of childhood.

Fifty years ago, and perhaps still today, a boy contemplating the tests required to qualify for "man" status had justifiable reason to curse the Y chromosome that made him male. Consider three absolute requirements:

Utter fearlessness. This forbade him to behave naturally by howling in terror and begging for lights when sent to bed in a room that became infested with monstrous horrors the instant night fell.

Zest for combat. This compelled him to accept foolishly all challenges to fistfights issued by boys who were certain they could easily blacken his eyes and loosen his teeth and who wouldn't have challenged him if they weren't.

Indifference to pain. This required him to abstain from dramatic

displays of discomfort after having three fingers caught in a slamming door or being struck in the head by a baseball bat and when
asked "Are you hurt?" to reply "I'll be all right."

These, among the first of life's lessons, taught that being a man
meant suppressing certain natural instincts, among them the instinct to behave sensibly.

Much later I understood the primitive wisdom that had created
such irrational standards for boys to measure up to. It sprang from
the fact that in perilous times a man may be required by his country to face death in battle. To fulfill that duty it helps if early in life
you have been taught that being a man often requires conduct that
is neither sensible nor natural, but is nevertheless honorable.

Honorable: it is peculiarly a man's word, as are its antonyms:
dishonorable, ignoble, base, vile, swinish, caddish. Such words are
rarely applied to women. Even the phrase "a woman's honor," re-
ferring to the high-toned sexual morality once demanded of the
American female, sounds like a man's invention for burdening
women with heavier moral luggage than men chose to bear.

In antique popular fiction, men fight duels for the honor of
women. In not terribly old newspapers, one reads of lynchings
committed to avenge feminine honor. There was even a code of
honor governing the etiquette of protecting women's honor. The
honor of the avenger required him to accept the risks of the duel if
the dishonored lady had fallen to a man of sound social position; if
to a plebeian, the lout could be left to the mob.

Men do dreadful, irrational and unnatural deeds under the ban-
ner of honor. Women, of course, can behave just as nastily, but
rarely, I suspect, in the cause of honor. Women are more apt to be
tigerish when the cause is love. This is doubtless because women,
unlike men, are not bombarded from infancy with demands that
they behave honorably. Or, to put it another way, "like a man."
Which is to say, like someone who believes there is a higher virtue
than doing the sensible and natural thing: to wit, doing the honorable thing.

The honorable thing may be foolish or just plain stupid, may be suicidal or homicidal, may be asinine or merely absurd, may be noble or beautiful. It is unlikely, though, ever to be natural or sensible. Men don't let on that they're afraid of ghosts. Men would rather have their eyes blackened and teeth loosened than let the whole world see that they hate being severely beaten. Men don't make a fuss if it hurts a little when somebody drives bamboo slivers under their fingernails.

I tell you, folks: it's not all roses and featherbed mattresses being a man. They lay that honor business on you when you're just a little boy, long before you guess what it's leading up to, long before you can possibly know that if you don't live by that little-boy code someday a general may slap your face and call you a coward or order a firing squad to dispose of you as a disgrace to your sex and hence a menace to your country.

So the idea of honor becomes a vital part of a man's boyhood experience. When women are little girls, at least in my observation, they are exposed to no such grim conditioning. I have been father and grandfather to both male and female children and know I should be ashamed to tell you the fact that while I lavished love, kisses and indulgence on the females, I played the Spartan general to the boys.

Yes, ladies of the liberation, I actually warned my sons that men don't cry when they hurt. Told them to act like men. When one suffered disappointment and came to me for comfort and love, I advised him to take it like a man. Never once did I tell the girls to "be a woman," to "act like a woman" or to "take it like a woman." Women were to be loved, men to be imbued with the burden of honor.

All sensitive people now recognize that I was deficient in child-rearing sensitivity. Yet I am not so sure we are ready for a society in which men no longer count honor rather high when making important decisions. Lately there has been a good bit of somber brooding among the more articulate men who dodged wartime military service in Vietnam. Now and then you come across one of them chewing on his guilt. The draft slot that he avoided had to be occupied by someone else, probably someone else without the cunning, the money or the influence needed to escape it. Was that Unknown Someone Else killed? And if so . . . but who can ever know?

These brooding middle-aged nonveterans did what they considered the sensible and natural thing years ago when they dodged the draft. Yet now you find them wondering if the sensible and natural thing wasn't also, alas, the dishonorable thing. Sure, the course they took had been the only course that made sense to them. But was it, after all, the course a man should have taken in that terrible predicament? Doesn't being a man sometimes imply an obligation to ignore what is natural and sensible and do the damn-fool thing for some damn-fool senseless and irrational purpose? Like honor . . . ? If no men did, there would be few poems, few novels and very little history that didn't put us to sleep.

Now, lest I leave the impression that the Vietnam draft avoiders are all suffering guilt neurosis, let me note a curious phenomenon among our most hawkish middle-aged politicians and polemicists. An astonishing number of them, though of an age to have served in Vietnam, managed to avoid military service. Nevertheless, they are not in the least embarrassed about proposing bloody onsets in which Americans other than themselves would have to do the bleeding. Obviously, a substantial percentage of the male Vietnam generation has learned to stay within the limits of what is sensible and natural and, thus, to rise above honor.

This sounds meaner about our political hawks than I feel. I am wishy-washy on the question of the honorable vs. the natural in men. Respect for nationalism tempts me to admire the clear-thinking fellow who, seeing the inescapable necessity of war, proceeds to talk the country into it while simultaneously, having acknowledged that he couldn't bear being shot at, arranging to have himself excused. He might conclude quite sensibly that a man who can't stand being shot at can only handicap the army and should be confined to civilian life for the good of the war effort. Thus he might justifiably take patriotic pride in being a draft dodger.

The gall of this rationalization appeals to that part of me which makes me feel like a second-rate man. I grew up refusing to cry when afraid of the dark, and I hated being afraid to cry. I hated having to be beaten up by boys who chose me only because I was obviously no match for them, but I went ahead and got beat up anyhow, because men didn't say "This is ridiculous; you're out of my weight class." Sissies said that. If there was a beating around, I took it like a man.

I love John Wayne movies for several reasons. One is that they make me laugh at the boyishness of what passes for manhood in Duke's movie world. When Duke is shot in the leg, he doesn't cry. When they cut the bullet out with a pocketknife and no anesthetic but whiskey, he still doesn't cry. Hardly a grunt out of him.

In these circumstances I would cry, groan and yell. I realize Duke is just a big, overweight boy playing a game that might be called Man, but even though I know it's only a game, the knowledge that I couldn't suffer the bullet and knife without yelling makes me feel like a second-rate man.

Duke is always enjoying a terrific fistfight. You can't blame him. I'd enjoy a good fistfight myself if I always won and never showed so much as a scraped chin or a split lip after it was over. Not being Duke, I avoid fistfights so successfully that I haven't had my nose busted with knuckles since 1938. I know Duke's fistfights are just boy stuff, yet the knowledge that I wouldn't enjoy them the way Duke does makes me feel like a second-rate man.

There are too many other things that add to this feeling. Evenings with the boys, for instance. I hate evenings with the boys. And telling dirty jokes. I don't know why, but I dislike dirty jokes.

Pushing people around also pains me. Apparently, to be a fully certified man you've got to push people around. As a kid you literally push around other kids, or they push you. Then you grow up and go to the office. It is a place full of oversize boys pushing each other around. The best pusher winds up with his photo in the financial section of the papers. Admiring gush is published about his ruthlessness. Somebody writes a book about him, maybe a movie is made with his brutish identity thinly fictionalized.

I know this pusher is just an overgrown broth of a boy who, when he was just a little nose-picker, was told that a man pushed people around. I know I shouldn't feel bad about not being like him, but I do. Although I know that pushing people around is childish, I can't help feeling like a second-rate man because I'm no good at all at pushing people around.

Which brings us back to where we came in. What I meant to say back there before getting sidetracked was that, no matter what the women have been saying lately, it's no picnic being a man either. A lot of men have tried to come to grips with the problem in the "About Men" column. How well they have succeeded I leave for you to judge.

A couple of them confess that from time to time they have actually cried. I want to congratulate them for that; thanks to the women's movement, crying men are very fashionable nowadays. Still, their confessions made me uneasy. Instinct urges me to blurt out, "Men don't cry, fellows." And if they persist, "Think of your honor, for heaven's sake!"

Discreetly, I say neither. If I did they might feel obliged to assert their manhood by blackening my eyes and bloodying my nose. No, it's not easy being a man.

RUSSELL BAKER

INTRODUCTION

In this age of women, what is there to say about men? To judge by the response to the "About Men" column, the answer is: plenty.

Four years after it was introduced as a regular weekly feature in *The New York Times Magazine,* the "About Men" column attracts some seventy-five manuscripts a week. This means that the editors sort through an astonishing four thousand essays a year. It also means that American men, in searching for an outlet to express what they think about themselves, have made the column an immensely popular cultural forum.

And the words keep pouring in, as many as 75,000 of them each week. They express pain, joy, confusion, sometimes barely concealed rage, but always the deepest feelings of men.

Wherever we go, we hear "About Men" discussed—either lavishly praised or hotly condemned—usually with words like "It's the first thing I turn to on Sunday morning." The mail reflects this interest; the "About Men" column elicits more letters to the editor of the Sunday *Magazine* than any other regular feature. And many of these comments and letters are from women, testimony that both sexes look to the column for insight into how the changes of the last two decades have affected the person who once "brought home the bacon," was "strong and silent," and who "knew best."

As those outdated phrases indicate, the changes have been profound. Not too long ago most men believed they brought home the bacon, were strong and silent, and knew best—or, at least, they thought they did. But the women's liberation movement changed all that and, as painful as the transition has been for men, it seems to have been a blessing as well. The manuscripts men send to the "About Men" column show that many welcome the chance to liberate themselves from the old stereotypes. It is not so much a case that they think less of themselves; it's that they now have an opportunity to be more. A contributor from Albuquerque writes in the letter accompanying his submission: "If About Men has done nothing else, it has coaxed us out of our male shells a bit."

Early in 1983, A. M. Rosenthal, then the executive editor of the *Times,* sensed that the women's movement had changed men in ways that remained uncharted, and he began to search for a way the paper could report regularly on this development. The Sunday *Magazine* was chosen as the forum for two reasons. The daily paper already had a column called "Hers" that dealt with women's issues, and it was felt that a column by and about men should not be an exact counterpart. The other reason was that the magazine, with its fashion, food and home design pages, was already full of material that appealed to women, and a men's column might provide a welcome balance.

The first "About Men" column appeared on June 5, 1983, an essay on male humor by Isaac Asimov, which is included in this book. In the weeks that followed, the column carried pieces on men's style, gear, sports and outdoor adventure. But it soon became clear that the essays on how men felt about themselves were what they really wanted to write and what our readers wanted to read. And so the personal-essay format became established as the trademark of the column.

The column's first editor, Abbott Combes, did not have the luxury of a steady supply by mail. His task, in mid-1983, was to call up well-known writers and try to persuade them to submit to a page that had yet to find its identity. Many writers in the beginning saw the column as a place to be nostalgic about their boyhoods or about eccentric characters they had met. Many, too, were flippant about women, comparing men, favorably, to women much in the manner of "Why can't a woman be more like a man?" Some of these pieces were published, and the reaction from feminists was not muted.

They hated the macho stance of some of the writers and could see no reason why *The New York Times* should devote a column to men in any case. In addition, they were displeased that the column was given a color page in the Sunday paper with its higher circulation while the "Hers" column ran on Thursday in black and white. This criticism, however, failed to take into account the fact that the *Times*'s overall coverage, daily and Sunday, of women's issues far outweighed the attention it paid to men.

Reacting to this and other criticism, the editors, for a time, may have overcompensated. The "About Men" essays seemed to enter a tender phase in which many of the writers proclaimed "I do the dishes and love it." After that, a better balance was struck between the robust and the lachrymose. The mail began to flow, and the column finally was able to mix the work of professional writers with the thoughts of physicians, businessmen, scientists, lawyers, soldiers and railroad engineers. The experiences of these men gave the page a dimension that a steady diet of professional writers could not.

Today, well-known writers are always welcome, but so are the thoughts of amateurs. What is regularly rejected is abstract and scholarly work by sociologists, psychologists and therapists who have studied men and wish to share their insights. The editors insist that the column be personal essays, raw material, perhaps, for the experts who study men. What is sought in each piece is the expression of honest feeling and clear thinking about an interesting situation that seems to be unique to men at this point in history. The feeling must be evident in the manuscript in order for an essay to be considered, but often the clear thinking takes a bit of doing. It sometimes comes about after give-and-take between writer and editor. One recent contributor wrote: "You have penetrated my defenses and gently forced me to look squarely at the dynamics of my emotional dilemma. The honest truth does feel good."

The subject men want to write about most, to judge from the essays they send in, is their fathers. More than half of the manuscripts concern, in one way or another, men's thinking about the men who gave them life—appreciations, complete with boyhood

anecdotes, laments that the son never knew the father well, observations that the aged father is now a child himself to whom the son
must act as father. If, as it has been said, some American men don't
think of themselves as "men" until they have finished thinking of
themselves in other roles, it is clear to us that they think of their fathers, right off the bat, as "men."

Being a father is another popular topic, although most men,
brooding about their sons or daughters, soon find themselves remembering how their own fathers coped. Malcolm Cowley's essay
is one of many we have received on the problems of growing old.
The death of a man's father forces him to face many emotions, and
the occasion has prompted hundreds of men to write about their
feelings of loss and change. In fact, eulogies of all sorts make up a
significant proportion of the submissions.

Men write about their hobbies and enthusiasms, often their obsession with sports, particularly baseball. They love to recount anecdotes from World War II. They write about divorce and how it
changed their lives.

The list of topics men don't write much about is interesting.
They compare men's lives to women's, for instance, far less often
than they used to. An indication, perhaps, that they have moved
beyond simply reacting to the women's movement. In fact, they
now write about women in general far less than might be expected.
The reputation of the *Times* as a "family newspaper" may deter
them from setting down much about their sexuality. Almost no
contributors, for obvious reasons, write about the love or hate they
have for their bosses or employees. Only a few write about work
and the corporate existence. John Kenneth Galbraith's piece is one
of the exceptions. About power and money, those allegedly male
obsessions, there is almost universal silence. A bit of editorial
prodding may change that in the future, however.

The column has had a number of critics, most of whom com-
plain that the essays favor wimps over red-blooded American
males who are still supplied with a firm Rocky-Rambo-Reagan
backbone. Such was the point of a parody in *Esquire*. An essay in
the *American Spectator* found a disturbing "avalanche of con-

fession" in the essays. A piece in *Vanity Fair* blames the emergence of musclebound post-feminist male heroes in popular movies and literature on Alan Alda and the "About Men" column.

When people start blaming a newspaper column for the state of American culture, you know it has finally arrived.

EDWARD KLEIN AND DON ERICKSON

FAMILY

STRAINS

RAFAEL A. SUAREZ JR.

Being a Jr.

There is a photograph in my parents' house in Brooklyn which never fails to grab a gaze as I pass by. It was taken in 1958, on the beach in Jacksonville, Florida. My father, trim, smiling, tan, holds his firstborn, a little over a year old. That's me. On that sunny day in Florida my sailor father is a few months past his twentieth birthday. I think of myself at twenty, a senior in college living in my first apartment, and laugh at the idea of my having had a child at that age.

My father looks happy in the photo. I look happy, too. Today I have a face something like his, a body much like his, and a name *exactly* like his. Exactly the same, except for two letters and a period on my birth certificate, diploma, driver's license and credit cards: Jr. At the risk of sounding a little syrupy, I'd say his name is one of the nicest things my father has ever given me. Rafael is one of the seven archangels, and he is known as God's healer for his role in restoring the sight of Tobit in that Apocryphal book. Thus Angel, my father's middle name, and mine, is fitting.

There are hundreds, perhaps thousands of names for men. There are plenty of other names in my own family that would have worked perfectly well. My brothers got them. My father and mother could have given me a different middle name. Then I would have been named for my father, but not a Jr.

When friends first see my byline, or look over my shoulder as I sign a register, and they see the "Jr." at the end, there are several reactions. "I wouldn't like that," said one. "I like having my *own* name." Some men say, "You're a junior? Me too!"

Only men get to say that, because only men get to be juniors. Women with feminized versions of their fathers' names don't get a legal tag to reflect the fact and neither do women named for their mothers. Besides, the attitudes that go with having "junior children" seem to be more closely associated with boys than girls. Though customs are changing, carrying on the family name is still something done by boys and very effectively done by "juniors."

In addition to the sexual exclusivity of juniorism, there is a cultural one. Though there is no religious reason for it, Eastern European Ashkenazic Jews will not name children for their fathers or mothers, except in the unlikely event that the father is dead at a boy's birth. There are exceptions to this generalization, but none of the guys with whom I played ball at the Jewish Community House in Bensonhurst were juniors. Most of my Jewish buddies are carrying a dead relative's initials around, or some rough English cognate of a Hebrew name. It seems a shame that not only dad but *all* of the living are excluded from the thrill of having a namesake.

I'm happy with my name, and I like being a junior, but there is a down side. Mail meant for me still somehow ends up at my father's house. When I still lived at home I got half my mail "pre-opened." I can still remember the look on my father's face when my friends on the phone, asking for me and getting him, would launch into personal conversation. Family members finally got into the habit of asking "junior or senior?" when callers weren't specific enough.

In the world of juniors, I was one of the lucky ones. I was never called "Junior" as a nickname. I knew one Junior for years without ever knowing his real name. He and many other Juniors will tell you that Junior is their real name and sign it that way on a greeting card or a letter. These are the guys people probably have in mind when they ask me if I have a fragile sense of identity because of my juniorhood.

Identity is not a problem. In addition to being me, I get the privilege of having my name attached to something longer-lived than just me. When I introduce myself, I don't say "My name is . . ." or

"I am called . . ." I say "I am Rafael." The difference is important, because a name doesn't only tell people what to call you, it tells them who you are.

I often think about my life as being not only a gift from my parents to me, but as being a gift from me to them. It must be a special gift for my father, since we have the same name. I think of the kick he probably gets when he sees my byline in a magazine or newspaper, or when he sees my name, *our* name, under my face when I report on television. He loves my brothers and is proud of them. But it can't be the same as seeing his name, his son's name, in a prominent place.

Of the three brothers, am I the most like my father? Maybe. I think that when I was named for my father, the intention was that my name not be simply a utile thing, not be just a handy sound to summon a boy when the garbage needs to be taken down. When a child is named, it is an attempt to define the child. And my definition is my father. I thank my parents for their vote of confidence, and I hope I live up to my name.

Still, there are complications of juniorhood, and they don't end at the age of majority or when a boy moves away from home. I will be a junior until the day I die, no matter how long my father lives. If I ever have a son, he can be named for me, but he can't be "Jr." We would have to begin the numbers game, which somehow doesn't have the intimacy of "Sr." and "Jr." This theoretical manchild would have "3d" (pronounced "the third") at the end of his name, and I'm not sure how I feel about that. My wife says, unequivocally, "No way." A friend suggested that the resulting name would be a "little too Waspy." But I don't think Rafael Angel Suarez 3d has to worry about being too Waspy.

JOHN WALTERS

Golden Gloves

The banks closed down, and people began throwing themselves out of windows. It was a strange time in which to be growing up. There were few psychiatrists, fewer welfare programs, and the word "depression" referred to an economic condition that saw grown men crying when they thought no one could hear them. I heard my father one afternoon when I came home from school. He'd been out of work for months, like millions of others. The sounds he made frightened me.

We'd recently lost our home and had moved into a smaller, rented, house. I'd also changed schools, leaving the private academy I'd attended and enrolling in a parochial school, most of whose students were from poor families. The adjustment was difficult. I was made to feel like a pariah. Worse, I was the only one in my junior high class who wore glasses, in those years the mark of a sissy.

One day, shortly after I'd begun there, the school bully picked a fight with me. I detested such physical violence and staggered home in a torn, frightful condition, made only worse when my father saw me trying to sneak upstairs.

I started to tell him what had happened, but he interrupted. "I don't want to hear all that. All I want to know is, did you win?"

"No," I said.

"Did you quit?"

"I guess I did."

He clenched his fists. He was a wiry, athletic man. Our relationship at that time in our lives was strained. He'd never been an affectionate man, and the Depression had driven him into a dark place, deep within himself.

A few days later, returning from the gym where he played handball several times a week, he called me aside.

"There's someone I want you to meet. At the gym. This coming Saturday."

The someone was standing with my father when I entered the locker room on the appointed day. "Meet Tommy Loughran," said my father. "Tommy, this is my son, Jack." The man who, a few years before, had been the light-heavyweight boxing champion of the world smiled, we shook hands, and after a few minutes' conversation, Loughran offered to supervise the boxing lessons my father had arranged for me.

I'd meet Tommy in the gym, usually before he and my father went off to the court to play handball. The room, that sweat-damp arena smelling of bodies, wintergreen oil and tired leather, was crowded with men and boys practicing the manly art, working out on punching bags and shadowboxing along the walls.

For the most part, I was left alone, and my early training consisted of imitating others. Eventually, I climbed into the ring for my first real lesson. Mickey, my sparring partner, was an Italian welterweight, considerably older than I, a semi-professional and a former Golden Glover. It must have been a curious dance, Mickey grinning encouragement, I flailing away, with Tommy and my father standing by.

So it went. I'd walk home those afternoons in the bleak fall weather, walking the four miles to save carfare, carrying my bag of gym clothes. Sometimes I'd jog home, the bag slung over my back, drifting through the park and enjoying sweet liberation from my troubles. The gym sessions, at first a bitter imposition, became in time a regular part of my life, and I began to like them. I felt myself growing stronger, taller and more confident. Relations with my father improved.

One day, Mickey pulled me off the heavy bag. He'd been building me up, matching me with more experienced fighters. "You're all right, kid. You wanna qualify for the Golden Gloves, you could. You're ready. Tomorrow I'm gonna put you in there with a guy I know."

Something in the way he said it told me it would be by far my toughest match. That night I couldn't sleep. Waves of anxiety swept over me as I kept thinking it could end in a repeat of the schoolyard incident.

I got up and went downstairs for a glass of milk. My father was sitting at the kitchen table, reading the newspaper and drinking a beer.

"What's the matter with you? Why aren't you asleep?"

"Thought I'd get a glass of milk."

"Milk, is it? Here, have a beer."

In my astonishment, I merely stood and stared at him. He poured a glass, and I carefully sat down across from him. By now, I was taller than he. He did not look too well, I thought. I knew that something important was happening.

"You're filling out, son," he said, and smiled. The sound of love in his voice caught me unawares. I started to say something, but choked. His hand lay near mine on the table, and I thought he was going to reach out and touch me.

He did not. In the silence, I could hear the clock ticking. "You reading any good books?" he asked.

"The Call of the Wild," I said, knowing he approved of Jack London.

"Ah, now there was a man," he said. We drank in silence, and he went back to his paper. After a while, I ventured upstairs. I cannot remember whether he returned my goodnight.

There is little to add. The rest is postscript. I won my match the next day by a knockout. Looking down at my opponent, I realized he was bigger and tougher than anyone I knew in school.

A few months later, my father died. I'd dropped out of school temporarily to go to work, with the help of a kind neighbor who worked in a factory still operating. We lied about my age.

Years later, I met the boy who had bullied me at school. He seemed to have shrunk and had forgotten all about our encounter.

I chose not to remind him. I heard still later, after completing my own odyssey in World War II, that he'd died in the Pacific.

I never again put on the gloves with anyone or felt the need to assert myself in such a fashion. But I often think of Mickey and Tommy. The gray light, and the way it fell through the narrow windows in that arena from which I graduated, returns in the nights.

Sometimes, unable to sleep, I will get up for a drink. The clock in the kitchen is electric and emits no sound. The table is bare, and I avoid sitting at it. The cat keeps me company by the refrigerator, as I tip a measure of milk for him into his dish under the sink. I stroke the soft, humming fur, waiting for God knows what to happen—a word, an adjustment, the righting of some ancient wrong. Straightening up, I raise my hands, clenching them, dropping my left shoulder in a feint, thrusting my right hand out as though to encounter something in the air . . .

MES C. G. CONNIFF

Manchild Coming of Age

My youngest son, Mark, has his suits and jackets fitted with extra care, because, five feet tall, he weighs more than 170 pounds and is built like a padded fire hydrant. He is dieting to fight that image, though, and has twenty-seven Special Olympics awards on his wall to prove it, right beside life-size posters of Michael Jackson, Kenny Baker and Barbara Mandrell. Mark is a powerful swimmer, and five of the awards are for first place in the category.

For thirty-one years, Mark has been a central fact of our family life, knitting us together, trying our patience, helping us laugh, probably making us better people than we would have been without him.

I remember the night call, hours after he was born, and the doctor's trying to be gentle as the darkness around me grew suddenly deeper: "I regret having to tell you your new son may be mongoloid."

They don't say that anymore. They don't call leprosy leprosy, either. Now it's Hansen's disease. And mongolism is Down's syndrome, or trisomy 21, a chromosomal abnormality that hinders the development of the mind. The growing brain signals its imprisonment in the smaller skull by causing erratic gait, slower growth, vulnerability to infections, clubfeet, other anomalies.

Knowing I was a medical writer, the doctor shared with me the details that left little room for doubt: the epicanthal fold of the eyelids at either side of the nose, excessive bone-flex even for a newborn, deeper-than-normal postnatal jaundice, clubfeet, the simian line across the palm of each hand. Later, one of many specialists we consulted would say of Mark: "Let's leave a door open for me to back out of. There are people in Congress less bright than he may yet turn out to be."

Nobody's perfect, in other words. Even so: *mongoloid.* The word boomed in my soul like the tolling of a leaden gong. No more sleep for me. Next morning, I entered upon a conspiracy of one.

"Why can't I see the baby?" was my wife's first question after the kiss, the forced congratulatory smile. The lie. "They're getting him ready" came with clinical ease. "He'll be up to see you soon."

Then the quick maternal discovery of his clubfeet, and my too-swift assurance that the feet were "only an anomaly" which remedial measures would correct. Worst of all, her tearful puzzlement at learning we would have to leave him in the hospital "for a few more days" to make sure his casts "weren't on too tight"—or some such double-talk.

Back home without him, I found myself unable to keep up the charade under mounting internal pressure. After a few miserable days, I blurted out the truth and endured her dry-eyed demand that we "Go bring him home, right away, so I can take care of him. Now. Today."

Caring for a baby with legs in plaster casts spread wide at the ankles by a rigid steel bar to straighten the growing feet can take its emotional toll. But from the start, Mark's older brothers, and especially his sisters, devoted themselves to helping us raise him. Under what I now look back on as a cascade of sunrises and sunsets "laden with happiness and tears," we overcame any misguided temptation we may have had to institutionalize him.

One undeniable result has been that he is much further along, and far better equipped to deal with life in spite of his limitations, than he would have been if we had done that to him. Today, as he stands poised to see whether he likes it in a group home, we take comfort in knowing we tried to do right by him. Another gain has been that he has done well by us; caring for him has matured us. Aged us too, no doubt, but that would have happened anyway.

The father of a retarded child wonders if in some unforeseeable way he may have contributed to the tragedy (in my case, possibly the case of mumps I had before Mark was conceived). Some men walk out on what they see as an impossible situation, a saddling of their marriage with an unending burden. Some come back. Each case is unique. No one outside it can judge.

Ironies abound. Long before Mark was born, I wrote an article on mental retardation. It helped, I'm told, to get federal funds for research into the causes. And when Hubert H. Humphrey's grand-daughter was born retarded, he and I wrote pieces pleading with readers to recognize that mental retardation is a totally different affliction from mental illness. "It's not contagious, either!" Hubert would shout at me, as if I needed convincing. Yet in my own extended family some still think Mark is contagious.

Harder to take is watching him strive, in a family of writers, to produce copy. Pages of hand-scrawled and sometimes typed letters, all higgledy-piggledy, spill from his fevered efforts to "follow in your footsteps, Dad!" And almost nightly, lonely and eager for an audience, Mark interrupts our reading or television watching to rattle off plots from reruns of "M*A*S*H." We try to look attentive, even though it drives us nutty. Shouting matches help ease tension, and I have on occasion threatened to work Mark over. But sooner or later he forgives me. With a hug.

Indefatigable, Mark has handsawed his way through storm-toppled tree trunks without resting, mowed lawns, backstopped me on cement-laying jobs. I repay him with prodigious hero sandwiches, which he seldom fails to praise.

At thirty-one, he still cannot read, but he does guess at numbers, at times embarrassingly well. When, here lately, he began to put a cash value on his toil and asked for pay, I offered him a dollar. He looked at me with a knowing grin and said, quite clearly despite his usual speech problems, "Five bucks, Dad, *five* bucks." I gave him five ones.

For signs like this that the manchild is coming of age, I am grateful. And for something else: I can't say we feel he's ready for Congress, but he has given us hope. Unlike the night he was born, in part because of Mark, I am no longer afraid of the dark.

FREDERICK KAUFMAN

My Father and Spencer Tracy

In *Bad Day at Black Rock,* a film my father wrote, Robert Ryan tells Spencer Tracy: "Nobody around here has been big enough to make you mad. I believe a man is as big as the things that make him mad."

I've never forgotten those lines. They are linked to one of my earliest memories of my father: Dad is pacing the living room, holding the phone under an arm like a football and screaming into the receiver, "Don't tell me how to write the goddamn thing!"

I can't remember exactly what was going on, but I do know that he was yelling at an agent, a director, a producer—one of the multitude in Hollywood who can torment a writer. I also know that I hated his rage, that I wished for a less angry father. "Writing," my father often told me, "rhymes with fighting."

One afternoon—I could have been no more than nine years old—my father and I were in the pantry. He was up on a ladder, trying to get his pliers into an obscure corner. It was my job to hand him the tools he needed. My attention wandered, and soon he was yelling at me. About an hour after his screaming subsided, Dad came to my room and apologized. "You are not the target," he told me. But I remember thinking that if I wasn't the target, who was?

Years later, my college writing instructor asked me to her office to discuss one of my short stories. As she critiqued my writing, I became full of rage. To calm myself, I repeated under my breath, "A man is as big as the things that make him mad." Finally I shouted, "Don't tell me how to write the goddamn thing!"

I was kicked out of my first writing course, and six years elapsed before it occurred to me that what had happened had something to do with my father.

By then, I was living in New York in a windowless garret, working at a small publishing house by day. At night, I typed on my Smith-Corona portable. It was a year of pounding out furiously whatever came to mind—damn the editors, damn the publishing industry. I had inherited my father's stubborn rage. When the year was over, I needed a new typewriter. When I looked at my vast, useless pile of paper, I had the feeling something was not right.

On my next visit to Los Angeles, I made a point of joining my father for a lunch of chicken hot dogs. He overcooks them in the broiler every day, and they emerge black and swollen with raised bubbles—the way he loves them. He covers them with mustard or ketchup or Tabasco sauce and eats them between slices of not-quite-yet-stale French bread. No matter who joins him—a producer, the gardener—the grub is always the same.

"Want some?" he asks.

"No, thanks."

But when they're on his plate, I ask for a bite. He gives me an annoyed smile, forks over half his meal and tosses a few more dogs on the broiler.

"Dad," I ask, "why did you decide to become a writer?"

He told me that after he had returned from the Marine Corps in World War II, he thought that the most sensible way to make a living, with the least expenditure of effort, would be to write theatrical motion pictures, about which he knew absolutely nothing. His first job was with United Productions of America, where he was teamed with the director John Hubley and asked to create an original cartoon.

My father came up with a character based on his Uncle Leonard, who was also known as Bub. I had met Uncle Bub when he was an old man, deaf and barrel-chested. The cartoon character needed a name; my father turned to California geography, which, he said, is full of inherently funny names. He loved the pretentiousness of Azusa ("Everything from A to Z in the U.S.A."), and Point Mugu, up the coast from Malibu. He decided to change the spelling and call Uncle Bub Mr. Magoo.

The cartoon was an immediate hit. But after my father had written the first half-dozen Magoos, he left United Productions. In Dad's opinion, writing cartoons was no job for a mature man, so even though he had hit the jackpot early, he told his agent to get him different work. The agent discovered that M-G-M was planning a picture about boot camp. At that time there were surprisingly few writers in Hollywood who, like my father, had been in combat. The agent went to Dore Schary, vice president in charge of production. "I don't know whether this kid can write," he told Schary, "but if he gives you nothing more than a few little things that are for real, at the end of the month you can him and you get a professional writer." Dad got the job.

A few weeks later, as Dad was leaving the studio, a voice hollered "Millard!" It was Schary. The head of the studio was charming, and apologized for not having seen Dad earlier; he was terribly busy.

"I tell you what let's do," he said. "It's so difficult talking around the office, there are always phones and one thing or another. Why don't you come over to the house tomorrow morning, and we'll talk while I'm taking a shower?"

"All the vicious and demeaning things I had heard about the treatment of writers in Hollywood kind of ganged up on me," my father told me. In a rage, he screamed at Schary, "And what the hell shall we do then? Play unnatural games?"

My father walked away.

I pictured Mom and Dad in the living room later that evening. Of course, Dad would have to find another job. He had had the chance to do what he had dreamed of and rage had spoiled it. But Mom said to hell with Schary, you're right.

So in the kitchen, over the remains of chicken hot dogs, I realized that no matter what the reward, my father wouldn't lick another man's boots. His rage had a lot of good in it: I, too, will never have to read my work to the vice presidents of this world while they soap their armpits.

And years ago, as my parents sat brooding, the phone rang. It was Mrs. Schary's social secretary, inviting them to dinner. My father stayed at M-G-M for eleven years, during which time he earned two Academy Award nominations, one for the second film of his career, that western starring Spencer Tracy and Robert Ryan with the lines I won't forget.

GENE LIGHT

My Father's Son, the Artist

Every family has its "in" joke. The standing gag in mine was that my father never quite knew what I did for a living. My father was a butcher. His father, uncles and brothers were butchers. He married the cashier at the butcher shop he worked in. Her brothers were all butchers. When I was born, my mother vowed I could be anything I wanted to be except a butcher.

As a youngster, I drew pictures all the time, mostly airplanes like all the other kids. Because of this, my mother decided I should go to art school. Before I knew what was happening, I was taking the test for the High School of Music and Art and then traveling an hour and a half from my home in Brooklyn to the school in upper Manhattan.

"My son, the artist" was the way my father introduced me to his customers. I worked in his butcher shop every Saturday all through high school. My father naturally assumed I would take over the store when I graduated. When I announced that I had won a scholarship to the Cooper Union School of Art and wanted to continue my art training, he was stunned. He suddenly realized that I was taking this art thing seriously. According to him, "Butchers, grocers, shoemakers . . . that was a way to make a living. Butchers especially . . . people always had to eat! Artists starved in . . . in . . ."

"Garrets, Pop."

"Whatever."

It was useless for me to explain that I was not going to be a

painter but a commercial artist. The nuances of my chosen profession escaped him. An artist was an artist—and they starved.

Ten years later, my father sold his butcher shop and retired. I
was an art director with *Life* magazine, married with two children
and moving into my first house in the suburbs. My father came to
see the new house, and I noticed a quzzical look on his face. He
simply could not understand how "the artist" managed to feed and
clothe his grandchildren.

I knew he was terribly proud of me. I heard it all the time from
the neighbors on the street in Brooklyn where I grew up. He was
always bragging about his son, "the artist who draws for *Life* magazine." Every week my father would get the magazine, and every
week he would call and ask, "What did you draw in the magazine
this week?" I'd explain that I didn't draw anything. I designed the
pages. I placed the photographs, picked the typefaces. He would
mumble to himself. Obviously, I was getting my paycheck under
false pretenses and would soon be found out.

In December of 1972, *Life* folded. Needless to say, I was upset. I
was at home watching the news reports of the magazine's death,
when the phone rang. I knew it was my father. Eventually, he came
out with it: "If you were a butcher, you wouldn't be out of work
now." He tried to say it lightly, but I knew he meant it. I never
loved the man more and was actually glad to hear it, for somehow
it meant my world was still intact.

"Do you still remember how to cut meat?"

"Yes, Pop."

"Remember, people always have to eat."

As I write this in 1984, I have been art director for the last twelve
years for a publishing house. Every month, my father gets in the
mail the twenty or so books we publish. He calls to tell me how
much he likes my paintings on the covers. I no longer explain that I
design the covers, choose and place the type and then commission
other people to paint them. I just take the credit and thank him. He
has pictures to point to and show the neighbors.

The family gag about my father's not knowing what I do for a
living hit home sharply a few months ago. My son called from Cal-

ifornia. He's a talent agent with a major agency in Los Angeles. He had had a great offer from a rival company, and he wanted my advice about changing jobs. I said something about "doing what's best for your career in the future," but I realized I didn't know enough about what he actually does to advise him.

I remembered eight years back when he called from college and said he had decided he wanted to go into show business. I mumbled the usual: "It's your life and your decision." But when I hung up, I turned to my wife and said, "Show business? What kind of a way is that to make a living?" Why hadn't he chosen medicine or law or engineering? "Or being a butcher," my wife said. "People always have to eat."

My son must have made the right decision. At twenty-eight, he's obviously successful. When I visited his office for the first time, I was impressed. His secretary kept interrupting, asking if he would take a call from this person or that. She was using names that anyone would immediately recognize. For a moment, I thought the little punk had set me up and that the woman was making up the names to impress me. I caught my son looking at me, and I'm sure I had the same quizzical expression I used to see on my father's face. I suppose that unless a man's children work at exactly what he himself does, a father never quite knows what they really do. The intense love, bordering on the painful, always makes a man slightly scared for his children. How could this kid, who couldn't pick up his own socks, be trusted with whatever the heck it is someone is trusting him with?

Someday my son's son will tell him what he is going to do with his life. I know my son will think, "What the hell kind of a way is that to make a living?" He will call me, and I will say, "Tell him to be a butcher. People always have to eat."

By the way, my father no longer says "My son, the artist." He now says "My grandson, the talent agent." He also subscribes to *Variety.*

SAMUEL G. FREEDMAN

A Mother's Presence

I have never visited my mother's grave. I know, of course, where
her body lies, in a cemetery along a road I have traveled hundreds
of times in the nine years since she died.

And even now, I can see the burial. There is my grandmother,
contorted and wailing, tossing herself on the coffin, seeming insane,
insane. There is my father, little tears falling out of unblinking eyes
and sliding down his cheeks; he does not wipe them. My brother
looks dazed, numbed, and my sister topples into the arms of my
mother's best friend, howls erupting from her like uncontrollable
heaves.

I am there, too, with raccoon eyes, eyes ringed black—black for
mourning, black from the night awake in a motel near an airport
waiting for a morning flight home. My eyes are dry.

It is not for the lack of love or longing that I could not weep then,
that I cannot visit the grave now, always promising I will, never
keeping my word. But something remains confused and contradictory, the way, perhaps, it always must be between a man and his
mother. Sometimes those two words—"man" and "mother"—seem
mutually exclusive; with his mother, a son, even a grown son, remains somehow a child. And so to become a man I had to hurt and
reject the woman who brought me into the world.

I realize that most acutely because my mother died when I was
nineteen years old, on the cusp of manhood, in the midst of leaving
home. Her illness tied me to home, yet I lived a thousand miles

away. Duty and love called me home, yet I chose independence and distance.

Had my mother lived longer, there would have been time for discussion, explanation, reconciliation. We could have outgrown the roles of adversaries and, as two adults, renewed and strengthened our friendship, savored it for years. As it is, we are frozen in a moment without resolution, and I am stuck with choices that I see now as both necessary and shameful.

Those choices, as I think back, had their precedents. On my first day of nursery school, I had cried—even as my sister, a year younger, did not. And so on the day I was to begin kindergarten, my mother decided to walk with me the three blocks to school. After a block and a half, I demanded she let me go on alone. Part of me, I think, simply wanted to show what a big boy I was. But another part, I am sure, wanted to leave my mother behind because she knew the little boy who had cried in nursery school, homesick only four blocks from home.

A few years later, in second or third grade, I brought home a painting I had done in art class. I was angry because I had had to rush to finish it before class ended. My mother looked at the painting and said it was nice. So angry was I with this unwarranted approval that I crumpled up the painting and threw it in the garbage. She rescued it and somehow straightened all the wrinkles. A few weeks later, she entered the painting, without my knowledge, in a children's art contest sponsored by some local department store. It won for me the first prize, a silver dollar.

How could I not love my mother for her patience and her faith, salvaging that painting and saving me from my moods. Yet years later, I still had trouble accepting her approval—this time for articles in my high school and college newspapers—because approval from a mother seemed tainted, not sufficiently objective and hard-won.

Nevertheless, our relationship was good and strong. I can envision a pennant of Chinatown from a day spent together in New York, a birthday cake baked by her in the shape of a football field, the books in the den we both read and discussed; I miss those talks, and I miss the sound of her voice more than any aspect of her presence. I know that a certain number of battles are normal with either parent, but I never had to rebel against my father, as I did against my mother, just to grow up.

I can still see her, asleep at the kitchen table, her face resting on an opened newspaper. I am sixteen or seventeen years old, and I am opening the front door quietly, because my friend Mark and I have been out drinking, splitting a six-pack of beer and a pint of Southern Comfort as we walked the streets of our hometown.

"Why did you wait up for me?" I ask my mother. It is 2 A.M. "I wasn't waiting up," she says. "I fell asleep reading the newspaper." "You were," I say. "You were waiting up." I pause. "C'mon. Go to bed. I'm home now."

I wait for my mother to climb the stairs, wait for her bedroom light to flick on, then off. I take some beers from the refrigerator and go outside to meet Mark again.

I knew my mother did not want me to go away to college, but I did. I knew she wanted to accompany me to the University of Wisconsin when I enrolled, but I would not let her. She might have sensed how intimidated and worried I felt amid the Norse farm boys and the bearded New York Jews; she might have seen me, homesick again.

All this time, she was getting sicker. She slipped on water the dog had splashed out of her dish and pinched a nerve. Reaching for towels on the top shelf of a closet, she lost her balance and fell off a stepladder, breaking two toes. And because of her cancer, nothing healed. I can never forget her attending my sister's high school graduation in a wheelchair, a virtual cripple, reduced and shamed in front of the people she knew. As she sat in the wheelchair, a teacher walked past her and accidentally tipped it. I saw her begin to topple, and thought that if she did, she might simply break into pieces and I might lose my mind right then. Somehow, she righted the wheelchair in time.

All the following fall at college, letters came from my father, invariably relating the latest diagnosis, the latest bad news about

Mom. It seems those letters always came on a Saturday morning, right before I was going to a football game, dashing my pleasure, ruining my good time.

She decided to visit me at college that fall. She took a motel room with two beds, just in case I wanted to spend a night. I did not. I hurried her in and out of my dormitory—what kind of guy has his mother visiting? She wanted to sit in on my classes, and I said fine, but she could not sit next to me. When I look back, I see myself walking out of the lecture hall at the end of class, putting distance between us, not acknowledging my own mother until we were a block or two farther along.

Such was the selfishness and mean spirit of my imagined manhood. I shrivel at the memory. I shrivel, and yet I can imagine it no other way. The twenty-eight-year-old I am would celebrate this amazing woman, his mother, show her off to friends; the nineteen-year-old I was tried to hide her as a vestige of childhood and dependence. And because she died soon after, there was never a time to change, or at least to apologize.

There was only one day, in Madison, Wisconsin, a few years after she had died. I was taking my girlfriend to dinner—a dressy sort of place, away from the campus—and on the way I remembered that it was the same restaurant at which mother and I had eaten one night during her visit. And I began to cry.

CLARK BLAISE

A Middle-Aged Orphan

I was thirty-eight years old when my father died. I am now forty-five, but I don't feel I had thirty-eight years of fathering. In fact, I've heard more from my father these last seven years than I ever did when he was around.

He's on my mind because of the smell of cigarettes. He was a lifetime three-pack-a-day smoker, and his smoker's musk lingered over everything he touched. I was living in a furnished apartment in Atlanta, as Emory University's visiting writer, and the person who preceded me in that apartment had left his traces in the air, on the walls and in cigarette burns on the rim of the plastic bathtub. The edges of the dining table and kitchen counters were nicked with little brown parabolas where a butt had smoldered to its filter. Careless, hard-smoking people will be gone in a decade—it's hard to see them now as Bogarts and Hellmans after the Surgeon General has put them on notice. But they embody to me the low-rent heroism of people who know, better than most of us, their weakness, their foolishness and the price they're going to pay. I look on smokers as I look on my father now: foolish mortals, with stories to tell.

Seven years ago, my father was in a New Hampshire hospital, where I visited him every weekend from Montreal. He'd left Canada years before, tried Florida and Pittsburgh and several marriages, only to end his days in the French enclave of Manchester. His veins had collapsed, his feet were icy, he would never walk again. I had him where I wanted him. Now we could talk. Now he could hold my books, perhaps even read them, and he would tell me, finally, about his life, the epic novel that he'd lived.

His was the voice that had spoken to me whenever I wrote. I wanted him to know that. Through him and his stubborn fatalism, I made sense of my own heritage. The best book that I would ever be able to write would be *his* story, and I wanted him to start telling it. About Frenchness and hunger and death. About being the youngest of eighteen, seeing six siblings die in a single week, about the medieval Roman Catholicism of old Quebec. About his rum-running days during Prohibition, his prizefighting, his marriages. Such a simple thing to wonder about: do I have brothers and sisters? What made Leo Blais run, what made him into Lee Blaise, respectable Pittsburgh furniture dealer for a few years at least?

He'd had marriages before my mother; the father I remember was always in his fifties, always gray and turning white, thin on top, as I am now. When I was young, I was my mother's son, and until now I can say I was never his—intellectually, morally, physically. So why, in middle age, should I feel only his encoding? The face I sense looking out on the world is his. At forty-five, I'm in better shape than I've ever been, nearly in his ex-boxer's condition, without the side effects. I wouldn't shame him; we're a credible father and son now.

Like him, I left Canada, accepting risk for the hope of security. Risks both of us found, security never. He moved the family around the corners of America thirty-five times in twenty years— he was caged, there's no other metaphor—and it's with a certain terror that I realize I've registered my car in four different states in the last three years. Perhaps late blooming is encoded in both of us, along with the DNA of wanderlust. Perhaps father and son had to try on several selves before settling on one they could live with.

I remember a day, long ago, on a central Florida street. We'd just come out of the bank, and I must have asked him for Coca-Cola money. He dug deep into the pocket of his high-waisted pants and came out with a handful of change. Forty cents or so. "That's it, son, that's all we've got." And it thrilled me; it was a sign. That meant we would make it, because that's how it turned out in the movies. You've got to be down before you can rise. All he had to do was hold on to his little house and the little job he had, and in ten years he would have become a millionaire, like all his friends. Six months later, he lost it all.

When he was nearly fifty, he began the lone successful operation of his life, a furniture store in Pittsburgh. We worked through a Pittsburgh summer converting a landmark restaurant into a furniture store, sealing up the old meat locker, boarding up the old fireplace. We presented the bank with a *fait accompli,* and they gave him a loan to stock the store. And the amazing thing, for a family that had known only insecurity and failure, was that for seven years it succeeded. It got me through college, before a new woman entered his life and, once again, he lost everything.

Besides the cigarettes, I remember now the lingering smell of stale meat and the acrid, encaked soot from the fireplace. That it should come down to this—a father, odors only! He died with his stories intact, and if I am to bring him back, I must reconstruct him from smoke and memories. As I enter my perilous years, I find that he is inside me, we are becoming one. His traces surround me, though his world is gone, or going fast. Middle age is the final orphanage.

L. SPRAGUE DE CAMP

Talking to Ghosts

For forty-odd years, I have conversed with ghosts. Perhaps you think that, as a longtime writer of fantasy (more than twenty novels and eighty short stories in that genre), I believe in ghosts in the usual, supernatural sense. I do not. These phantoms of mine are "No things of gauzy mist, or rattling bones, / Or clanking chains, or marrow-freezing moans. . . ." They dwell only in my mind; they are memories of my parents.

My mother died in 1927, my father in 1945. Although I am thrice a grandfather, these specters still beguile me into conversation. I argue with them, boast to them and defend myself against their ready, if imagined, reproaches. When I travel, I mutter: "What do you think of this, Dad?" or, "Too bad you never saw that, Mother; you loved travel!" Ever, I strive against my ghosts' belief that I would never amount to much.

In 1939, when I married my incomparable Catherine, I asked my father: "What do you think of her?" He replied: "Wait five years and ask me then." Five years later, I repeated the question. He said: "Wait five years more and I'll tell you." The following year he died. Now that my superwoman and I have been married for forty-five years and still have a wonderful time together, I tell the paternal shade: "You must admit I've done at least one thing right!" When my hundredth book appeared, I subvocalized: "Come on, Dad! Aren't you a little proud?"

While I have no doubt that my parents loved me, they let me know in little ways that they, especially my father, thought me too

47

vague, unworldly and impractical to make it on my own. Unknowingly, they gave me a lifelong drive to prove them wrong. They made me a workaholic, an overachiever, an obsessive self-improver. When, on rare occasions, I relax—say, sitting beside a son's backyard pool to enjoy the sunshine—I have a guilty feeling that I ought to be lifting weights or studying my Portuguese.

My father was an upstate New York businessman, in real estate and lumber. He was basically an introvert, nervous, irritable, who for the sake of the business forced himself to assume the manner of a genial, gregarious extrovert; but the mask often slipped.

My mother was a daughter of my one distinguished forebear, Colonel Charles Ezra Sprague, a minor Civil War hero, president of a New York bank, professor at New York University, author of books on finance, inventor of the first bank-book calculating machine and a linguist who spoke seventeen languages. His wife was a noted headhunter of the "Upper West Side set," who proudly snared Oscar Wilde as a dinner guest on his 1882 American tour. An older relative once told me: "As usual, he insulted everybody." Although my mother had all the virtues but common sense, she and my father were divorced when I was in my teens. They remained friendly, however. She moved with her children to California, where she died at forty-four of an overdose of faith healing.

Both parents were heavy-handed disciplinarians. I got countless spankings. One that rankled for years was inflicted around 1913 for failing to find a drugstore on Columbus Avenue, whither my perfectionist mother had sent me on an errand. The store had put up a new sign, which I did not recognize. Long afterward, a psychologist told me I had a minor neurological handicap: low figure-ground perception. This means that if something I seek is out of place, I have a terrible time seeing it even in plain sight. Hence, I am fanatically neat and orderly, because that is the only way I can quickly find things when I want them.

Older kith and kin have said that my father treated me cruelly. So it might seem; but when I think what a high-strung, gabbling, generally obnoxious child I must have been, I cannot altogether blame him. One must bring up children of one's own to appreciate the travails that one put one's parents through. Therefore, I do not resent mine. In fact I loved them, not to the point of idolatry but with a certain cold-eyed realization of their faults and blunders.

Less excusably, my father never got around to treating me as a grown man. When Catherine and I were engaged, we lunched with him in New York. He talked to her as an adult but continued to allude condescendingly to me, aged thirty-one, as "the boy." I shriveled visibly. Perhaps that helps explain why, silly as it seems, a healthy septuagenarian with a happy home life, a decent professional standing and some grounds for self-satisfaction should still feel he must earn his parents' approval.

In senior high, I wanted to become a paleontologist and spend my days digging up dinosaurs. On his annual Christmas visit to his family, my father took me to a university professor to ask how to go about it. When, on our return, I happily announced my plans, my mother said: "I am dreadfully disappointed." Her reasoning was that scientists did not command enough income and social prestige.

After a conference about my career, my father proposed a sensible-seeming compromise. I was also interested in aircraft, so he said: "Why not send him to engineering school, so he'll always be able to earn a living? Then if he wants to go on with this science thing, we'll see."

So I graduated from California Tech as an aeronautical engineer—this was in the early 1930s, when the Great Depression lay upon the land and engineers were being fired, not hired. After some minor jobs, I got into freelance writing; save for the Hitlerian War, I have been at it ever since. Writing has enabled me, besides earning a living, to ride my boyhood fossil hobby by paleontological articles, books and stories.

My father lived to see my first two novels, a textbook, and forty-odd stories and articles in magazines. He seemed to take a quiet satisfaction in these, and told me of a comment by one of his friends on the humor in my tales.

Praise from Lyon de Camp, however, would have been quite out of character. So my youthful yearning for parental approval has never been slaked. Family ghosts still haunt my cortex and will do so until I "join the majority." Will our own two sons in turn feel that they must justify themselves to our wraiths?

JOHN BOWERS

King of the Hill

When a man has a brother, he is forced from the start into a deep rivalry that may well prepare him for some of life's later great battles. But a brother may also mire him in preadolescent squabbles. A brother makes a boy grow up fast but, in certain ways, keeps the man a child forever.

My earliest memory is of my brother throwing me on top of a tent, letting me roll down while I giggled in great glee, and then catching me a few feet from the ground. Even in diapers I knew we were involved in some sort of vital, complicated game.

My brother, Howard, was twelve when I came yelping aboard in Tennessee on a gray, windy morning. He came grumpily down the stairs in our frame house (where I was born in a chintz-curtained, second-floor bedroom) to report to a visiting neighbor, "They got a boy, I think."

He had been king of the hill before that—a dynamo touted for his ability to climb the highest tree in the county, dive off precipices into the deep, muddy Tennessee River, and survive typhoid fever when a country doctor had given him up for dead. He had lost all his hair with the fever, became as bald as a cue ball, and then had willed a mass of black curls to sprout. My first image of him was of a broad face, a wild shock of hair and two rows of white teeth—someone whose sole purpose was to keep me ever smaller and whipped back. When I began swatting baseballs with my pee-wee crowd, I could count on Howard ambling up, demanding the bat, and then slugging the ball over a line of tall oaks. "Run get it," he'd say, "so I can hit another."

We engaged in combat in wide and diverse ways; we continue it still, which isn't surprising. Freud himself, Ernest Jones reports, felt "guilty all his life because of his death wishes, based on jealousy, which he had cherished against his own little brother."

Many people get along quite well without a sibling, though. I watch a six-year-old boy, an only child, fill up an entire living room on a rainy day with a complicated Lego construction. I marvel at his self-sufficiency and power of concentration. I witness with a shudder my own son of five fling himself into a tantrum when his seven-year-old brother sneaks in an impromptu dance with his mother. I am mystified by siblings who have never competed, who get along magically—or, stranger still, do not have an influence on one another. A friend of mine in New York has a couple of brothers who live here, and he goes years without seeing them, without thinking of them, it seems. But then, he claims to have hated his mother—and perhaps that's why he had no reason to struggle with his brothers and get to know them.

I certainly got to know my brother, and I learned early what I had to compete against. He was one of upper east Tennessee's great athletes; he "lettered" in five sports—a fact he never ceased casually alluding to. I remember sitting in a bone-chilling rain watching him star in a championship football game. I walked home with water squirting out of my Thom McAn shoes. I can see him bringing some of his teammates by the house later while my teeth still chattered. He is swaggering, smoking a wooden-tipped Roi-Tan, and my mother is chiding him affectionately. "But we won the championship," he's saying, hugging her and getting her to act coquettish. My father is quoting statistics from the game, and I'm looking at my big brother in wonder. If I could ever stand there in such glory!

I tried—Lord, how I tried. My brother's nickname was Tiger during the football season and Trickshot for basketball. I was called Bones all the time—and that tells you everything. I was terribly proud of my brother, but never above sabotage. Once, when he was compelled to baby-sit for me while our parents were out, he arranged a date with a golden-haired goddess in an angora sweater and took me along. He parked by some woods and went off with her and a blanket, leaving me in the car to look at the moon. "You'll be okay, kid," he said. "Just sit still."

A few minutes later, alone, I bellowed his name. I kept howling until he returned in a white fury, the girl a pace behind, and drove away.

He made sure to tease me about girls when my turn did come to date. He made sure, too, that I couldn't best him at any sort of game whatsoever. When he went away to become a naval officer in World War II, I put up a basketball hoop in the side yard, practiced trick layups till past dark, and challenged him to one-on-one when he came home on leave. I was ahead—until he began holding my belt. I next learned a deadly maneuver in hand-to-hand combat from a U.S. Army Ranger. When my brother paraded into the house in a Navy officer's brilliant white, cronies in tow, my mother and father in attendance, I said, "Howard, could I show you this wrestling hold I just learned?"

"Sure, kid—and I'll show you how to break it."

I took his hand, and a second later he was flopping on the floor like a fish, screaming that I'd broken his arm and begging to be released. My father, in his last days, was still talking about "the time you threw old Howardie to the floor with that jujitsu hold."

My brother and I competed for our parents' affection right up to their very last moments on earth. After my brother's black shock of hair had long since turned wispy and gray, after I had taken to wearing reading glasses, we argued as if we were teenagers over the disposal of books from our old home when it was closed. To this day my brother teases me about June Loudy, a pubescent next-door neighbor of long ago, and I go through the motions of being angry.

But the lines are blurred now—like my eyesight—between rivalry and affection. No one makes me laugh the way he does. No one can make me madder. Our mother romanticized New York, and every Monday in Tennessee a fat copy of the Sunday *New*

York Times was in the mailbox. Is it any wonder that Howard lived for stretches in the city and that I do now permanently? He's retired from coaching football and lives in Tennessee, but he returns to New York occasionally. I think I can sense him by the time he reaches New Jersey.

DAVID SHERWOOD

Discarded

My younger brother, Andy, lives in Paris and I in Hartford. Neither of us ever has any money to speak of, so we hardly get to see each other or even to talk on the phone. We keep in touch by sending letters back and forth across the Atlantic.

Judging by the letters, I think of Andy as a fine, fine writer. But lately, he has been writing a book, and, based on the chapters he's sent me, I'd say that publishers won't be encouraging. Andy's book is about our small family and, most especially, Andy's unhappy childhood some forty years ago. What happens, I think, is that as Andy writes about his childhood, he sort of becomes again the child he once was—a child having a hard time of it. The change he undergoes changes his writing for the worse.

Andy was a boy whose father seemed to show him next to no sign of love or respect. "Next to no" will allow for signals of affection and esteem perhaps apparent at the time, but of which we have no recollection. We had the same father, but he was not the same with the two of us. He was all I could ever have wished for, but he never took a shine to Andy.

Andy liked to try on women's clothes; he would draw picture after picture of plume-hatted hoop-skirted women; his favorite playmates were girls; his gestures were effeminate. It was all beyond endurance for our father, who, aside from being the schoolteacher to whom a Class of 1945 yearbook was dedicated, was a graceful athlete, a deadpan poker player and a man who had a way with the ladies. His small son's achievements—good comportment, words spelled right—were, so far as one could tell, scant source of pleasure to him. Our father had a wry sense of humor and a quick-silver laugh, but he seemed to lose his light touch in my brother's presence. Altogether then, Andy found little to assure him that he was in any way precious to his father. When we were still kids, our father, barely forty, died.

We'd been raised in Delaware, on a boarding school's campus, among people we'd known forever: teachers, support staff, their wives and children. Nobody there made an issue of Andy. But once our father died, we moved to Wilmington so our mother could find work. And in the Wilmington of 1945, among my new seventh-grade pals, Andy seemed suddenly exotic. What had bothered my father about him now bothered me. So I was glad we were enrolled in separate schools, glad that Andy was away at piano lessons when my friends dropped by, glad not to have to introduce him or even have them see him. I remember once meeting a boy who'd just transferred to my school from Andy's. The name Sherwood regis-tered with him right off. "You got a fairy named Andy for a brother?" he asked.

I kept Andy at more than arm's length for years thereafter. But once I'd become the father of a boy myself, we became brothers again. What happened, I think, was two things. Andy liked being Uncle Andy. It gave him a valued mainstream credential. And I, living a humdrummish life, found myself now pleased to tell friends about this gay brother of mine who lived in New York, as he did then, with an illustrator of medical textbooks and relaxed at restaurants like Max's Kansas City. In those days I wished to seem more interesting than I knew myself to be. Acknowledging Andy and visiting him was a way to do it. More than that, I'd be in his living room watching him amusing my son, and I'd feel shame for having never been an older brother to him. One day, I called up two of his former friends and threatened to rip their place up if they didn't quickly return to Andy some furniture they owed him money for. It was the first favor I'd ever done him.

Andy's adult life, in my eyes, has been one of accomplishment. He tutors private pupils in voice and piano; he once taught harpsichord; he has sung countertenor with chamber groups, and these are not his primary endeavors. Mostly, he teaches English to French adults whose tuitions are paid by their employers. The head of his school, he wrote in 1981, "has told me I'm her best teacher. She's been putting me with new students who've come to test the school out for their companies, so that, if they like it, more will follow. I, then, have to create the most favorable impression, a sort of . . . seduction. . . ."

My brother, in fact, has fashioned for himself a life that leans often on the seducer's art. Apart from his classroom role, he is a photographer whose prints are, once in a while, exhibited and sold in galleries, and he must coax from acquaintances who pose for him a certain moroseness of expression that flavors his photographs and causes the public and an occasional magazine or museum to buy them. Engaged in the 1960s for anonymous bit parts in opera—no singing, no dancing—Andy was reproved sometimes for diverting attention from the principals. "Mr. Rudel at the New York City Opera," he said, "told me everyone was watching me in *The Flaming Angel* instead of the heroine. Mr. Bing at the Met told me the same thing in *Andrea Chenier*."

"I turn many fewer heads than I used to," he now writes. "A friend and I have a pastime we call 'Existing,' which consists of guessing if a stranger is aware of us, and if so, of which one, or whether we obviously don't 'exist' and are looked through, not at." These strangers, by whom Andy and his friend define their "existence," are boys and men first seen from afar, then from up close as they pass one another on the sidewalk. "When we do get a glance," he adds, "it is usually for Patrice, who is 15 years younger."

Andy can handle the increasing absence of glances from strangers. But he is encumbered by having never seduced an affectionate glance from our father. I want to believe that, had our father lived longer, he'd have made his peace with Andy. Their love of music and language, their storytelling skills, their parallel teaching careers—there is common ground there now. But I also know, as a father of five, how tough it is to look with new eyes upon a child who baffles you, disappoints you.

Andy will live out his years not knowing how things might have worked out between them. Each draft of his book that arrives shows how punishing his recollections are, how infirm they make him, and how hard it is to get out from under the shadow of a father who hasn't loved you.

BRENT STAPLES

A Brother's Murder

It has been more than two years since my telephone rang with the news that my younger brother Blake—just twenty-two years old—had been murdered. The young man who killed him was only twenty-four. Wearing a ski mask, he emerged from a car, fired six times at close range with a massive .44 Magnum, then fled. The two had once been inseparable friends. A senseless rivalry—beginning, I think, with an argument over a girlfriend—escalated from posturing, to threats, to violence, to murder. The way the two were living, death could have come to either of them from anywhere. In fact, the assailant had already survived multiple gunshot wounds from an accident much like the one in which my brother lost his life.

As I wept for Blake I felt wrenched backward into events and circumstances that had seemed light-years gone. Though a decade apart, we both were raised in Chester, Pennsylvania, an angry, heavily black, heavily poor, industrial city southwest of Philadelphia. There, in the 1960s, I was introduced to mortality, not by the old and failing, but by beautiful young men who lay wrecked after sudden explosions of violence. The first, I remembered from my fourteenth year—Johnny, brash lover of fast cars, stabbed to death two doors from my house in a fight over a pool game. The next year, my teenage cousin, Wesley, whom I loved very much, was shot dead. The summers blur. Milton, an angry young neighbor, shot a crosstown rival, wounding him badly. William, another

59

teenage neighbor, took a shotgun blast to the shoulder in some urban drama and displayed his bandages proudly. His brother, Leonard, severely beaten, lost an eye and donned a black patch. It went on.

I recall not long before I left for college, two local Vietnam veterans—one from the Marines, one from the Army—arguing fiercely, nearly at blows about which outfit had done the most in the war. The most killing, they meant. Not much later, I read a magazine article that set that dispute in a context. In the story, a noncommissioned officer—a sergeant, I believe—said he would pass up any number of affluent, suburban-born recruits to get hard-core soldiers from the inner city. They jumped into the rice paddies with "their manhood on their sleeves," I believe he said. These two items—the veterans arguing and the sergeant's words—still characterize for me the circumstances under which black men in their teens and twenties kill one another with such frequency. With a touchy paranoia born of living battered lives, they are desperate to be *real* men. Killing is only machismo taken to the extreme. Incursions to be punished by death were many and minor, and they remain so: they include stepping on the wrong toe, literally; cheating in a drug deal; simply saying "I dare you" to someone holding a gun; crossing territorial lines in a gang dispute. My brother grew up to wear his manhood on his sleeve. And when he died, he was in that group—black, male and in its teens and early twenties—that is far and away the most likely to murder or be murdered.

I left the East Coast after college, spent the mid- and late 1970s in Chicago as a graduate student, taught for a time, then became a journalist. Within ten years of leaving my hometown, I was over-educated and "upwardly mobile," ensconced on a quiet, tree-lined street where voices raised in anger were scarcely ever heard. The telephone, like some grim umbilical, kept me connected to the old world with news of deaths, imprisonings and misfortune. I felt emotionally beaten up. Perhaps to protect myself, I added a psychological dimension to the physical distance I had already achieved. I rarely visited my hometown. I shut it out.

As I fled the past, so Blake embraced it. On Christmas of 1983, I traveled from Chicago to a black section of Roanoke, Virginia, where he then lived. The desolate public housing projects, the hopeless, idle young men crashing against one another—these reminded me of the embittered town we'd grown up in. It was a place where once I would have been comfortable, or at least sure of myself. Now, hearing of my brother's forays into crime, his scrapes with police and street thugs, I was scared, unsteady on foreign terrain.

I saw that Blake's romance with the street life and the hustler image had flowered dangerously. One evening that late December, standing in some Roanoke dive among drug dealers and grim, hair-trigger losers, I told him I feared for his life. He had affected the image of the tough he wanted to be. But behind the dark glasses and the swagger, I glimpsed the baby-faced toddler I'd once watched over. I nearly wept. I wanted desperately for him to live. The young think themselves immortal, and a dangerous light shone in his eyes as he spoke laughingly of making fools of the policemen who had raided his apartment looking for drugs. He cried out as I took his right hand. A line of stitches lay between the thumb and index finger. Kickback from a shotgun, he explained, nothing serious. Gunplay had become part of his life.

I lacked the language simply to say: Thousands have lived this for you and died. I fought the urge to lift him bodily and shake him. This place and the way you are living smells of death to me, I said. Take some time away, I said. Let's go downtown tomorrow and buy a plane ticket anywhere, take a bus trip, anything to get away and cool things off. He took my alarm casually. We arranged to meet the following night—an appointment he would not keep. We embraced as though through glass. I drove away.

As I stood in my apartment in Chicago holding the receiver that evening in February 1984, I felt as though part of my soul had been cut away. I questioned myself then, and I still do. Did I not reach back soon enough or earnestly enough for him? For weeks I awoke crying from a recurrent dream in which I chased him, urgently trying to get him to read a document I had, as though reading it would protect him from what had happened in waking life. His eyes shining like black diamonds, he smiled and danced just beyond my grasp. When I reached for him, I caught only the space where he had been.

LOVE AND

MARRIAGE

FRANK MacSHANE

Love Letters

"Call me!" says the telephone company ad, so after their weekend together, he does. At first the line is busy, and he wonders whom she's talking to, but after a while he gets through. "Hello, darling," he says. "How are you?"

"Okay. I was hoping you'd call. How was the traffic?"

"Terrible," he replies. "Also, it's pouring rain here."

"Rain? Here it's just cold."

"Well, it's raining here. And also pretty cold."

So the conversation limps along until finally he says, "Take care of yourself. I'll see you next week." She replies, "I love you," and he says, "I love you, too." They hang up.

He feels disappointed. The expected intimacy of the telephone has produced so little. But today, what is a man to do? Had he been John Keats, living two hundred years ago, he would have sat down at his desk and written these words to Fanny Brawne: "I never knew before, what such a love as you have made me feel, was; I did not believe in it, my Fancy was afraid of it, lest it should burn me up."

Keats's message is clear, but for all its vaunted pretensions about communication, the modern age seems to have deprived men of one of the greatest pleasures of being in love, the writing of love letters. Parting is such sweet sorrow because the pleasure of memory remains, along with the desire to write about it. Keats said that he looked "upon fine phrases as a lover," but the reverse is also true: love makes phrasemakers of us all.

They have spent the weekend in New York, and in his letter afterwards, he reminds her of their dinner together at the Plaza and how they walked along Fifth Avenue, looking at the shop windows. "It was a magic moment for me," he writes, "alone but together in the crowd, with your arm in mine. I want it to be that way from now on."

She writes back, "I am wearing the bracelet you gave me. It sparkles under the lamp, and I think of our nights in New York with the lights of the city shimmering all around us."

These exchanges sound all right on paper, but they wouldn't do on the phone. Passionate and intimate messages seem unsuitable these days when they are spoken. But, crazy in love, he may write, "My love for you grows every day, like flowers bursting forth in spring. Every morning there are new things about you to admire, and you have become an enchanted garden in which I live. I no longer love you. I adore you."

Yet sometimes, even on paper, reticence can be more effective than hyperbole. He reminds her of another time they were together, but instead of being explicit and detailed, he writes, "I miss waking up with the azaleas." She will remember the bedroom, their first night together, and her own fantasy will provide the particulars. This approach has other merits as well, for since love letters are documents, they can fall into the wrong hands. Lovers in the Middle Ages avoided this kind of trouble by inventing a language of flowers to express their feelings.

Since no love affair always runs smoothly, the letter is often more politic than the telephone. The words spoken may give one message, but the tone of voice will give another. Also, letters are less impulsive. There is no literary equivalent of slamming down the receiver. Time, distance and good manners modify the anguish of lovers' quarrels; second thoughts can be expressed rather than be left in the lover's throat after he has hung up.

Love letters reveal unexpected qualities in the writer, transforming curmudgeons and cynics into gentle pushovers. Who would guess the name of the author of this letter, which is addressed to "my darling"? It ends: "I don't at all regret the haphazard, unhappy life I've led up till now because I don't think that without it I could love you so much. Goodnight my blessed child. I love you more than I can find words to tell you." The author? Evelyn Waugh.

Writers have long acknowledged the need for inspiration, but love letters allow them to exercise talents they may have buried under the demands of their professional careers. John O'Hara was known for cool and dispassionate books such as *Pal Joey* and *Appointment in Samarra,* but he also wrote this in a letter: "I am so in love with you it is a wonderment, a word which I just now looked up in the Concise Oxford and it doesn't mean what I thought it did, so my love is not a wonderment. The Concise Oxford does not make sufficiently clear what wonderment does mean, but I know what I mean. I mean it as a wonder, like the wonder of the world, and I could have said so in the first place. I don't often use words I don't know the meaning of. Well, then, let me say it's no wonder I love you."

In love letters a man can make little jokes, he can tease in a way that is difficult or unnatural in person or on the phone. "Love me, love my dog," she has intimated when they were together. He didn't love the dog, and for good reason. But knowing that nothing could be accomplished by his saying so, he writes: "I spent yesterday afternoon trying to repair the socks that Mocha chewed. I hope he didn't suffer any indigestion or wool poisoning, for as you know, I am interested in his health. In more ways than one. Sometimes he seems to have been attracted to the heels of my socks, sometimes to the tops. Like his mistress, he has varied interests. At any rate, I'm glad he preferred the extremities, because my shoes cover up the holes in the toes and my trousers hide the ragged tops. I hope you'll tell Mocha how much I appreciate his consideration."

Like everything else, writing love letters can be dangerous. Men who use love letters as a vehicle for philosophizing are headed for trouble. To write about values, the future, even death is tempting, because the lover wants to protect his beloved and plan for their years together. Unfortunately, letters on such abstractions tend to become prolix, windy and pretentious; the envelopes grow fatter

and heavier, the intervals between the lady's replies grow longer.
Then, inevitably, she lets him know it's all over. A postcard arrives
with a four-liner by Dorothy Parker:

> Whose love is given over-well
> Shall look on Helen's face in Hell;
> Whilst they whose love is thin and wise
> May view John Knox in Paradise.

JOHN TIRMAN

Romance by Commute

Carol received the telephone call on April Fools' Day, the day I began a new job in Cambridge, Massachusetts, and she called immediately with the news. The editor of a new magazine in New York, an exciting new magazine, wanted her to fly down for an interview. The thrill in her voice was palpable. The encouragement I gave her was limp. A month later he offered her the job, and by the time summer arrived our three-year romance had added another adjective: "commuting."

For the ensuing year, we traveled to one place or another to meet every weekend, arranged to spend our vacations together, schemed to get the extra Friday or Monday away from the office and argued about who would give up which job and move. We enriched Amtrak, the Eastern Air Lines Shuttle and Ma Bell. We thought about buying a place in between and settled for a summer rental in the Berkshires. We kept stiff upper lips.

Soon enough we learned that, although the traveling was tiresome, it was manageable. We had lived in both cities and enjoyed their different pleasures, and, as much as possible, we created two homes. About once a month we'd meet at some third location—the Connecticut shore, Saratoga Springs or Vermont—to break the routine. Not surprisingly, the weekends together were warm and exciting. The pettiness and boredom that can creep into any relationship were vanquished in our weekly trysts. Even the most fearsome ogre of separation—jealousy—never ensnared us, though the opportunities for cheating were apparent. Once in a while an irrational, unfounded suspicion would surge through my body like an electric jolt. But the trust was implicit—no 6 A.M. calls, no "Where were you when I phoned last night?"—and rewarded.

Away from Carol five days and nights a week, I inevitably changed, however, and did so in unexpected ways. The elements of the separation I most feared in advance—loneliness, jealousy, a breakup—never threatened me seriously. But I was thrust into a new and different condition of manhood: attached but alone, part of a couple whose other half was absent most of the time. As a result, my appreciation of friendship sharpened. A half-dozen friends freshened me with dinners, conversation, after-work drinks or sporting events, and I found I was re-creating the kinds of attachments I had before meeting Carol: old-friend couples to whom I confided everything, tennis and drinking buddies, gossipy office-mates, and women with whom my friendship was platonic. To my dismay, I also discovered that many of the friendships Carol and I had formed as a couple didn't work for me as a part-time single. It was as if we had divorced and they were forced to avoid me.

There is an intrinsic value, I found, in friends unrelated to one's couplehood. One evening I entertained three friends from college in the Harvard Square apartment I rented after Carol went to New York. We had just finished dinner and were recalling old times when I suggested, "Let's name names, just list people we haven't seen or thought of for a decade." We did, and it became a kind of game, a catharsis even. Laughing, we shouted the names and each loosed a flood of nearly forgotten stories. It was something I wouldn't have done had Carol been present.

What I didn't foresee was how my being alone would affect me. At first I thought of absorbing myself in activity to chase away loneliness. I vowed to sign up for Chinese cooking classes, learn a foreign language and sit in on lectures at Harvard. I did none of these. I promised to work out intensively at squash or swimming and joined a nearby YMCA. I never went. My failure to consummate these earnest time-fillers derived not from laziness alone, but from a stronger, more basic and healthier urge—the attraction of solitude.

My solitude was like a warm cocoon, woven from the simple desire to enjoy myself. Days were filled with the social chatter and business meetings of the office, so evenings were a chance to escape from the calisthenics of human interaction. The solitude I naturally gravitated toward was not one of painful isolation and pining away for Carol; it was robust, amused, careless. On a typical night alone, I would shop for myself at the grocery, then spend the first half-hour at home splitting wood out back. The fire in the wood stove would be kindled, supper would be slapped together, the radio news might be played, a Dick Francis mystery would be opened, and I, alone, would drift into that exquisite languor of dreaming, planning, remembering—unencumbered by the needs of a partner, unbothered by the social graces demanded by guests, and, most important, free from the instinctual mate-hunting urge that dominates the night and day of the single man.

That solitude, the nightly, casual exploration of the self, gave me, although no earth-shattering revelations were uncovered, a fresh sense of self-reliance and self-comfort. Inevitably, I carried these qualities with me into the part of me that was half a couple.

Carol's dream job turned out to be not so paradisiacal after all; she left after a year of turmoil and moved back to Cambridge. I felt no more than a moment of ambivalence. I wanted her back—the strains of travel and the cost were becoming intolerable—and it was fortunate that no divisive decisions had to be made about our careers.

The pleasure of solitude and my newly shaped friendships did not vanish upon her return, though they diminished as the daily constituents of my life. Yet the effect of that year is lasting. When the commuting started I would say to friends, "Well, it's a chance to find out if we're for real." That was a cavalier comment, and, finally, it anticipated only half of the coming challenge. The commute was the test of our love, and we passed it admirably. But the year proved something else, that *I* was for real, that I could thrive as a solitary man. And, as a result, I have become a better man apart and together.

ERIC LAX

Wedding Rings

Before things got serious with my wife, I didn't think much about wedding rings. They meant trouble. In my youth, I spent many Saturdays robed as an acolyte helping my father, an Episcopal clergyman, marry couples. Among the things I saw were a lot of wedding rings getting stuck on swollen, clammy knuckles.

For me, jewelry was something other people wore, many of them women. I did have a college ring that my parents bought for me. It was very big. It had an amethyst in the center and made me look like a bishop. I got it just before joining the Peace Corps and going to an island in the Truk lagoon, but I never wore it there. I kept it in a toilet kit, which I left in a pension in Rome on my way back to the United States in 1968. I discovered the loss several hours later when I unpacked in Florence. I called the Roman pension, but they not only hadn't seen the toilet kit or the ring, they hadn't heard of me. It was the last time I thought about having a ring until, as I said, things got serious with my wife.

That was two and half years ago. I was thirty-seven and had never married. One day I woke up and realized that my thirty-eighth birthday would be my last as a single man. I liked the idea. I was aware that I had become very adept at being alone while still conducting a full life. I was a very good one-man band, which is precisely the point. A one-man band has rhythm and displays a remarkable dexterity, but lacks harmony. And it turned out that I had come to the point where making music with someone else was preferable to making it by myself. Besides, I was wildly in love.

So there I was, faced with all those big decisions that follow *the* big decision: where to live; how to afford to live there; whom to invite to the wedding; and, immediately at hand, whether both my intended and I would have rings.

It wasn't long before I knew that I wanted to have one. Not wearing a wedding ring, it seemed to me, was pretending that you weren't really married, which never works. People "look" married. It leaves its mark. Among other things, a ring acknowledges that. Sometimes it does so in ways people would prefer it didn't. The most self-deceiving example of this is a man who takes off his ring when flying on a business trip. I've seen this dozens of times. A major flaw in this strategy is that a ring shields the skin from the sun, and thus its image is there even when it is not. A white band on an otherwise tanned hand stands out like Las Vegas at night. There would be none of that for me, I decided. The ring would go on and stay on.

The next question was: What would the ring look like? My first thought was that it would be a simple, thin band, neither ostentatious nor obtrusive—slim, delicate, elegant, yet substantial. Little did I know.

Having obtained the name of a man who creates quite spectacular rings and bracelets, my bride-to-be and I went to see him. It was a few hours before the traffic for the Fourth of July weekend broke loose, but we figured there was plenty of time to order two gold bands and then to get on an early train to Connecticut for the holiday. We mentioned this to the jeweler, who told us that *he* was spending the weekend in Scotland. He was taking the Concorde.

I described the ring I had in mind. He shook his head. "It will disappear on your hand," he said.

I looked skeptical, and he produced a ring similar to the one I had described. I tried it on. It disappeared on my hand.

"How about something like this?" he said, pulling a very wide band from a drawer. "It was my grandfather's." It looked like a piece of gold pipe. I slipped it on. My hand disappeared. But to my surprise, the idea was right. He put masking tape over part of it and asked me to imagine the ring as slimmer. I held out my hand and looked. I put it down by my side and looked. I wasn't sure what I saw.

"Take a look in the mirror," the jeweler said. I sat at the desk, turning my hand. Then I stood sideways and tried to be dispassionate about what I was seeing. It was no use. I have trouble looking at shoes in a store mirror and deciding whether they look right or not. Trying that approach with a ring put even more distance between me and my objectivity. I felt silly. An hour after beginning, we had turned to making paper rings of varying widths. I was still trying both to be natural and to imagine gold in the place of foolscap.

And then it happened. After the latest model had been taped on, the three of us exclaimed, almost in unison: "That's it." "It" was huge. My slim band had become a chunk.

I had visions of its ripping through my best man's coat pocket, but when the time came, my ring passed from hand to hand without a problem. It cleared my knuckle like an Olympic hurdler and came to rest as if drawn by a magnet.

A wedding ring is an ancient symbol, but one that has always been contemporary. The band my wife gave me, like the one I gave her, is an expression of continuity and wholeness, the closed circle of our vows and bond. It is a subtle, constant reminder of them and of the special relationship that is a marriage. It is particularly good at doing that during tough moments. There are times, after we've exploded over something important or insignificant—it doesn't really matter—when I've looked at my ring and my anger has been swept away. All that the ring means floods my mind.

For a while after we were married, when friends asked to see my ring, I would stick out both arms in front of me, the left hand a little farther out than the right, as if the weight of the ring had stretched my arm. The fact is, the ring is a token of my stretched life. I think of this often. I also like to think that as our single-digit anniversaries pass into the teens, then into a score and greater, I will continue to remember this. I hope it won't be simply because, as happened to a man I know, my finger will have enlarged so that the ring is embedded in it. My ring comes off, but seldom—only when I do messy chores around the house. One of those came up recently, a repair job on the washing machine. For some time afterward, I had an odd sensation, a feeling that I couldn't quite explain. Then I looked at my left hand and knew. My ring was still off, and I felt naked.

ANTHONY GIARDINA

Competing with Bruce

Not long ago, my wife began an obsession with Bruce Springsteen.

I tried to overcome my initial jealousy—it was no small thing—by an effort of understanding. She was working as a baker at the time Springsteen's album *Born in the U.S.A.* was released, and the radio stations could not play enough of him. All day long she pounded bread in a hot bakery, a job she had long ago become bored with, while a sexy voice came over the airwaves, asking her to come out onto the front porch, to hop into his car and let the wind blow through her hair, to allow him to drive all night just to buy her some shoes. So all right, I reasoned. Who in the midst of tough, hot labor wouldn't be enticed by such sentiments? I waited, with a kind of testy patience, for her to outgrow her summer infatuation.

In September, a well-connected friend was able to get us tickets to Bruce's concert in Hartford. I thought it might be a good idea if she went without me. Too easily I could imagine myself sitting there, arms folded, an oppressive presence keeping her from getting up and carrying on to her heart's content. Underneath, I did not really want to be present when the woman for whom I had, until recently, been romantic object enough first laid eyes on the man who, I feared, was coming to replace me. I went. It wasn't as difficult as I'd imagined it to be, but neither was I swept up by the force that is Bruce. I tried hard, but I could feel her disappointment beside me. I wasn't, after all, going to be able to follow her down this road. It was then that I had my first inkling that something larger than I'd guessed was going on, but it would be several months before I fully caught on.

There are extenuating circumstances that go a way toward explaining some of this. Two years ago, we moved from Manhattan to a town in western Massachusetts for reasons no more complicated than I thought it would be a good place to write a novel. That kind of decision has not been untypical: we have generally done things, made decisions, because of my needs, not hers.

When I met my wife, she was an actress, but over the course of time, and at least in part because of the demands of becoming a wife and mother, she made baking a profession, honing her skills at restaurants and bakeries but never taking those skills too seriously. There was our daughter to take care of, and the vicarious excitement of seeing her husband's plays produced or a book published. Something changed when we moved here: the filter put up by living in New York was removed, and there it was, just plain *life,* for want of a better word, all around us. For maybe the first time (we were lovers even before she left home), she was faced with the removal of all the roles, all the ways of defining herself, that had been standing between her and the singularity of what she was actually going to do with her life. Her husband, the writer, and her child, growing up, melted a little into the landscape; her own image had started to come scarily forward.

The questions she's been confronting for the last year or so are different from mine. In a more direct way than I am yet able to, she deals with aging and mortality and simple dailiness. She endures work that is unchallenging, and tries, in an honorable way, to come to grips. She is preparing to go back to school, for a long hitch, to study midwifery. In so doing, she's facing the fact that she will probably never be the actress she once wanted to be, that youth and beauty are only on loan, and that plans must be made for the days of their absence. Then suddenly here's this voice on the radio, saying *"Don't surrender, don't give in,"* all it takes to keep the future from happening is a kind of wild resistance. Face it, girl: we were born to run.

He offers the thrill of the boy who comes along and says the opposite of what a husband in his mid-thirties can't really help saying, even subliminally: it's time to settle down and take our place among the others, the good but somehow boring people who raise children, work at jobs and lead unexceptional lives. *Forget* that, Bruce insists. Come into my car. Let's ride fast. The moment is all.

Of course, he's saying a lot more than that. His message goes deeper, and I know she hears him in his entirety, hears the sympathy and despair as well as the escape. But it's the escape that started it, no question. I know that, in a very real way, she wants to get into that car and run away from the future she has chosen. The man she married is a slow driver. Cautious. He stops at lights.

The day Bruce got married, she was silent at dinner, as I imagined women all over America were silent, and I made the mistake of laughing at her reaction. When I asked her about it, she gave me an answer I hadn't expected. It wasn't, after all, that she'd been secretly harboring the wish that he'd come and sweep her away. It was simply that she saw his life in heroic terms and took comfort from the fact that he seemed to exist in such a pure, unfallen state. His marrying a well-to-do model had knocked him clean off the pedestal.

For the last several months she has been trying to get adjusted to having a tarnished hero. In a way, this has made me feel closer to Bruce, more accepting. I've been tarnished myself, in her eyes, too many times to count. But in the last year, I think maybe I've learned some valuable lessons about the separate dignity of the woman I love, about her quest, separate from mine. And how, along with those things, there goes the necessity for separate heroes.

LANCE COMPA

The Faithful Desperado

I just completed seven years of marriage without having to scratch the famous itch. It's not something I dwell on, but when I speculate—usually idly—on having an affair, I'm surprised at having been faithful since my wedding.

Fidelity doesn't fit a self-image shaped by the sportings of a normal young adulthood. There were different loves of varying lengths and passions, some of them concurrent, before my wife and I got married. When that happened, at thirty, I felt like the Desperado in the Eagles ballad of that name: come down from my fences to let somebody love me, but still a hard cowboy at heart.

I suppose my marriage vows were sincere, but good intentions were tempered by skepticism. I didn't see myself as Dagwood Bumstead, or Ralph Cramden or Chester Riley. I still wanted to be Archie Goodwin or Travis McGee. In the normal course of work that brings me together with interesting, attractive women, surely I would one day succumb—not entirely a victim—to the fever of an affair or at least a fling. It hasn't happened.

Publicly confessing fidelity is a risky step, hard to do without sounding sanctimonious. The supposed return to traditional values is the last bandwagon I'd want to ride. Then there's the risk of hypocrisy. I can't guarantee that this streak of fidelity won't end. The only way out is to confess ambivalence. I'm not so sure I want to be faithful. With both of us working, raising kids and running a household, married life takes on a draining routine. Lingering mornings of love play are long gone now; little feet and little stomachs and quirky faucets and job deadlines see to that, just as they lengthen the intervals between loving nights.

I know this is a normal, healthy, happy life that I'm intellectually committed to not betraying. But emotionally, it's not easy. In a busy home, the relentless demands of keeping things organized bring a hankering for an uncomplicated liaison. This isn't just a male trip, either; my wife feels the same pressures. Will neither of us again know the helpless thrill of a new love? It's an unsettling thought only halfway through life.

Fortunately for fidelity, it's not a simple contest of intellectual constancy versus renegade emotion. There's no such thing as an uncomplicated affair. Besides the excitement, I remember the lies, the sneaking and remorse that accompanied extra-relationship affairs when I was single. Even when I wasn't serious about a steady girlfriend, I could barely face her after seeing someone else.

If I felt so bad when I was uncommitted, I can't see myself now being faithless, then coming home, without dying of shame. My wife and I share the bundle of big and little intimacies that make up our life together—making love when we get the chance, understanding unspoken signals, saying "I love you" and meaning it, teaching our two-year-old "Star Light, Star Bright," sharing the successes and frustrations of our work, trading our standing jokes and our standing arguments. If I violated any of this I'd feel as if "Cheater" were etched across my teeth every time I tried to force a smile. Avoiding that distress is a powerful emotional check on infidelity.

And yet, I'm still drawn to someone who seems special. Sometimes speculation moves beyond the idle and banter beyond flirting. There it is on the horizon and moving closer: involvement. But you can tell when the person and the setting and the moment for an affair are nearing coincidence. Maneuvering is fun, like walking along the edge of a cliff. The contemplation is thrilling, the prospect is daunting, the leap might be liberating, the consequences disastrous. Better to step back in the end. Better to step back early on.

On the other hand, maybe my reasons are more practical. For one thing, who has the time? We go flat out all week with kids, work, meetings and chores from six thirty in the morning until eleven at night, when we crash for a half-hour of reading and talking. I couldn't squeeze in any extracurricular activity even if I wanted to. Then, too, being born ten years too soon to be caught in the herpes scare is a relief. Why risk the security that comes with being married and monogamous?

It could be I'm just slowing down. I can still remember some driving moves to the hoop playing basketball in my twenties; now I settle for midrange jump shots. Does the hankering settle, too? I didn't find any substance to the seven-year-itch business; year seven wasn't much different from year one. But maybe it happens so gradually that it's not noticed.

Maybe, too, all this is an exercise in reverse braggadocio, a responsible adult's version of locker-room disclosures. From appearances, most of my men friends are unperturbably faithful. Am I the only one who gives it a thought? Hell, maybe their wives are doing it. Maybe my wife is. She has all the temptations I do, and being beautiful, smart, sexy and funny, she's more eagerly sought. Kidding each other about conquests is one of our inside jokes; who knows for sure when there might be something to it? Maybe many older men who felt in their late thirties as I do now are smiling and saying "Sonny, just you wait." For my part, I can't see why the next seven years should be any different, either for happiness in marriage or opportunities outside of marriage, than the last seven, and I made it through them.

In the end, the surprise at being faithful is topped by another surprise: it's the very ambivalence that makes fidelity and marriage work. That tension means we're not taking each other for granted; we're sticking together, itch notwithstanding. It boils down to feeling special, not just that my wife loves only me, but that this vulnerability of mine belongs only to her. The joke is on the Desperado: he came down from his fences and let himself love somebody. I may wistfully rue the opportunities missed, but I'll have a deeper satisfaction, and at bottom, I think, a supreme excitement, in the love we share. Will it stay like this? I hope so.

STEVE TESICH

An Amateur Marriage

Everyone told me that when I turned sixteen some great internal change would occur. I truly expected the lights to go down on my former life and come up again on a new, far more enchanting one. It didn't work. Nothing happened. When asked by others, I lied and said yes, I did feel a great change had taken place. They lied and told me they could see it in me.

They lied again when I turned eighteen. There were rumors that I was now a "man." I noticed no difference, but I pretended to have all the rumored symptoms of manhood. Even though these mythical milestones, these rituals of passage, were not working for me, I still clung to the belief that they should, and I lied and said they were.

My twenty-first birthday was the last birthday I celebrated. The rituals weren't working, and I was tired of pretending I was changing. I was merely growing—adding on rooms for all the kids who were still me to live in. At twenty-one, I was single but a family man nevertheless.

All these birthday celebrations helped to prepare me for the greatest myth of all: marriage. Marriage comes with more myths attached to it than a six-volume set of ancient Greek history. Fortunately for me, by the time I decided to get married I didn't believe in myths anymore.

It was a very hot day in Denver, and I think Becky and I decided to get married because we knew the city hall was air-conditioned. It

An Amateur Marriage   83

was a way of hanging around a cool place for a while. I had forgotten to buy a wedding ring, but Becky was still wearing the ring from her previous marriage, so we used that one. It did the job. She had to take it off and then put it back on again, but it didn't seem to bother anyone. The air-conditioners were humming.

I felt no great change take place as I repeated our marriage vows. I did not feel any new rush of "commitment" to the woman who was now my wife, nor did I have any plans to be married to her forever. I did love her, but I saw no reason why I should feel that I had to love her forever. I would love her for as long as I loved her. I assumed she felt the same way. The women I saw on my way out of city hall, a married man, did not look any less beautiful than the women I saw on my way in. It was still hot outside. We walked to our car carrying plastic bags containing little samples of mouthwash, toothpaste, shampoo and aspirin, gifts from the Chamber of Commerce to all newlyweds.

And so my marriage began—except that I never really felt the beginning. I had nothing against transforming myself into a married man, but I felt no tidal pull of change. I assumed Becky had married me and not somebody else, so why should I become somebody else? She married a family of kids of various ages, all of them me, and I married a family of kids of various ages, all of them her. At one time or another I assumed some of them were bound to get along.

Marriage, I was told, required work. This sounded all wrong to me from the start. I couldn't quite imagine the kind of "work" it required, what the hours were, what the point was. The very idea of walking into my apartment and "working" on my marriage seemed ludicrous. My apartment was a place where I went to get away from work. The rest of life was full of work. If marriage required "work," I would have to get another apartment just for myself where I could go and rest. Since I couldn't afford that at the time, I said nothing to Becky about working on our marriage. She said nothing about it herself. We were either very wise or very lazy.

We were led to believe that the harder we try, the better we get.

This aerobic-dancing theory of life may apply to certain things, but I don't think marriage is one of them. You can't go to a gym and pump marriage. It can't be tuned up like a car. It can't be trained like a dog. In this century of enormous scientific breakthroughs, there have been no major marriage breakthroughs that I know of.

Progress junkies find this a frustrating state of affairs. They resist the notion that marriage is essentially an amateur endeavor, not a full-time profession, and they keep trying to work on their marriages and make them better. The only way to do that is to impose a structure on the marriage and then fiddle and improve the structure. But that has nothing to do with the way you feel when the guests have left the house and it's just the two of you again. You are either glad you're there with that person or you're not. I've been both.

This need to improve, the belief that we can improve everything, brings to mind some of my friends who are constantly updating their stereo equipment until, without being aware of it, they wind up listening to the equipment and not to the music. You can do the same thing to friendship, to marriage, to life in general. Let's just say I have chosen to listen to the music, such as it is, on the equipment at hand.

The best trips that I have taken were always last-minute affairs, taken as a lark. When I've sent off for brochures and maps, the trips always turned into disappointments. The time I invested in planning fed my expectations, and I traveled to fulfill my expectations rather than just to go somewhere I hadn't been. I consider my marriage one of those trips taken as a lark. I have become rather fond of the sheer aimlessness of the journey. It's a choice. I know full well that people do plan journeys to the Himalayas, they hire guides, they seek advice, and when they get there, instead of being disappointed, they experience a kind of exhilaration that I never will. My kind of marriage will never reach Mount Everest. You just don't go there as a lark, nor do you get there by accident.

I'm neither proud nor ashamed of the fact that I've stayed married for thirteen years. I don't consider it an accomplishment of any kind. I have changed; my wife has changed. Our marriage, however, for better or worse, is neither better nor worse. It has remained the same. But the climate has changed.

I got married on a hot day a long time ago, because it was a way of cooling off for a while. Over the years, it's also become a place where I go to warm up when the world turns cold.

HARVEY J. FIELDS

On-the-Job Training

It is 6:30 A.M. and my wife just left for work. Three months ago, she launched a new career as a stockbroker. Together we concluded that it was a good idea. It would boost our income; perhaps more important, it would provide a creative outlet for her talents. "We have a solid marriage. You are young and capable. Look around," I advised. "There are all kinds of opportunities."

We reasoned that her time had arrived. Two of our children are at college; a third is a self-sufficient high school student. For the last twenty-two years, my wife has cared for our needs, run thousands of errands, driven millions of car-pool miles, kept our family finances, been there when the plumber arrived to fix our leaking faucets, and at my side, looking radiant, for a constant stream of professional-social obligations.

Now all of that has changed. And it is not as easy as I thought it would be. Accommodations have to be made. Worries, doubts, little aching jealousies and resentments, and big ones as well, have emerged. Then, while driving to my office and brooding over this transformation erupting in my life, I happened to hear a commentator announce that new research has determined that husbands with working wives have a shorter life expectancy than those with traditional homemaker wives. Icing on the cake, as they say.

During the first few weeks, certain tasks just fell into place. She could no longer deliver and pick up at the cleaner's, or make it to our bank. They were out of her way, but happily right on my route to the office. So were the pharmacy and supermarket.

86

The supermarket. I love the supermarket, but on Sundays. Never during the week, all dressed up in a business suit. Sunday is when a man is supposed to visit the supermarket and fill his cart with all sorts of whims and his favorite beer.

Did I feel queasy pushing a cart around on Tuesday afternoon, holding a long list written on a pink sheet of paper, and with all those women and children staring at me? I did. And I wanted to evaporate when Gwen Sommers cornered me holding a large box of Tide in one hand and a big bottle of Era Plus in the other. With sympathy pouring from her compassionate brown eyes, she asked, "Is everything all right with Sybil?" By that she meant: "You are supposed to be at your office doing a man's job, and Sybil should be here shopping." Of course I wanted to explain, defend, send her home to read *The Feminine Mystique,* but I didn't. Instead, I headed for the checkout line gripping my six-pack of beer, hoping to indicate that all the boxes, cans, fruits and vegetables in my cart were simply the unbridled enthusiasm of a mad male on a shopping spree.

When I reached home, her car was not in the driveway. Another trauma. She was always there to greet me at the door with a warm hug and kiss. Now she was late getting home. The house was dark and empty. No sweet aromas of dinner prepared. Just silence, and all those groceries to bring into the house and put away, and bothersome doubts about how our emerging new arrangement will affect us.

It already has, but you grin and bear the first frustrations. A week after she was hired, we sat down to talk about vacation time. I am tired. It's been a tension-filled year. I need a few weeks to unwind. We have always vacationed together. We would never have considered going off alone. Not us. We are "together" kind of people.

But she is committed to a training program, sixteen weeks of rigorous study. She is flowering with new enthusiasm, and her career demands most of her energy, time and attention. So what about me? A vacation alone? By myself? It hurts, fills me with resentment. What are we married for, anyway?

"What about coming up for long weekends?" I suggest. "I will have to check with my boss." It's an innocent remark, but I want to explode. Her boss? I am supposed to be No. 1 in her life. Now, suddenly, she has to get permission from someone else to spend time with me. The gall starts to ooze. I whine inside: "Are we giving up too much? Are we to become roommates sharing the conveniences of a home, the warm memories of rearing our kids, and nothing else?"

One evening, she tells me: "I had lunch today with Tom, George and Steve. We went to this fancy sushi bar. Tom suggested I try it. George says we are going to make a dynamite team. Steve says this. Tom . . . Steve . . . George . . ."

I am not listening to what she is saying. All I hear are male names. All I see are new men in her life: associates, partners, colleagues, customers. All male. All aggressive. All with claims on her.

"Do you know what Jim asked me the other day?" she inquires. I want to stuff my ears, pretend nothing has changed. "What?" I answer, already angry at what I might hear. "I was shocked," she says. "He asked me what I was going to do when the first client came on strong with a proposition and made it clear that, if I wasn't willing, he would take his business elsewhere."

My stomach tightens into an ache. I feel as if I have been hit in the groin. Creeping doubts rumble inside me. I am silent, reflective about it all. The propositions won't be that straightforward. They will come subtly, twisted into all sorts of temptations. The devil always wears angel's garb and his voice is sweet and innocent, even naïve.

Later, I laugh at my fears and anxieties. All those years, all my trips, conventions, speaking appearances, alone in hotel rooms in new cities, did she have the same flurry of doubts? Did she wonder about whom I was meeting, and where? How did she make it through all those years, and I can't seem to bear all the questions and confusions for even a month?

And there are other questions. Whose number should be given at the high school in case of emergency? Who is responsible for banking, cleaning, shopping, cooking? How much help can I expect from her when it comes to attending functions related to my career? And is she expecting me to go out and be nice to her clients, rub elbows at office parties with her associates? How shall all of these be sorted out? Who calls the shots?

My stress level is rising. I liked the way we were. We had negotiated a comfortable arrangement. It was smooth, seldom a surprise. Now it's all in flux, and I am scared.

I see myself being stripped of my masculine, dominant, father, success image. There it is. I have said it. We were programmed by parents into believing that the male was the breadwinner. His job was top priority. He was to earn, protect and preside over his family. He was the senior partner; she was the junior partner. But the curtain has fallen on those old assumptions, and it's painful and bewildering.

So I am afraid for us. Human relationships are delicate affairs. Their circuitry is complex and bewildering. They jam, overload and burn out in the most inexplicable ways. The future is no sure bet. That may be tough, but it is the truth.

Who knows, if we are lucky, and do our job at communicating, sharing, listening and loving, the fact that my wife just went to work may not shorten my life at all. It may add qualities and dimensions that surprise and enrich us. Let's hope so, because I have just rushed home at lunchtime to meet the plumber, and something has got to make that worthwhile.

GORDON MOTT

Following a Wife's Move

My wife's announcement was not dramatic. She walked into the house after work and said, "They want me for the Paris job." The offer was not unexpected nor unattractive. The bank my wife works for was giving her a promotion and transferring her to its Paris office. I reacted with excitement. I imagined all the wonderful aspects of a life in Paris: springtime, restaurants, the Louvre and weekend jaunts to quaint country inns.

The announcement did not violate the set of rules established by our two-career couplehood. Seven years ago, I ambushed her outside a New York City squash court with the declaration that I'd been transferred to Mexico. She made the move and began work in her company's Mexico City office. Ever since, I have been reminded that living in the third world had been my idea and that the next move, in our two-career couple jargon, was "hers."

But within days of letting "Sure, sure, sounds great" slip out, I succumbed to second guessing, reluctance and terror. This wasn't for play. We were moving. My rationalizations about the career flexibility of freelance journalists crumbled. I was forced to face the reality that I would be throwing away a network of contacts in Central America that I had built up over the years; I was also abandoning work as a stringer for *The New York Times* after months of struggling to get my freelance writing off the ground. I envisioned weeks of inactivity, huddled with my dog, Nica, in a Paris apartment, waiting for my wife to return from her job.

Then it struck me where my fears came from. The man in the

family—me—was putting his career at the mercy of his wife's. In the starkest psychological terms, I was following her and abdicating my traditional male role.

I can't deny that special factors, some sounding exotic and glamorous, distinguish a move between Mexico City and Paris from, let's say, a move between New York and Boston. However, the same emotions, career concerns and the reactions of colleagues are probably common to most professional men confronted with making career choices dictated by their wife's job.

My psychological reactions are the toughest to understand and verbalize. My generation—men and women in their thirties and forties—had the rules switched. I grew up believing that I would be the breadwinner and those little girls across the schoolhouse aisle would be housewives and mothers, not professional competition or providers. Although I have embraced the notion of career women for the last ten years, the move opened mental cubbyholes in which the idea of a working woman just didn't seem right. Even though I cringe at the admission, I've had strong emotional responses that I'm less of a man for not putting my foot down and saying, "Stop this career stuff, woman, and get into the kitchen." That reaction is probably unavoidable because of my background and expectations. But the anxiety also undermined my resolve and led to arguments with my wife about whether we would leave at the same time, about where we'd live in Paris.

Professional colleagues and acquaintances betrayed their own prejudices and unease. Innocent queries such as, "Well, isn't that nice, but what are you going to do?" rang with not-so-subtle implications. The questioners' tone suggested that I was giving up the rest of my professional life and denying my own personal desires for my wife's career. The offhand, joking remarks about "How does it feel to be a kept man?" or "What will you do in your spare time?" revealed inflexible attitudes about the best way to pursue a career and an unwillingness to accept women as equal partners.

On the other hand, not many men have the opportunity to explore alternative career options or take a break from the career-ladder syndrome. My wife's move is giving me that chance. Even though I know I will now be forced to devote long and difficult hours to establishing a new network of people and publications, the freelancer's lifeblood, there also will be time for improving my French, visiting and writing about the eight countries in which my wife will be traveling for business, immersing myself in European politics and finishing a novel.

I'm also glad that I've opted for what is perceived as the uncommon choice. I've heard complaints from many single women that they can't trust any man's willingness to promote their careers. At least I know I'm not in that category. My worries about losing my self-worth or masculinity are offset by feeling courageous.

Another benefit has been the strengthening of my marriage. I think my declaration that being with my wife is more important than anything else is an absolute expression of love. I think she understands my commitment more clearly because of my willingness to take a chance with my own career. In addition, our ability to work out the problems caused by the stress of moving has deepened the bond between us.

A subtle shift has occurred, too, in our perceptions of each other. I've always been the one to initiate change. This time, it was her turn, and I'm the one enjoying the results of our belief that it's good to be adventuresome in our lives, jobs and relationships. That has enhanced my trust and respect for my wife.

Finally, I've experienced something broader. Like the characters in the movie *The Big Chill,* I've been dismayed as many ideals espoused by me and my friends in the early 1970s slipped quietly out of vogue. One thing that didn't change was my relentless support for women's rights. But until now my advocacy existed in the abstract. It was never tested, even as I enjoyed the benefits of a two-salary family and a dynamic, involved partner.

The issue of women's rights is real for me now, although it's still not easy for me. I know my fears are not going to disappear magically, nor is this move the last time we'll have to juggle our careers. But I'm actively challenging my assumptions about traditional male roles and forcing myself to live the beliefs about women that I've held for the last ten years. That seems right.

AND THE

BABY

CARRIAGE

———————

CHUCK BARRIS

A May-December Marriage

A friend of mine once told me the most beautiful marriages of all were the May-December kind. My sister agreed. She pleaded with me to marry the young redheaded woman I had been living with for five years in California, the one who was twenty-two years my junior. She was afraid I would procrastinate and lose the Redhead and, with her, any last chance for happiness.

My mother disagreed. May-December, Shmay-December was her attitude. Older men, she said, married young women to satisfy some not-so-stable itch, a wobbly vanity, a retarded ego—not such good reasons. Then you know what happens? The man *really* gets old. All of a sudden, his stomach pops out. His hair drops off. His teeth are in a glass. And "other things." She asked if I had seen the great foreign film classic *Knife in the Water*. Some great May-December marriage *that* was, she said. My mother reminded me that in the movie, soon after the wedding, the old husband was fixing a sail on their boat, while—behind the old husband's back—a young handsome crewman was fondling the young bride's toes. Behind the old husband's back! In my mother's view of May-December marriages, everything ends up behind the old husband's back.

Not so, said my friend, standing firm. May-December marriages were the most beautiful marriages of all. Look at Bing and Kathy Crosby. Arthur and Cynthia Koestler. Sam and Bettye Jaffe. Lee and Anna Strasberg. Charlie Chaplin and Oona O'Neill. Xavier Cugat and Abbe Lane. Georgie Jessel and Lois Andrews. And

weren't all those couples happy? Didn't they have beautiful marriages? I didn't know. My friend assured me they most certainly
did. "The Redhead is wonderful," my sister said. "Don't lose her."

Still, I had this persistent unease that the Redhead was too wonderful. I was also worried that, as a December bachelor, I had lost
the touch. I was now unable to tell a good prospect for marriage
from a bad one. (Hadn't I failed to do so once before, when my
brain was young and alert?)

I married the Redhead anyway, we moved to New York, and, to
my unabashed delight, nothing horrible happened. My young May
bride—who had been uncommonly good to me during our extended courtship—did not turn into a monster the moment we became man and wife. On the contrary, she continued being
uncommonly good to me. She tended to all my elderly fetishes and
my old December hardened ways. She pampered me, ministered to
me, watched over me, aroused me, made me laugh and never
seemed to mind my many bad moods and grouches.

It's true that acquaintances thought my wife was my grown-up
daughter, and that at first this embarrassed and angered me. Eventually, however, the blundering indiscretions of others became an
inside joke for my young wife and me to share. Equally unperturb-
ing was the disparity between my wife's age and those of the other
wives in the company I was used to keeping. Everyone seemed to
get along just fine. "Didn't I say it would work like a charm?" my
friend said after our first anniversary. "I said it would work, too,"
said my sister. She added, "And she doesn't even make any demands." My sister was wrong about this. The Redhead made one
demand, and it was a whopper. She wanted a baby.

I didn't. I had been through all that. But there was no way of
being unaware of my young bride's rampaging maternal instincts.
In Central Park, she would often let loose a scream that would turn
me rigid with fear until I saw she was shrieking with delight at two
passing ducklings on the lake, or a baby girl with a pink bow
wound through her three hairs, or a two-year-old toughie in sweat-
pants. Once, in a crowded elevator, a small child toddled over to
my wife and held on to her leg. My wife's eyes welled up. I capitu-

lated. How could I do anything else? And so began, for me, the only real problem of my May-December marriage: the making—at my age—of a baby.

Granted, I am not a high school quarterback anymore. But I'm not dead yet, either. I can still fulfill certain responsibilities—and with gusto. But, with respect to late-in-life babymaking, I had never considered the debilitating and frightening problems caused by the requirement to perform at any time of day or night. Nor had I ever contemplated the violent alarm a simple oral thermometer can produce in a December husband when his warm May wife beams and declares, "Wow, honey, my temperature's at an all-time low!"

When a woman's body temperature is low—it dips during specific hours of the month—she is more susceptible to becoming pregnant. Hence the thermometer and the declaration; a horrific team, always working their tandem terror at the most inopportune times, such as the afternoon of my corporation's annual stockholders' meeting, or during one of my raging head colds. And then a frantic race home across town with the weight of the world on my shoulders. The quiet disappointment at the end of twenty-eight days—for my wife, the certainty that she was not pregnant; for me, the harrowing realization that I would be facing the infamous thermometer and numbing declarations for at least another four weeks.

All of that combined with the other restrictions and superstitions my young wife and her well-meaning friends inflicted on me. Gone were my evening steams at the Friars Club (weakens the sperm, I was told). No dairy (makes girls). Eat protein (makes boys). Once I discovered my wife under the covers with a box of candy, a twenty-dollar bill and a pound of boiled ham beside her (so the child would be sweet, rich and never hungry). No child has yet been forthcoming.

Yes, I confess it has been rough, this late-in-life responsibility of making a baby. Maybe, if I had it to do over again, I would have tried to resolve the question of whether or not to have a child after we were married *before* we were married. But that resolution would most likely have produced two very unappealing scenarios: (1) the possibility that we might not have married at all, and (2) that we might have married but never added to our May-December joys the experience of planning for a kid of our own to love and raise. Obviously, it was never written that life's decisions were to be simple. Meanwhile, my wife is absolutely convinced she will become pregnant any day now, and for some unexplainable reason, I think she will, too. That settles it.

PHILIP TAUBMAN

Doubts in the Delivery Room

"You're doing natural childbirth, aren't you?"

A friend asked me that question when my wife, Felicity, was two months pregnant. I hadn't given much thought to childbirth. I knew Felicity would go into labor someday, I would take her to the hospital, and a baby would be born. It would be her show, not mine. I wasn't doing childbirth, natural or any other kind. Natural childbirth conjured up images of a midwife ministering to Felicity in the bedroom while I boiled water downstairs.

A few months later and wiser, I found myself enrolled in a natural-childbirth class with my wife and a half-dozen other couples. "Don't forget to bring the pillows," the teacher had said. There we were, resting on the pillows in the basement of the instructor's house, bending our bodies like pretzels to simulate the sensation of childbirth.

By then, I had become somewhat accustomed to, if not enthusiastic about, the idea of natural childbirth, also known as the Lamaze method or, in medical jargon, psychoprophylactic childbirth. In theory, I wanted to help Felicity master and eventually use the various breathing and relaxation techniques that were designed to help her cope with the pain of labor and delivery without the use of sedatives. Being at her side in the hospital, helping her remember how to use the controlled breathing to divert her attention from the pain, seemed to be reasonable ways of bringing a husband's love and involvement to a physical and emotional ordeal, one that most women for years experienced alone in hospital rooms while fathers waited nervously down the hall, if they were present at all.

When I was born in a Manhattan hospital in 1948, my father was listening to the Boston Symphony at Tanglewood. He and I didn't meet until a day later. My mother, later recounting the experience with some pride, said she never felt a thing as I was born, because she was under anesthesia. "Why do you want to go through all the pain?" she asked Felicity.

Part of the answer, which I didn't suggest at the time, seemed to be drawn from a mixture of Marine boot camp and Vince Lombardi football: no pain, no progress. That, of course, was putting it crudely. But the basic idea was that women should experience the full agony and exhilaration of childbirth because it is one of the seminal events in their lives. Medically, I was told, it was also preferable if the mother and child could get through the birth without being heavily drugged.

Still, it didn't seem quite natural to be sitting on pillows doing exercises designed to strengthen the vagina.

Now that I have been through two births, I know that some of my initial doubts were right. I wouldn't want to take off for Tanglewood, or even retreat to the waiting room, but I think I can do without some of the *cinema verité* sights and sounds, not to mention some of the volatile emotions, that went with the natural births of our sons Michael and Gregory.

Felicity's screams, for one. Months later, I still remember them. In the final hours of labor they were desperate, plaintive appeals for relief, cries that seemed to reverberate through the corridors of Sibley Hospital in Washington. I had seen my wife cry before, I had seen her in pain, but never like that, gripping the bed railing, her muscles straining, her face convulsed. It is never easy to watch someone you love suffer, but it seemed particularly cruel to join her doctor in denying her requests for a sedative until the final minutes.

That was my job. In natural childbirth, the role of the father during labor is to help his wife manage the pain as contractions intensify. Try telling your wife that, ultimately, despite efforts to keep her mind off the labor, the only thing you can do to relieve the worst pain she's ever experienced is to coach her on breathing fast and wipe her brow periodically with a wet washcloth.

I was also frightened. It was the lack of control. Someone should have taught me breathing exercises to manage the fear of being in a situation where every instinct to take action, to do something to protect and help my wife, was stymied by the principle that her suffering was necessary. Felicity seemed to enter a zone of pain beyond my reach. Was her safety or the baby's in jeopardy? When the fetal heart monitor started showing an erratic heartbeat during the birth of our second son, I wondered whether natural childbirth was going to kill our child.

Witnessing the birth itself was like no other experience I have had. Even in a hospital delivery room, with all the bright lights, shining surfaces and sterile equipment, the first sight of the living being seemed like a primeval vision. Felicity insists that when, at the doctor's direction, I cut the umbilical cord, my smile was so intense she could see it through the surgical mask that covered my face. I was truly astonished and awed. Yet, I wasn't sure I wanted to see my wife that way.

We've talked about it since. Felicity says that the exhilaration and pleasure she felt when the boys were born were the most thrilling moments of her life, and they more than compensated for the pain. Yet she says she understands my ambivalence. She made an effort during the second birth to spare me some of the harsher sights, including the pelvic examinations by her obstetrician during the height of labor. Neither of us would, for a moment, consider the latest trend, which is to take one's children to see a sibling being born. I don't think we could afford the subsequent psychoanalysis—for them or us.

But just as I cannot fully appreciate the feelings she experienced during the births, I suspect she cannot completely understand my doubts. In a way, I think, the problem is that natural childbirth forces a man to live suspended somewhere among the roles of husband, lover, partner, protector and father, not knowing which way to turn.

JOHN DARNTON

A Vigil Worth Keeping

I have spent New Year's Eve in some strange places, but I never thought I would be sitting with a plate of grapes in the children's intensive-care ward of a Spanish hospital.

Our youngest child, fourteen-month-old Jamie, had been stricken. His throat seized up in a spasm of inflammation, cutting off his breathing. It was the third such attack in six weeks. Twice before, he had stopped breathing altogether, and this time it was clear, from the frenzied expressions of the doctors who crowded around his crib to insert a tube down his windpipe, that they were fighting for his life.

We were lucky that our hospital, Ramón y Cajal, was one of the best. And so, once the tube was inserted, we were allowed to put on backward-fitting pale green surgeons' gowns and push quietly through the double set of swinging doors into the ward itself. There we found other parents, all in green, bending over tiny cribs plugged into banks of medical machines.

As time wore on, we became habitués. We got to know all the nurses, wooing them, as one does in such situations, with anything—sycophancy, assertiveness, helpfulness—that might mean an extra bit of attentiveness for Jamie.

We got to know the other parents, too, and, this being Spain, all the relatives and the friends of the relatives. Outside the ward was a permanent encampment. At night my wife, Nina, found the women's bathroom festooned with newly washed lingerie from the women sleeping on plastic couches.

We soon found we had a vigil of our own, from our Spanish friends Juan, Teresa, Augustín and others who came night after night just to sit with us. Shelly, Augustín's American wife, said this was customary, part of the culture: "Americans behave differently. It's not that we don't feel the same things. It's that we're always afraid of intruding on someone's privacy or grief. Spaniards just assume you want other people around—and, you know, they're right."

In the crib next to Jamie was José Enrique, a nine-month-old born with two holes in his heart. He was no bigger than a squirrel and made a soft sound like a cat's meow when he cried. His mother, an eighteen-year-old Galician, was at his side every waking moment. When other children cried, she would rock their cribs.

Across the way was a twelve-year-old girl, suffering from Down's syndrome, who had contracted, it was feared, meningitis. "Our child's not normal," said the mother. "But we've accepted her, and we love her. And I only pray, now, let her live."

This family came into the ward one at a time. A sister-in-law brushed the child's hair. One brother play-wrestled. Another carried on with speech lessons.

Presiding over it all was Dr. Barrios—first name never offered—a man with more than a touch of monomania. He bounced through the ward like a whirlwind, checking supplies, barking orders, reading and rereading temperature charts. He called in, on his off hours, to ask about the babies. I loved him.

A solidarity developed among us parents. The greetings became not *"Buenos dias"* but simply "How is he today?" They enjoyed telling us about Spanish customs and about New Year's Eve, when everyone waits for the chimes of the clock at the Puerta del Sol and eats twelve grapes, one for each stroke of midnight.

To be with Jamie was both better and worse, harder and easier. He was strapped down, spread-eagled on his back, inside an oxygen tent. He could not speak or make any sound, because of the tube, but he still cried, and when this happened, silent tears flowed down his cheeks. I caught them one by one, with my finger, and he wrapped his hand around my thumb and stared upward.

As often happens with babies, there were problems with the intravenous feeding. The needle became dislodged from an arm, and the arm swelled to twice its size. Then his head was shaved, and it was put there. But the needle came loose again, and his head swelled like a hydrocephalic's. This wasn't dangerous, but it filled us with terror. Finally, the IV was placed directly into a severed vein in the foot.

Then there were the machines to monitor heart rate and respiration through wires strapped to his chest. If you wanted to design a torture chamber for parents, you could do no better than this, to sit them before a panel of screens with constantly changing numbers that mount suddenly, inexplicably, until they fall back within the normal range, and squiggles of green lines that should be even and rectangular like New York skyscrapers but often lapse into jagged waves like the Pyrenees.

From time to time, the machines go berserk. The numbers keep mounting, and an alarm bell sounds. It means nothing, you learn—a conductor has loosened on the chest or some such thing—but each time your own heart rate rises up, keeping pace, in hysteria. As hateful as the machines were, they were addictive. It was much worse when they were disconnected.

The medical care that Jamie got was excellent, I have no doubt of that. And there was even something more. It was there in the conversations, the friends who came, even in the sad spectacle of the lingerie in the women's room. My wife felt it when a nurse who worked all night took her shopping the next morning to find just the right humidifier.

It was there when a doctor gave up his office for us to sleep in. And when the newspaper salesman outside, perceiving that I was upset, suddenly and wordlessly put his arm around me as he handed me a paper. Whatever this quality is, which runs so deeply in the Spanish character, I hope they never lose it. It is the perfect antidote to the machines.

And so it was that on New Year's Eve, with Jamie sound asleep, tube and all, Nina and I found a group of nurses motioning us into a side room. There was a white tablecloth and candles, spread with a feast of chicken and shrimp and champagne. The TV set was tuned to Puerta del Sol. We were handed paper plates, each containing twelve grapes. And when the big clock struck, we downed them, one by one.

"My wish for you," said a nurse, raising a glass, "is that you never have to spend another night in a place like this." Weeks went by. Jamie was safely home. We sneaked in at night to check his breathing. Some of the bad memories, especially the one about the silent tears, don't go away. But when they come, I find I can almost push them aside with other memories, of that champagne toast and of the grapes.

CAREY WINFREY

Fatherhood Postponed

My first wife and I were out of sync when it came to children. When I wanted them, she didn't, and vice versa. Perhaps that should have told us something, though even now, I'm not sure quite what. In any case, the marriage was over before I knew it— literally—and once we were separated, people kept saying wasn't it fortunate there hadn't been any children. I couldn't argue with that.

For a while, after my divorce, I didn't give the idea of kids a lot of thought, though somewhere at the back of my mind lay the assumption that I would someday have them. If pressed, I would have said that being a father was not something I wanted to miss out on but that I was in no rush. There were still things I wanted to do before I got tied down.

By the time I got married again, at the age of forty, I was more than ready to be a daddy. It was as if some slow-release time capsule had suddenly gone off in my psyche, unleashing a pool of paternal yearnings. And when Jane and I had twin sons, most of our close friends our age were having babies, too. As much as I hate to think of myself as a part of any trend, it seems undeniable that Jane and I have become soldiers in the growing army of late-blooming urban parents.

The thing I was always warned against about waiting a long time to have children was that I wouldn't be able to throw a ball with them. Well, I'm here to say that I don't think it's going to be a problem. Either I'll throw balls with the best of them and that'll be that, or I won't and it won't matter a damn. Three-plus years into this fatherhood business, I know at least that what kids require of their fathers is a lot of attention, a lot of love and, I suspect, if mine ever reach the age of understanding, a lot of that, too. They can find other people to throw balls at them.

I like being a father. I *love* being a father. And I think I'm a better one for having waited. Though no number of years can ever adequately prepare one for the enormous delights and anxieties of fatherhood—worry and fear for his child's well-being will never be far from any father's consciousness—I also believe that coming late to it has some real pluses. One of them is the rejuvenating way kids force you to experience the world anew, a world filled with Dr. Seuss and showing off and funny animals and marching bands. Maybe some younger fathers get just as big a kick as I do vicariously viewing the world this way, but I wouldn't be surprised if it takes a bit of mileage on the old odometer fully to appreciate what Wordsworth was getting at with his line about the child's being father of the man.

I know I resent the dramatic way my kids have circumscribed my life less than I would have a decade or more ago. I can hardly say I did it all, but I did enough—read enough books, saw enough movies, went to enough parties—not to mind much the degree to which those activities have been curtailed. I'm often even grateful to my children for providing the excuse, as well as the reason, to stay home. I don't want to make too much of this because certainly there are times my wife and I would (and do) pay any price to escape "the boys" for a little while (and then, inevitably, we spend most of our precious time alone talking about them). But nine nights out of ten—okay, four out of five—our sons (and whatever happens to be on the tube in the hour left to us after getting them to bed) provide sufficient diversion.

Of course, truth also compels me to confess that, lacking the energy I once had, my tyros can grind me exceedingly fine, particularly when they have a full day to do so. Many Saturday and Sunday nights find me close to tears from exhaustion (around *our* house, it's T.G.I.M.—"Thank God It's Monday"). But when morning comes around, assuming the boys have not awakened too many times in the wee small hours to wail for "appa juice," or "Mommy," or both, I'm again ready to give them as much of me as they want.

Then there's the money part. Admittedly, twins cost more than single babies (about double, roughly), but even one child these days creates financial burdens better borne by mature than by starting salaries. Though the financial plateau I've reached after twenty years of for-the-most-part-gainful employment remains modest by almost any objective standard, it is nonetheless proportionally higher than it was a decade or so ago. It is not hyperbole but fact that the woman who takes care of our children while Jane and I cavort at work makes as much money as I did not many years ago, even when the dollars are adjusted for inflation. But even if she didn't, children would have taken a much greater share of my expendable income just a few short years ago. More important, I almost certainly begrudge them the financial drain less today than I would have in all my yesterdays.

Recently, for example, my wife and I took out an amount of life insurance that makes each of us far more valuable as a dear departed than in the here and now. In my salad years, that money might have gone quite effortlessly into travel or clothes or cameras. I signed the insurance checks, if not joyously, with a satisfied sense that few expenditures could ever feel as warranted. It's hard to think of a better use for money than my sons' welfare.

Once the insurance was taken care of, Jane and I made out new wills. Since embarking on my fifth decade, I've given what she considers an indecent amount of thought to my own mortality; still, nothing so focuses the mind on the subject as the making out of a will. Sitting in the lawyer's office, listening to the stream of whereases and parties-of-the-first-parts, it occurred to me with the force of revelation that the expectation of being survived by one's children is yet another unanticipated pleasure of parenthood postponed. The thought of my sons carrying on after I'm gone is probably about as close to a belief in an afterlife as an aging pagan like myself is likely to get. But curiously, it's close enough for comfort.

TIM PAGE

Life Miscarried

It was early one June morning when the doctor called and confirmed Vanessa's pregnancy. I had been listening to the Brahms F Minor Piano Sonata—to the rapturous descent of melody that opens the second movement—and the soft, still sense of wonder I felt will follow me forever, with this tender andante a soundtrack for the memory.

The remaining four months of the pregnancy more closely resembled a Mahler scherzo: a grimacing series of phantasms that shattered hopes and balance. For it was obvious, almost from the beginning, that something was wrong. Days blurred together, a confused mixture of tears and blood, centered only by visits to the obstetrician. Any joy in the pregnancy was always tempered by fear; I cooled our loved ones' enthusiasm with mumbled admissions that there were problems along the way.

After Vanessa was confined to bed, we endured the New York summer as near prisoners in our apartment, the leaden heat relieved only by an occasional breeze off the Hudson. Finally, in late September, it was over. My wife, nearly four months ahead of schedule, entered the hospital for a sixteen-hour labor—the most excruciating pain, it is said, that a human being can bear—all to produce a half-formed visitor, a child that could not stay.

Every manual provides a different statistic: one out of four, five, seven or ten pregnancies ends in miscarriage. By any standards, it is a common occurrence. Yet miscarriage is a subject that few men can easily discuss. One is tempted to pretend it didn't happen, to relegate the experience to the safety of nightmare. During an era when every intimate human phenomenon has been catalogued, dissected and analyzed in clinical detail, it is perhaps revealing that there should be such wide, expert disagreement about the prevalence of miscarriage.

It is not merely the numbing, animal sense of loss that causes us to flinch from the subject; it is the abstract quality of that pain. For an unborn child could be anything at all: it is ours, it is us, but we know little more. We can only imagine the color of its eyes, the chime of its laughter, the breadth of its dreams. There is nothing concrete to mourn, only a negation of infinite possibility.

Men are physically excluded from the birth process; no matter how many Lamaze classes we attend, no matter how much of the burden we wish to shoulder, our knowledge of motherhood is necessarily vicarious. Still, if I could not ease Vanessa's physical pain, I wanted to provide a base of love and support. So, assuming a well-meaning boosterism that I now fear may have seemed roseate and superficial, I found reassuring answers to all of my wife's complaints and relayed tale after tale of disastrous pregnancies with happy endings.

And, at times, I thought we had a chance. During those occasional days when everything seemed, however temporarily, to be progressing smoothly, we would talk for hours, meticulously planning our first twenty years of parenthood—discussing nutrition, religious training, sex education, even college tuition.

But the pains returned, with increased severity, and optimism ebbed. The doctor confessed his helplessness: there was probably a healthy baby inside Vanessa, he said, but we could only watch, wait and hope that she didn't go into premature labor. It became my duty to keep her comfortable—adjust the television, fetch some ice water, cook an amateur meal, and occasionally kiss her swollen abdomen and beg our baby to hold on for just a few more weeks.

It was not to be. The agonies of childbirth are usually assuaged by anticipation, but Vanessa entered into labor without hope, full knowing that our child could not yet live outside the safety of her womb, but unable to stop the impending expulsion.

What may I write of my firstborn son that will neither demean nor romanticize his brief life? Born after sunset, dead by daybreak, his eleven-hour scrap of existence was little more than a shuttle down fluorescent hallways, a tour of wards and laboratories. He surely felt the violence of his birth, may have sensed a few flutterings of human consciousness when they placed him in the incubator, and then fell back into darkness.

The decision to become a father is, in some ways, a *memento mori.* It is an admission of our own mortality. We resign our supremacy in the vanguard, and take up the good fight for somebody even newer, even more helpless than ourselves. Yet it is also a supreme affirmation. I have heard it said that all young men believe in their primacy, but it sometimes seems that the members of my age group came to maturity believing—silently but profoundly—that these were the final days; that we were to have no sequel. Our fear of immediate extinction has caused many of us to pass through life as though it were an endless Sunday brunch, grasping out halfheartedly at trends and textures. I have spent my share of time mouthing the platitudes of nihilism, while secretly frightened of caring too deeply. If you hold on to nothing, little can be taken from you.

I will never again subscribe to this philosophy; a conscious decision has been made—not merely to survive, but to live. Vanessa and I fought—failed, to be sure, but fought hard all the same—and discovered a new selflessness, even a peculiar glory, in the struggle. We hope to become parents soon, with as little pain as possible. But, come what may, we are now caught up in life's intensity and gifted, for the first time, with an awareness of our fragile place in the continuum.

MEN

WITHOUT

WOMEN

———————

RODERICK THORP

A Wary Bachelor

When asked why he dates young women, George Burns, patron saint of Los Angeles, where I live, explains, "They tell shorter life stories."

As another bachelor, but with forty years' less experience, I know what he means. I've heard my share of all-too-long, all-too-tragic tales of lost intimacy, madhouse marriage and duel-to-the-death divorce. The sight of glazed eyes never stops the outpouring. But simply, there are certain people who cannot keep themselves from digging up dirt from their distant pasts and dumping it on the dinner table.

The fact is, all adult singles have been hurt by love. It's how we got to be single. But most of us have learned to live with the scars, and a few of us have even learned from our mistakes. We know we're in trouble when we find ourselves with someone who can't make the hurting end. One woman I know won't date a man if he has been out of a long-term relationship less than a year. When I'm trapped for an evening with a woman who won't stop crying into her avocado slices, I quietly whisper the magic word taught to me when I started dating again:

Next!

Los Angeles is a city full of adult singles, and the singles scene is very big business. Ads for dating services clutter the classifieds, the landscape is dotted with dating bars, and the weekends are crowded with the dances, meetings and lectures of Parents Without

Partners and lesser-known groups. This isn't a world of fresh-from-the-campus, first-job, partying kids, but one of single parent-hood, grueling responsibility, sniveling lawyers and hateful former spouses. Perhaps because they think they don't deserve it, most of the players in this game regard their participation as only transitory, like a brief stay in jail in Monopoly. Sometimes the conversation can turn abrupt and cutting. I heard:

He: What sign are you?

She (warily backing away): Resume Speed.

She was doing him a favor. After I told a mixed discussion group that my ideal woman can read a racing form, one of the women slipped me her phone number. She turned out to be a nonsmoking health nut who ran five miles a day. Three dates later, as I declined an invitation to a rock climb, I asked why she had wasted our time, energy and emotion. She had taken a chance, she said.

I could understand; I've done it myself.

It took courage for me to try the dances, lectures and mixers. I thought that sort of thing would be a little too cornball and slow-moving for a former New Yorker. What didn't enter my mind was that not attending a singles dance in thirty years had left me ill prepared for asking a stranger out onto the floor. That first time, I stood frozen against the wall for an hour until a really nice woman walked up and said hello. We saw each other once after that, but the spark between us was only a false alarm. After twenty-five years, she was still working for her first employer, which was as frightening to me as the insecurity of my self-employment must have been to her.

In this period after the sexual revolution, except for a few bozos of both sexes who haven't heard of herpes or AIDS, the sleeping around of the 1960s and '70s is over. After twenty-five years in two successive long-term relationships, I know that achieving real intimacy is a slow, arduous process that has nothing to do with bed hopping or sexual conquest or deception. I am cautious; I go slow. If my position is in the middle ground—as I want to believe, but have no way of telling—then the middle ground is often an empty place, because I'm alone a lot, and sometimes it's depressing. Other people have told me that it's much the same for them. A little loneliness seems to be part of acting responsibly toward oneself.

Or maybe it is the consequence of self-defense. I wished I was home when a woman announced in a single evening that she didn't like: sushi, theater, dogs, her lawyer, lima beans, the house she lived in, Groucho Marx, or the fun teens have with clothes these days. Sociologists who want to understand our divorce rate, and the wife-, husband- or child-abuse fueling it, should take a look at those living outside the family. Without anybody nagging them, an awful lot of people are running around who are just plain *angry*.

Despite my wariness, I believe, like any horseplayer, that my day will come. In the meantime, a certain eccentricity is setting in. Being alone makes it inevitable. I see eccentricities in all the single people I know. A bachelor friend was surprised to discover that I have real furniture, pictures on the walls, even a cat. At forty, he has a bed, a pinball machine and a life-size plastic statue of Darth Vader. The milk in a woman's refrigerator turned out to be twelve weeks old—she forgot about it, she said, as we laughed.

You have to maintain a good attitude. We have to do right by ourselves no matter what. For all his joking about young women, George Burns told us long ago that, after Gracie's death, he didn't begin to sleep again until he got into her bed. The woman who taught me the magic word (Next!) recently gave up her search for Mr. Right to have a baby out of wedlock. Her gynecologist told her she had to do it now or never.

Perhaps the happy thing is, you don't know what's coming tomorrow. After she told me she was to be a mother, the woman asked if I had heard the news about her homely friend—"You know, the one with the stringy hair and bad skin?"

I remembered bowlegs, too. No, I hadn't heard the news.

What she told me still has me spinning, but it was no lie. I just saw the homely friend on television, and she looked terrific, her attitude even better. She was standing next to her new husband, who was being interviewed about his latest project. Being interviewed goes with being a movie star, which is what he is. But he is a shy and self-conscious man, uncomfortable with hoopla. He was holding on to his bride as if he had been looking for her all of his life.

Exactly. That's the feeling I'm looking for.

NOEL PERRIN

A Part-time Marriage

When my wife told me she wanted a divorce, I responded like any normal college professor. I hurried to the college library. I wanted to get hold of some books on divorce and find out what was happening to me.

Over the next week (my wife meanwhile having left), I read or skimmed about twenty. Nineteen of them were no help at all. They offered advice on financial settlements. They told me my wife and I should have been in counseling. A bit late for *that* advice.

What I sought was insight. I especially wanted to understand what was wrong with me that my wife had left, and not even for someone else, but just to be rid of *me*. College professors think they can learn that sort of thing from books.

As it turned out, I could. Or at least I got a start. The twentieth book was a collection of essays by various sociologists, and one of the pieces took my breath away. It was like reading my own horoscope.

The two authors had studied a large group of divorced people much like my wife and me. That is, they focused on middle-class Americans of the straight-arrow persuasion. Serious types, believers in marriage for life. Likely to be parents—and, on the whole, good parents. Likely to have pillar-of-the-community potential. But, nevertheless, all divorced.

Naturally there were many different reasons why all these people had divorced, and many different ways they behaved after divorce. But there was a dominant pattern, and I instantly recognized my-

119

self in it. Recognized my wife, too. Reading the essay told me not only what was wrong with me, but also with her. It was the same flaw in both of us. It even gave me a hint as to what my postdivorce behavior was likely to be, and how I might find happiness in the future.

This is the story the essay told me. Or, rather, this is the story the essay hinted at, and that I have since pieced together with much observation, a number of embarrassingly personal questions put to divorced friends, and to some extent from my own life.

Somewhere in some suburb or town or small city, a middle-class couple separate. They are probably between thirty and forty years old. They own a house and have children. The conscious or official reason for their separation is quite different from what it would have been in their parents' generation. Then, it would have been a man leaving his wife for another, and usually younger, woman. Now it's a woman leaving her husband in order to find herself.

When they separate, the wife normally stays in the house they occupied as a married couple. Neither wants to uproot the children. The husband moves to an apartment, which is nearly always going to be closer to his place of employment than the house was. The ex-wife will almost certainly never see that apartment. The husband, however, sees his former house all the time. Not only is he coming by to pick up the children for visits; if he and his ex-wife are on reasonably good terms, he is apt to visit them right there, while she makes use of the time to do errands or to see a friend.

Back when these two were married, they had an informal labor division. She did inside work, he did outside. Naturally there were exceptions: she gardened, and he did his share of the dishes, maybe even baked bread. But mostly he mowed the lawn and fixed the lawn mower; she put up any new curtains, often enough ones she had made herself.

One Saturday, six months or a year after they separated, he comes to see the kids. He plans also to mow the lawn. Before she leaves, she says, "That damn overhead garage door you got is off the track again. Do you think you'd have time to fix it?" Apartment life makes him restless. He jumps at the chance.

She, just as honorable and straight-arrow as he, has no idea of asking for this as a favor. She invites him to stay for an early dinner. She may put it indirectly—"Michael and Sally want their daddy to have supper with them"—but it is clear that the invitation also proceeds from her.

Provided neither of them has met a really attractive other person yet, they now move into a routine. He comes regularly to do the outside chores, and always stays for dinner. If the children are young, he may read to them before bedtime. She may wash his shirts.

One such evening, they both happen to be stirred not only by physical desire but by loneliness. "Oh, you might as well come upstairs," she says with a certain self-contempt. He needs no second invitation; they are upstairs in a flash. It is a delightful end to the evening. More delightful than anything they remember from their marriage, or at least from the later part of it.

That, too, now becomes part of the pattern. He never stays the full night because, good parents that they are, they don't want the children to get any false hopes up—as they would, seeing their father at breakfast.

Such a relation may go on for several years, may even be interrupted by a romance on one side or the other and then resume. It may even grow to the point where she's mending as well as washing his shirts, and he is advising her on her tax returns and fixing her car.

What they have achieved postdivorce is what their marriage should have been like in the first place. Part-time. Seven days a week of marriage was too much. One afternoon and two evenings is just right.

Although our society is even now witnessing de facto part-time arrangements, such as the couple who work in different cities and meet only on weekends, we have no theory of part-time marriage, at least no theory that has reached the general public. The romantic notion still dominates that if you love someone, you obviously want to be with them all the time.

To me it's clear we need such a theory. There are certainly people who thrive on seven-day-a-week marriages. They have a high level of intimacy and they may be better, warmer people than the rest of us. But there are millions and millions of us with medium or low levels of intimacy. We find full-time family membership a strain. If we could enter marriage with more realistic expectations of what closeness means for us, I suspect the divorce rate might permanently turn downward. It's too bad there isn't a sort of glucose tolerance test for intimacy.

As for me personally, I still do want to get married again. About four days a week.

MARK KRAMER

Waiting for Next Time

I'm driving along the crowded highway and obeying the speed limit. It's Sunday, and I've seen four police cars along the verge of the road, each behind a motorist. Then the blue light is flashing behind me. I see my speedometer drop down from 65 as I pull over, too.

"I just figured out why I was speeding," I say, glancing out at the wholesome, red-cheeked officer who reads my documents. He doesn't appear puzzled, much less conversational. What I wanted to say next would have gone something like this:

"I'm single, right? Used to be married. I'm out for supper with this woman tonight. We get on real well—been out before. We're saying very personal things. Outside, we have to go separate ways, and it feels like the right moment, so I kiss her. She turns her head, like in high school, so I kiss her cheek. It felt awful. I guess I was just driving along, Officer, and remembered that scene—and down went the pedal . . ."

What I really say to the policeman is merely, "Sorry, must have taken my mind off my driving." He delivers what he calls a "verbal warning," and I allow how I'll be much more careful from now on, which I will.

The first months—in fact the first year—after my wife left were nasty. She had made one of those surprise departures, one that started on a random afternoon with "Guess what, sweetie?" I finished writing a book that fall. Working sustained me. The book seems blacker than I'd make it if I had it to finish again.

123

I followed the patterns predicted in the grief-and-mourning manual I read on a visit to my mother's bookshop. I rehearsed the trauma until I became bored by my own fury. I extinguished fury, internalized the good relics, healed and grew cheerful again. I experienced these emotional states on schedule, like some beaver building a dam. I ceased believing in free will. Time is relentless, but also merciful, air-brushing harsh events. After two years I can, as the book suggested, write up an inventory of the brighter side:

Found out wonderful loyalty of friends.

Had entrancing romantic interlude, part of cure, that would not have had otherwise.

Learned am tough and can take it.

Refreshed sense of independence and adventure.

But things aren't back to normal, even though I am. What is not normal, for me, is being single. I do it well enough, but, quite literally, my heart isn't in it. I indeed read books in restaurants, actually like to go solo to films, and have traveled alone industriously. I again have freedom that my married friends say they miss. (I missed it, too, a few years back.) I've fallen in with a circle of single people of wit and warmth and adopted a proxy sister—we grow a garden together and listen to each other's social news. We keep track of the continuity of each other's lives, for the moment, and there's comfort in that.

Yet the gain rarely seems worth the loss. Being one of a pair alters everyday life luxuriously. I liked joking in the supermarket, holding hands unthinkingly on the dull drive to Boston, bothering to sprinkle paprika on the breakfast omelets. Most of all, I liked being known—having the harrowing work of getting-to-know done. I liked sharing an emotional and narrative history.

Now I date. To "date" is a calendar metaphor for when meetings are anticipated—isolated and special. But it's the habit of meeting, and then of not even having to set the next time to meet, that's nicest of all. When dates happen well, I may begin to "see" someone—and that's quite tender, as euphemisms go, singling out one's new love for special vision. The prospect of new love balances the weight of separation, but admitting to myself that I wish love again shifts daily life to treacherous ground. If a key to happiness is not to want, awaiting new love eases one into paradoxical nonendeavor.

For when one "sees" someone, there are anecdotes to relate. (Some cast the shadow of their last retelling.) There are vulnerabilities to edge in upon. Even the giddiest chat may negotiate the structural stuff of real relationships: independence, trustworthiness, specialness, intimacy. It's hard enough to traverse this ground with someone who has given and taken with you for years. But it's wearing, and thrilling, to do it willfully with the occasional likable near-stranger. The puzzle of such times has no answer: how to want, but not need. "It's supposed to be fun," says my proxy sister, shrugging. It's a time for jokes.

In spite of knowing that one's prospective next eternal companion is in the same fix, one has to keep alert. What attracts people to each other seems to coincide only by luck with what keeps them together for the long haul. Combining the two happens flukily. That it happens at all makes me believe in Cupid, if not in God. I felt a twinge of longing for the mail someone's receiving from a personal ad in *The New York Review of Books.* The ad sought a self-assured, sane, pretty nonsmoker, twenty-eight to thirty-five, accomplished at something and wishing a child or two. Although I might trade off some sanity for advanced Scrabble skills, that's who I want, too.

But who's attractive? Who's sane? Love comes by chance. The timing must be fortuitous. Laura met David in an elevator. Shirley met Bob in traffic court. You can hardly articulate, much less ask for, the things that turn out to count most. Lovers have to smell right to one another. My next true love will be someone interesting, confirming, admirable, familiar—which are, of course, the most idiosyncratic and personal of traits, the ones that allow any lovers to declare that their partners' ordinariness is fetching. Love probably can't be advertised for, but it surely happens, has happened to me before. And I wish it would again next week.

MARTIN GOTTFRIED

Single Again at Fifty

Getting divorced was bad enough without becoming unmarried in
the bargain. Fact was, it was embarrassing to be single again at
fifty. I was too old for it. As my father had once said of a crooner's
singing, it was no fit thing for a grown man to do. Single was for the
exuberant fellows in the beer commercials, the ones who slide
down the dunes with lobsters and six-packs. Single was not for a
man of earnestness and serious purpose, a fellow who had made
something of himself and had an establishment to prove it: a wife,
a child, a car, a home with carpeting and sofas and lamps and
armchairs; the complete Beethoven quartets. Was that not evidence of a life lived? Was it not absurd for such a man to live in a
high-rise apartment with an L-shaped living room and a butcher-
block table from Conran's? Square one is fun only the first time
around.

There is a difference between being single and being alone, and
everyone knows the difference. Single is good. Single is not a fresh
start but *the* start. It is for the young and promising, the young and
looking for action, the young and impatient. It may be solitary, but
it is solitary with all the options; that is, it's up to the single person
whether or not to have company. On the other hand, alone is
alone—old, ill, self-pitying—and it's true: *nobody* wants you. A
family man is not faced with such issues, but as the old psychiatrist
had told me, "You don't have a family now; do me something." I
couldn't do him anything.

There are men my age who seem elated by second bachelorhood.

They jog, they grow beards, they drive sports cars, they bring tall girlfriends to East Hampton where they all slide down the dunes with lobsters and six-packs. I can only buy four-door sedans—the dealers reserve them for me—and whenever I try to grow a beard, it comes out as though I have no business walking around in need of a shave. I may be a scientific marvel, genetically conventional. I could not imagine myself single again, I felt merely alone, but the beard and car were apparently secondary issues for the two ladies in chenille robes who sit at a Formica kitchen table stubbing out Chesterfields in their coffee saucers while they classify the newly divorced. They nod their heads in weary unison: You single, you alone. I was too young to be alone. It was the only thing I was too young for.

Truth was, I wasn't alone. Not only did I have a daughter, but I actually spent time with her. Not for me a Sunday afternoon fatherhood at the Central Park Zoo, and, lest I forgot, she kept reminding me. There is a generation of divorce lawyers growing up in grade school. Instead of playing with toys and whispering sexy stories back and forth, they are becoming knowledgeable about separation agreements, alimony and visitation rights. My daughter's classmates, half of them from divided homes, were teaching her divorce law, and she would repeat the lessons to me. The litany related mainly to joint custody, even though my wife's lawyer had threatened me on the subject and my own attorney had advised me to avoid it. However, even this issue was made temporarily subordinate to the immediate one of finding a place to live, since my home, I was informed, was no longer my home.

The nests of my life had been feathered by women. I believed, without thinking about it, that no home I made for myself could ever really be a home, and in that conviction I found a furnished apartment, which was doubly advantageous: it was made by someone else, and it was perfectly temporary. There was a sofa bed for my daughter in the living room, and when I found a new nest-featherer, there would be no lease to break and no furniture to dispose of. For the duration, I was sheltered, an L-shaped roof over my head. I was ready for dates.

Dates. At fifty. It took a few weeks just to swallow the idea and keep it down.

People kept telling me that the man who is single and straight can have the women of New York at his feet. The ratio of unmarried women to men, they said, was a full harem for every adolescent fantasy. Unfortunately, living out an adolescent fantasy requires that one be an adolescent. My father's remark resounded ever louder in my mind's ear: adolescence was no fit thing for a grown man. Was I actually to make a boy's telephone calls? Are you free Tuesday? Would you like to go to a movie? Was I to make small talk and then lunge for the blouse buttons? It is fun to flirt, but ludicrous to do anything about it, once past the age of honest skinniness. The only adolescence I could summon up was the pimply fear of female rejection.

I did meet one woman who seemed to know how to reduce the pressure of opening gambits. She approached me at an arts benefit, a black-tie dinner dance, quite grand. Unprompted, but not without warmth, she wrote down her telephone number and slipped it into my tuxedo pocket. Not a word had been exchanged between us. I felt very romantic, extremely attractive. I felt so attractive, in fact, that I was only slightly nervous when I called her. She remembered me, of course. "I think I ought to tell you," she whispered intimately and huskily on the telephone, "that I am in the home entertainment business."

Now that is a euphemism.

The ego survives. I made plans and filled the evenings when my daughter wasn't there. The plans did not have to be amorous. I could have male friends. I could even have female friends. I learned that a woman could come for a sleep-over while my daughter was there and I didn't have to feel guilty about it. My kid was healthy—as she put it, she had won joint custody—and an overnight wouldn't bother her unless it bothered me.

I even assumed the lease on the apartment, buying my own furniture and walling off the leg of the living room's "L" as a second bedroom. Why, the day even came when I walked through the

front door, gloomy as usual in anticipation of emptiness and silence and instead found myself glad to be home; content enough,
and even if single and sometimes alone, still *home*.

Now I'm afraid of getting used to it.

WINSTON GROOM

Alone and Not Married

A few years back, a young woman and I had reached that precarious stage of romance at which we had to decide either to "get involved" or not. There were some good and some bad times, but things seemed to be flowing smoothly until one weekend when she arrived at my house in the country, tense and distant. Three days later, I discovered the reason.

I had arranged for her to ride out from the city with a close friend, a widow with two grown children, who had been happily married to a famous writer. During the drive, my friend, meaning well, had treated the young woman to a lecture on the importance of marriage—specifically, marriage to *me!* The young woman was frightened. Suddenly, she faced the specter of total commitment: a lifetime of children and responsibilities. After that, our relationship went downhill. Nothing I could say could erase the specter and, predictably, our relationship ended soon after.

It happens all the time. Not long ago, I was standing with my date at a cocktail party when a person with whom I was barely acquainted came up. His face beamed with sincerity as he said to us: "Well, don't you make a lovely couple. When are you getting married?"

I could have strangled him.

We mumbled some cute reply, and there it should have ended. But of course it didn't, because questions like "When are you getting married?" cover an occasion like a pall. What, until then, had been a casual dating relationship took on serious dimensions. The "big question" had been raised, and each of us then had to admit that at least the possibility of marriage existed. From then on, things were strained, and we finally just drifted apart.

I wish people would stop asking when I'm going to get married, or, more precisely in my case, when I'm going to get married again. If I knew, I'd make an announcement like everybody else.

I think a lot of people are just plain curious when they ask questions like "Why hasn't some lovely young thing hooked you?" Perhaps they're probing to find out about sexual proclivities, inasmuch as a free heterosexual man about town is supposed to be scarce. There are others who simply think a man should be married because *they* are. If their match is "for better," they want you to join in the fun; and if it's "for worse," they resent your having a good time when they aren't.

A few months ago, I shared a conversation with my father, a gentle octogenarian who practices law in a historic Southern city. Even *he* asked me why I hadn't married again.

Now if anybody has a right to such a question, I suppose he does. So I told him. My answer was simple enough—I just hadn't found anybody I *wanted* to marry.

Having handled his share of divorce cases, he was sympathetic, but went on to lecture me on the way to find a wife. The analogy he used was of buying a car: one must look to cost, durability, comfort, design, economy, speed and handling. All must be reasonably balanced. To concentrate, for instance, on design exclusively would most likely result in the selection of a bad model—or a bad wife.

This lawyerly and practical advice seemed to make sense until it occurred to me that one normally trades in a car every few years. It is more difficult to trade in a wife. It followed that if one were to find a wife with all the attributes of a "lifetime car," one would be looking for the equivalent of a Rolls-Royce, which is a very expensive proposition. Probably, too, there would be a waiting list.

When I brought this up to my father and also pointed out that he hadn't dealt with the matter of love, he peered at me over tortoise-shell glasses and said, "I do not think you *want* to get married."

Maybe he's right.

The question of whether one *should* be married aside, there's the additional matter of whether one is *ready* to get married. I've watched, fascinated, as acquaintances of mine suddenly became ready. They often marry the first person of similar desire who comes along, like people who turn on the television just to watch it. Lightning courtships ensue. Frankly, I haven't seen much evidence that these couplings turn out any better or worse than other kinds. But what seems to cause them is that the freedom and excitement of being single suddenly loses its glitter; fear, loneliness and the need for security begin to dominate.

It's not as though I haven't felt this myself from time to time. Being unattached in New York City can be terrific if you fall in with good people and have a sense of humor and a little money. But I remember sitting alone once on a terrace in Jamaica. My feet were propped up, I had a cool tropical drink in my hand. I had just written the last pages of a novel, and I was watching a marvelous sunset. And I suddenly found myself thinking, "Why am I doing this? I've worked hard, done well, but what good is it if there's no one to share it with?"

The moment was somewhere between self-realization and self-pity, but it became evident to me then, I think for the first time, that the natural order of things was for a human to share his life with another human—permanently, if possible.

So why am I not married?

The fact is, it just isn't as easy to get married as it used to be, not when half of one's friends are grieving and splitting up. To add to the confusion, women have changed their concept of marriage in the last decade or so. Recently I asked a woman point-blank what kind of man she wanted to marry. "He has to make me laugh," she said.

So we shall return, my colleagues and I—men and women—to the cocktail parties, dinners and dances; the women dressed in their tuxedos with clip-on ties, talking of Proust and other interesting things, and the men listening, trying to figure out what the deal is—everybody sort of nervous, nobody really much wanting to be there. But everybody half-hoping to meet Mr. or Miss "Right."

I was having lunch at a sidewalk café the other day, watching a woman walk by with a dog. Both seemed happy, especially the dog.

"Do you know what?" my luncheon companion said. "You need to find a nice girl and settle down."

I stared at him.

"There's this cast party tonight," he said. "It'll be great . . ."

"Sorry," I cut him off. "*Casablanca* is on television at ten."

MICHAEL BLUMENTHAL

No Big Deal

I am sitting around the kitchen table of a house in Ithaca, New York—kind of a spectator to this gathering, being an out-of-towner—when it dawns on me, in a way no longer at all abstract or metaphorical, how much the situation of men and women has changed in the fifteen or so years of my maturity.

Besides myself, there are eight others gathered around the table—six women and two men. The women are uniformly attractive, articulate, intelligent, good-humored and opinionated, actively engaged in their community. All of them, insofar as I can tell, own their own homes—as single mothers, married women, single women or part of a lesbian couple. As I walk in and am introduced to Natalie, the owner of the house, and to the others by my friend Marjorie, the women's attention to me is merely friendly and polite, benevolently disinterested in any "romantic" or flirtatious sense. That there is a new man in the room is of no particular interest: there is business to be taken care of.

The meeting's purpose is to discuss a new four-lane highway that the Department of Transportation has proposed building to alleviate congestion. The gathering lasts for about two hours, during which time several alternative proposals and reroutings are bandied around the table. There is no particular sense that anyone—or any gender—dominates the meeting. Everyone seems to have one or more interesting proposals, everyone is heard, everyone seems to

134

know what the issues are. Finally, when Marjorie and I get up to leave, the adieus are much like the hellos were—cordial, genuine—"Nice to meet you, good night."

We walk down the block to Marjorie's house, where she lives with her two pre-adolescent boys. Having asked her husband of thirteen years to move out of their previous home several years ago, she has, just recently, asked the man she has been living with for the last two years to do likewise. When she first told me, the other day, of their separation, I replied—almost Pavlovianly—"That must be hard." "No, not really," she responded. And the few evenings I've spent with her since bear out that reply. She seems happy to be alone, her saying so having not so much an air of rationalization as of truth. To the fact that I—reasonably bright, reasonably attractive, clearly interested—have just walked into her life, there is little more reaction than a mildly pleased amiability, like that of someone who has found an extra anchovy in her Caesar salad. My entrance into her life, as into Natalie's kitchen, is—my none-too-subtle wishes notwithstanding—no big deal.

This disappoints me. And I suspect I would hardly be alone among American men in this disappointment. For the analogy made by feminists between men and our patriarchal nation itself is, it seems to me, rather apt. Because, as men, we *have* been like America itself—and still often are. Accustomed to immediate respect, attention, deference, flirtation when we walk into a room full of women (or, by analogy, into a foreign country), it still comes, I think, as a shock to many of us that we are, in some measure, "no big deal"—in fact, are at times perceived as the enemy. Just as we find it, abroad, a sort of jarring injustice that Americans are not only not automatically welcomed everywhere with open arms, but are occasionally shot at, hijacked, kidnapped, ambushed, even (God forbid!) sometimes ignored, so we men (no matter how "feminist" we may claim—or wish—to be) are often still taken aback by the fact that the earth does not cease its turning by our merely walking into a room.

The fact is—as I was reminded in Natalie's kitchen and Marjorie's living room—that women no longer "need" men the way we men who came of age in the late 1960s and early '70s were once trained to believe they did. As did the women around that kitchen table, many of them have their own homes, their own careers, their own values, their own "network" of women friends, their own sense of security—even, in many cases, their own children. And if, indeed, they "need" men, those needs are, clearly, of a different genre—for partners, not protectors; for equals, not oppressors; for someone to look *across* at, not *up to*.

We all love—and covet—the easy, unearned respect that comes as an automatic appendage of certain genders, nationalities or jobs—be it Man, America, Doctor, Professor, Athlete, Movie Star or Indian Chief. Such respect asks nothing of us—other than that we fit into some preordained (and, largely, not of our making) category—and gives a great deal in return. And it is something that we, as men, have been trained to expect. The absence of that often undeserved confirmation of our own importance comes to be seen not as a kind of justice, but as a deprivation.

I still haven't quite grown used to the new sense of my initial unimportance (or, at least, neutrality) in the eyes of women, to the fact that they can (and do) live very well without me or other members of my once-benighted kind. All the studies I've read on the subject, in fact, suggest that, of the four possible heterosexual categories (married men, single men, married women, single women), single women and married men tend to fare psychologically the best, married women and single men worst. What this might say about who "needs" whom the most I leave for you, gentle reader, to decide.

Someday, of course, the hope—and the expectation—is that we will all come to be beneficiaries of this change in the equation of power and need between the sexes, as many of the men and women of my students' generation, and even of my own, seem already to be. Meanwhile, it's back to Marjorie's house tonight—perhaps merely as another small surprise in the mixed metaphor of what Yeats would have called her "crazy salad," perhaps to be greeted, when I enter, not with a combination of reverence and romantic longing, but merely with that benevolent disinterestedness—some small sign of a man's new place in the world, something he may have to *earn* the right to turn into a smile.

FRIENDSHIP

PAUL GOTTLIEB

The Reunion

My two best friends from college days are Hugh and Charlie. Hugh and I have remained close for the intervening quarter of a century, but Charlie is another matter altogether. Fifteen years ago, he disappeared completely from our lives. Last December, Hugh and I rediscovered him, and in so doing rediscovered the power of early friendships.

We three first met some thirty years ago, in my first week at Swarthmore. I had just turned seventeen, a nervous Brooklyn Tech graduate entering a small Quaker college at the start of everybody else's second semester. In the cavernous commons room of the main building, I spotted two boys who struck me as representing everything college was supposed to be. Hugh was discoursing on the metaphysical poetry of John Donne. Charlie was blowing smoke rings. I could do neither. They were older than I by two years and seemed vastly more knowledgeable. Though Hugh looked like a young Marlon Brando, there was never any question in his or anyone else's mind that he would become a writer. Charlie wore his wavy red hair in a tousled arrangement, as if he had more important matters to think about than his appearance. He would later become a psychologist, but in those days he aspired to the lifestyle and talents of F. Scott Fitzgerald.

In the ensuing months, the three of us talked incessantly—about God, about great and not-so-great literature, about our relatively brief past lives, about the nature of man—and we talked an awful lot about girls. That talk at all hours has, I think, something to do

141

with the intensity of friendships formed in early years. Such friendships demand an investment of time that one can rarely afford later, as well as a willingness to be vulnerable, to reveal oneself and to be receptive to new ideas.

Hugh and I, both New Yorkers, sprang from relatively similar, stable Jewish backgrounds. Charlie was the only child of a Boston Irish Catholic family: his mother a fragile woman who worked as a nurse and communicated rarely with her son; his father already in the mental hospital that he was never to leave. Over the coming years, Hugh and I were to become variations on the themes of our cultural pasts. Charlie's accomplishment was more awesome: he had to invent himself almost completely. He was the first of us to marry and have a child. In 1955, still in his F. Scott Fitzgerald phase, Charlie wed a Southern debutante. I was best man. Hundreds of elaborately dressed people filled the bride's side of the aisle; on the groom's side, there was Charlie's mother, one aunt and uncle, my family and Hugh.

Five years later, Charlie, now recovering from the end of his first marriage, came to New York to do research in psychology. Eventually, he married again, an elegant, reserved woman who seemed uncomfortable with our boisterous behavior. As we each began to raise our own families, Charlie's new wife gradually drew him away from our orbit. We were all too busy to notice what was happening, until one day Charlie and his family simply disappeared from New York. They left no forwarding address. We didn't know where to look for him. Besides, I suppose, Hugh and I were hurt. Charlie, after all, had chosen his new family over our old "family." We went on with our lives. Charlie was now part of our vanished youth.

Fifteen years passed. Hugh became a successful novelist; I became a publisher. Then, late in the fall, at a cocktail party, I ran into a woman who knew us all from the old days. "Have you heard about Charlie?" she asked. "He's divorced again and living in Annapolis."

Immediately, I knew what I wanted to do. I put my drink down, went into an adjoining room and called Hugh. We agreed that we were going to visit Charlie whether or not he wanted to see us. I managed to get his Annapolis telephone number and nervously called. "Hugh and I are coming to see you," I stammered. "When?" the familiar voice answered, as if we had spoken only the day before.

Early one Friday morning last December, Hugh and I took off for Annapolis. The small plane flew not far above the ground, and we fell into silence watching the landscape below. Would our meeting with Charlie be simply a reliving of past associations, or would there be more? Could we get beyond nostalgia for our lost youth and move into a future friendship as well?

We arrived at the Baltimore-Washington airport, and as we passed through the landing gate, there was Charlie looking for us. "Oh," I thought, drawing in my breath and my gut, "we are middle-aged for certain." Considerably heavier now, hair thinning, gray mixed with red, Charlie flashed us a familiar grin. We burst into excited shouts like small boys winning a Little League championship. We seized each other joyfully, jumping up and down, whooping, laughing, hugging and kissing. Arm in arm, we felt invincible, a reunited troika. We raced to the car, hopped in and drove off. Charlie was so excited telling us of his life over the past fifteen years that we completely missed the highway turnoff and had to drive thirty miles out of the way before we came to Annapolis. His parents had both died, he explained. He had gambled everything on his second marriage, hoping it would give him the roots he sought, but, while he had two more children, it had not worked out. He was alone again.

We pulled up in front of the hotel where we were to stay. Hugh and I checked in and chose beds as college roommates do, flipping a coin for first choice. Charlie smiled. "Hey, I bought us something." Three identical gift boxes contained three identical knitted ties, maroon with jaunty blue stripes. We laughed and put them on, three aging musketeers in the highest spirits despite the gray and drizzling day.

We linked arms to roam the streets of Annapolis. At a restaurant, we began drinking large quantities of wine from pewter tankards. I realized that Hugh and Charlie were sitting side by side as they had been the day I first met them, rattling on about the work of a writer, while I sat quietly, the disciple listening to my elders. We drank more wine, and then reeled from shop to shop, trying on hats, looking at paintings, browsing through antique galleries and bookstores. We flirted with a barmaid who invited us home to bathe in her large zinc tub. (Hugh and I were flattered; to Charlie the invitation was commonplace.) We drank beer and ate dozens of oysters; and, surrounded by the young people from the local college and from the Naval Academy, we briefly found our own youth again, found our young voices and our young minds.

That night, Hugh and I lay awake in our hotel beds as we had so often in our college dormitory. We speculated about the nature of our relationships and particularly wondered how we had all influenced each other so many years ago. As we drifted toward sleep, we agreed that the principal quality we had absorbed from Charlie was a sense of wit, that ironic edge that adds zest and spice to thought and language.

The next day, we had breakfast with Charlie, admired the view from his small apartment and took turns trying out his water bed. I told him of our conversation the night before, and he laughed.

Hugh looked up and said quietly, "Charlie, if we learned wit from you, was there anything you learned from us?"

Charlie looked at both of us. "I thought you knew," he said. "Love."

STEVE TESICH

Focusing on Friends

When I think of people who were my good friends, I see them all, as I do everything else from my life, in cinematic terms. The camera work is entirely different for men and women.

I remember all the women in almost extreme close-ups. The settings are different—apartments, restaurants—but they're all interiors, as if I had never spent a single minute with a single woman outside. They're looking right at me, these women in these extreme close-ups; the lighting is exquisite, worthy of a Fellini or Fosse film, and their lips are moving. They're telling me something important or reacting to something even more important that I've told them. It's the kind of movie where you tell people to keep quiet when they chew their popcorn too loudly.

The boys and men who were my friends are in an entirely different movie. No close-ups here. No exquisite lighting. The camera work is rather shaky, but the background is moving. We're going somewhere, on foot, on bicycles, in cars. The ritual of motion, of action, makes up for the inconsequential nature of the dialogue. It's a much sloppier film, this film that is not really a film but a memory of real friends: Slobo, Louie, Sam. Male friends. I've loved all three of them. I assumed they knew this, but I never told them.

Quite the contrary is true in my female films. In close-up after close-up, I am telling every woman who I ever loved that I love her, and then lingering on yet another close-up of her face for a reaction. There is a perfectly appropriate musical score playing while I wait. And if I wait long enough, I get an answer. I am loved. I am

145

not loved. Language clears up the suspense. The emotion is nailed down.

Therein lies the difference, I think, between my friendships with men and with women. I can tell women I love them. Not only can I tell them, I am compulsive about it. I can hardly wait to tell them. But I can't tell the men. I just can't. And they can't tell me. Emotions are never nailed down. They run wild, and I and my male friends chase after them, on foot, on bicycles, in cars, keeping the quarry in sight but never catching up.

My first friend was Slobo. I was still living in Yugoslavia at the time, and not far from my house there was an old German truck left abandoned after the war. It had no wheels. No windshield. No doors. But the steering wheel was intact. Slobo and I flew to America in that truck. It was our airplane. Even now, I remember the background moving as we took off down the street, across Europe, across the Atlantic. We were inseparable. The best of friends. Naturally, not one word concerning the nature of our feelings for one another was ever exchanged. It was all done in actions.

The inevitable would happen at least once a day. As we were flying over the Atlantic, there came, out of nowhere, that wonderful moment: engine failure! "We'll have to bail out," I shouted. "*A-a-a-a-a-!*" Slobo made the sound of a failing engine. Then he would turn and look me in the eye: "I can't swim," he'd say. "Fear not." I put my hand on his shoulder. "I'll drag you to shore." And, with that, both of us would tumble out of the truck onto the dusty street. I swam through the dust. Slobo drowned in the dust, coughing, gagging. "Sharks!" he cried. But I always saved him. The next day the ritual would be repeated, only then it would be my turn to say "I can't swim," and Slobo would save me. We saved each other from certain death over a hundred times, until finally a day came when I really left for America with my mother and sister. Slobo and I stood at the train station. We were there to say goodbye, but since we weren't that good at saying things and since he couldn't save me, he just cried until the train started to move.

The best friend I had in high school was Louie. It now seems to me that I was totally monogamous when it came to male friends. I would have several girlfriends but only one real male friend. Louie was it at that time. We were both athletes, and one day we decided to "run till we drop." We just wanted to know what it was like. Skinny Louie set the pace as we ran around our high school track. Lap after lap. Four laps to a mile. Mile after mile we ran. I had the reputation of being a big-time jock. Louie didn't. But this was Louie's day. There was a bounce in his step and, when he turned back to look at me, his eyes were gleaming with the thrill of it all. I finally dropped. Louie still looked fresh; he seemed capable, on that day, of running forever. But we were the best of friends, and so he stopped. "That's it," he lied. "I couldn't go another step farther." It was an act of love. Naturally I said nothing.

Louie got killed in Vietnam. Several weeks after his funeral, I went to his mother's house, and, because she was a woman, I tried to tell her how much I had loved her son. It was not a good scene. Although I was telling the truth, my words sounded like lies. It was all very painful and embarrassing. I kept thinking how sorry I was that I had never told Louie himself.

Sam is my best friend now, and has been for many years. A few years ago, we were swimming at a beach in East Hampton. The Atlantic! The very Atlantic I had flown over in my German truck with Slobo. We had swum out pretty far from the shore when both of us simultaneously thought we spotted a shark. Water is not only a good conductor of electricity but of panic as well. We began splashing like madmen toward shore. Suddenly, at the height of my panic, I realized how much I loved my friend, what an irreplaceable friend he was, and, although I was the faster swimmer, I fell back to protect him. Naturally, the shark in the end proved to be imaginary. But not my feelings for my friend. For several days after that I wanted to share my discovery with him, to tell him how much I loved him. Fortunately, I didn't.

I say fortunately because, on reflection, there seems to be sufficient evidence to indicate that, if anybody was cheated and short-changed by me, it was the women, the girls, the very recipients of my uncensored emotions. Yes, I could hardly wait to tell them I loved them. I did love them. But once I told them, something stopped. The emotion was nailed down, but with it, the enthusiasm and the energy to prove it was nailed down, too. I can remember my voice saying to almost all of them, at one time or another: "I told you I love you. What else do you want?" I can now recoil at the impatient hostility of that voice, but I can't deny it was mine.

The tyranny of self-censorship forced me, in my relations with male friends, to seek alternatives to language. And just because I could never be sure they understood exactly how I felt about them, I was forced to look for ways to prove it. That is, I now think, how it should be. It is time to make adjustments. It is time to pull back the camera, free the women I know, and myself, from those merciless close-ups and have the background move.

HERBERT GOLD

In Each Other's Company

These days, in California at least, the men I know seem to drink less and spend more time in coffeehouses telling each other how young they look. The child-custody fathers can bring their kids and find others of their species. The kids drink hot chocolate and eat oatmeal-raisin cookies. The fathers say: "Well, I didn't think it would work out like this. But it's working out okay." I sit there and guess that we are all in this thing together. Yes, we are getting older. No, we're not alone. We have our friendships.

Twisting and diving, loping and attacking—plainly grunting and sweating—a young textile tycoon and I play racquetball. With devout concentration, we hunt and roam in a closed arena. Evenly matched, we have learned not to be too cast down when we lose, although we chortle with joy when we win.

My partner's metabolism requires risk and the expense of inventive agility. I am struggling to understand why this fast play with a hard rubber ball and a short-handled racquet seems to rank with love, children and art as one of the great pleasures of life even if I lose—in fact, a pleasure without grief, which I can't say for love, children or art.

The tycoon and I are not intimate friends, but the game has made a bond between us. The racquet is a weapon, like the gun or the bow and arrow. Hunters also know this comradeship that springs up between men who share the ancient rituals of exertion, risk, competition. There are women in the club, but my partner and I share a bit of disdain for those who treat it merely as a singles'

149

meeting spa. For the moment, we are content in each other's company.

A few years ago I was interviewed for a book about "male bonding," which is a pompous way to say "friendship between men." The writer and I discussed how old friends are the dearest, perhaps because of self-love: they have witnessed one's life. And then we speculated that sometimes new friends are the best, because one is free to proclaim any self-inventions one likes, and the new infatuation makes credence easy and agreeable. So those occasional new friendships also imply self-love. You are whatever you seem to be at the moment, whatever the friend sees in you.

We were enjoying a meeting of minds about the deep matter of friendship, and I thought we understood each other. Then he asked, "Do you kiss your friend?"

"What?"

"On the lips?" he asked.

I began to laugh, and he looked hurt. I was laughing because I had thought we understood each other and we didn't; he was hurt because he had in mind a model for friendship based on a credo of his former wife's women's group, and evidently I didn't have that in mind.

So that other mode of association between men began to assert itself: hostile banter. I accused him of not attending to friendship, not listening to me, but merely going by the current politically correct feminist notion. He replied that women have a lot to teach men about friendship. We parted in mutual suspicion.

Now when we meet, a few years later, we recall the incident with a sense of the shared past, irritation and disappointment—emotions!—which amount to a curious friendship. We went through something together. Talk may not be as true as racquetball, but discussion can sometimes arrive at understanding.

My concert promoter friend, Bill, seems to live with telephones stuck in his ears. To get his attention, one must participate in his current deals, his angers, his frantic triumphs. Mostly this is a lonely sharing. Yet we are friends. I had the idea of hiking with him in the California woods and suggested to this obsessed talker that we take a vow of silence as we walked to the Tassajara Zen Monastery. He agreed, but before we could go he telephoned to say, "Something has come up."

"Something always comes up," I said.

Shamed, he put our hike back on his schedule. Our vow of silence lasted ten minutes, until the first bug bite. Then came his steady stream of cursing—un-broken-in boots, insect nips, poison oak for sure. So we talked. Then we were silent. We climbed and panted and forded streams. We learned something it was unnecessary to discuss: a difficult sharing affirms friendship. Planned and formal as a cross-country hike might be, fitted into a schedule, it nevertheless serves to define and establish the facts of feeling.

The great model for friendship is the lifeboat. Classically, war has occasioned these moments of unscheduled danger and sacrifice. No matter what good company I find in a man in a bar or on a commuter train, there remains that secret need to know: Will he pull me into the lifeboat when I am in danger of swamping at sea? Playing games, competing, confiding, long sharing of work or opinions, even the borrowing of money, provide only a shadow of the test. Is this a friendship that would survive the ship's going down, one of us in the lifeboat, the other in the sea and reaching out? Will he carry me back to safety under fire? These urban palships of mine don't put this ultimate ideal to the test.

In Just Desserts, a San Francisco coffeehouse, there is, nevertheless, a sense of shared risk among single men—or men only delaying their return to the marital bed. Yes, finally the ship is going down. But meanwhile there are talk, compassion, jokes along the way.

And raising a child demands almost as much concentration as climbing into that half-swamped lifeboat. Now that my sons are old enough, they try and try to beat me at racquetball. One day soon they will. I'll try to take it good-naturedly, garrulous afterward, hoping they will be as philosophical with me, as gentle in the ancient round of things, as the hunter appreciating the prey slung over his shoulders for the trek homeward.

KEITH G. McWALTER

Hitting the Road

Several years ago, a good friend and I set out, without pretext of grand purpose, on a trip by car from a university town in northern California to Aspen, Colorado. Two guys, a black Scirocco, the open road. It was mid-August, and we took turns driving across the immense lunar deserts of Nevada and Utah.

When men travel, they try to do it in pairs. It's a fine tradition. Butch and Sundance, Lewis and Clark, Kerouac and Cassady, a million patrol-car cops. For mutual protection, for companionship, for fun. But for something else as well. When I was a teenager, the most impressive show on television was a meandering, male-bonding epic called "Route 66." Two guys, a convertible Corvette, the open road. The possibilities were limitless.

When men gather in groups, their friendship tends to degenerate into macho posturing, excessive drinking and other nervous tics. Left to themselves, a group of men will find a way to form into teams and engage in some form of competition. Men in pairs, though, often turn introspective and philosophical. If they are relatively footloose and of a certain age, the wistful subject of travel will inevitably arise, and if the stars are right and a vehicle available, they will be on their way, the act of traveling itself a vehicle for the act of sharing. Between men, travel by car is a wonderful excuse to continue a conversation for longer than it takes to down a beer or two (the natural half-life of the male exchange).

Our first night found us in Fernley, Nevada, less a town than a strip of asphalt bounded on one end by a gas station and a bar at the other. Against my better judgment, my friend chose to slake his highway thirst in that bar, and, moreover, chose to do so wearing a white Givenchy shirt. Bolstered by malt and hops, he danced with local womenfolk to country-and-western music on the jukebox. The boys at the bar were not greatly amused. Danger lurked. Eventually my lobbying prevailed and we escaped, having made no friends in Fernley.

Escape is central to the mythology of male travel. Strengthened by another of our kind, we leave behind wife, lover, kids, mortgage, office and routine, and light out for the territories, exempted from guilt by the righteousness of the myth, the inalienable human right to be a jerk in the company of another jerk. Beer cans fly out the sun roof; we weep at the beauty of the desert dusk. Where we stop nobody knows.

We hit a lot of slot machines in a lot of gas stations and bars across Nevada, kept the winnings in a big Styrofoam cup on the dash and paid for gas out of it. Thus we did conform perfectly to the spirit of the land we traversed: gambling and gasoline, inextricably linked. We took from the land and we returned our takings to it. So passed Nevada.

Utah was more puritanical, more fiercely desolate. It was there, in the vacuum grip of a die-straight highway, that we exchanged tales of betrayal and failure, loves misguided or denied, women we missed and women we mourned. Women, truth be told, were never far from our thoughts, but the chance of romantic encounter on this, our own Route 66, was a possibility we neither courted nor abjured.

Men in pairs are the quintessence of their sex. Reassured of their own natures by mutual example, and strengthened in the furtive conviction that it is not (despite the feminist complaint) a nature to be ashamed of, male friends try together to decipher the conundrum of sex and love without the false self-confidence that they are trained to exhibit in public and before the alien gender. We know full well how difficult we are, how much we need to be forgiven, how rare forgiveness is. Or so it was with my friend and me, both of us divorced parents of female children, there in the vastness of the

Utah night. As I sped us toward the receding dark, he wailed for a
woman he had recently forfeited because she had wanted more
commitment than he could then manage; I wailed for a woman I
wanted and could not have. Lust for freedom, lust for intimacy: the
inveterate yin and yang of the male psyche. Never a better time to
weep for lost love than when you've put your fool self a million
miles from nowhere in a hurtling machine.

Aspen was gained in due course, and late afternoon in that
Rocky Mountain August found us in a bar and restaurant, soaking
in the smug satisfaction of our completed journey. Large vertical
windows opened outward to scoop up cool evening breezes. The
women in the room were resplendent in their high-altitude reserve.
The chatter was of jobs, shrinks and real estate development.

Two men entered and sat at a table near the bar, their clothes
well tailored, their eyes avid. They were gay, I think. Talk at the
bar lowered. A couple of dudes in leather vests shifted uneasily on
their stools. My friend and I exchanged looks. He is just noticeably
older than I, and throughout our trip we had caught people eyeing
us oddly, no doubt certain that we, too, were gay city slickers on
some back-road sojourn. My one regret about the going public of
male homosexuality is that it casts all men in pairs in a new and
ambiguous light, before the world and before themselves. I don't
mind being mistaken for gay, but I do mind the crowding out from
the general consciousness of a kind of love between men that is neither romantic nor sexual, but is nonetheless terribly hard for most
men to acknowledge to one another.

I regret that development because, in the course of the long
drive, the friendship that my companion and I had long shared
matured into love in the usual way: through talk, horsing around,
vulnerability, fun, shared times. But we needed certain trappings to
make it happen; we needed the car, the myth of the nomad, the
bars, the road. That men must go to such distances to achieve
closeness with one another, that they are forced to such perambula-
tions of the spirit in order to come home to the simple truth of mutual caring, that is the message I had missed when "Route 66"
rolled off into a sunset of credits on my TV way back when.

I can't remember the return trip. Maybe it was too monotonous to leave much impression. Anyway, it was beside the point, a mere retreat from the territory we had made our own. It was the outward push, the dream of the shared unknown that propelled us, as surely as the gas fund in our Styrofoam cup, on that long mutual journey of the heart.

MICHAEL E. McGILL

A Female Best Friend

It was a summer's-end cocktail party. My wife, Janet, and I were enjoying an evening with friends, sharing vacation highlights, anticipating the return of children to school and fall's events. Late that evening we were with Tom and Sharon, close friends of ours for years, when Sharon asked Janet, "How do you feel about Mick's plans to take next summer off?" As soon as I heard where her question was going, I tried to jump in to change the conversation, but it was too late. Janet glared at me and said coldly, "He hasn't said anything to *me* about his plans for next summer." Then she turned and walked away.

I knew that when I caught up with Janet I would be in for cross-examination. "Do you know how humiliating it is to hear about what you're doing from another woman? What else have you told her that I don't know? Why can you talk to her when you can't seem to talk to me? What exactly is going on between you two, anyway? Just how close are you? Have you thought about what we're going to do for money if you take the summer off?" Janet legitimately asked that I explain why my best friend was another woman.

Sharon *is* my best friend. We make time to be together to talk, just the two of us; I often tell her things that I haven't told Janet or tell her things before I tell Janet. I am closer to her than I am to any of my male friends. Our relationship is not unusual, I've discovered. In a two-year survey of nearly two thousand men and women for a book on male relational behavior, I learned that one out of every three men knows a woman, other than his wife, with whom he feels he can "talk about anything." She is usually his mother, sister, a work associate or, as in my case, a friend.

My wife's reaction was not unusual either. Knowing that her husband is close to another woman can be threatening to any wife. Even for unmarried couples a man's relationship with another woman is a serious issue. A close relationship between a man and a woman is almost always viewed as a sexual involvement, and most, no doubt, are. But sexual relations are not the métier of best friendships. I know that it is possible for a man and woman to be close without having a sexual relationship. They may lack sexual interest in each other, or fear for their marriages, or, as Sharon and I did, mutually and consciously decide not to become sexually involved. Sharon and I are intimate but sexually innocent; our interest in each other is relational, not romantic. Some observers might say that this is our own particular brand of romantic involvement, but I don't see it that way. Sharon is my best friend not just because of *who* she is but because of *what* she is—another woman. Given the state of male friendships, at least as I have known them, I think every man needs both a wife and another woman.

In my opinion, men make poor best friends. Among ourselves, we men have functional friendships, alliances that serve specific purposes—tennis partners, business associates, drinking buddies. In those friendships we share no more of ourselves than the activity requires. We use interaction with one another to prove ourselves, following conventional rules of commerce and competition, ever aware that if we get too close, confide too much, it may be used against us.

But women use interaction as a way to improve relationships. It is little wonder that whenever we men feel a need to communicate something of ourselves, we seek out a woman for the purpose. Men have always found it easier to talk to women about the things that are really important. When I was a child my father always listened proudly to my small victories. He pitched in when I needed help on a task. But when I wanted to talk about how it felt to lose or when I was embarrassed or ashamed, he grew uncomfortable and pulled away. It was Mom who listened to my feelings and empathized. As a young boy, smitten with a playground crush, I was taunted and ridiculed by the boys in my gang, but girls my own age understood how I felt. In college, my fraternity brothers were great for philosophizing over beers, but when one of our number took his own life we looked to girlfriends to help us deal with our grief. Recently, when a close male friend got divorced, he turned not to me but to a woman friend for solace. Finally, as close as I am to Tom, we have never talked about how I feel about Sharon or about his feelings about my relationship with Sharon. We men don't talk about these things. In times of crisis and in times of caring, women make the best friends—and we men have always known that.

Wives can answer a man's need for friendship, but I am suspicious of descriptions of wives as a husband's best friend. In certain circumstances, a wife simply cannot act as a best friend. With Sharon I can, for instance, be totally revealing without risk. Her distance allows her to be objective. She can listen and understand what I'm experiencing without having a personal stake in what I say. If I say to my wife, "I'm thinking of taking the summer off," her immediate worry is how we're going to pay the bills. My friend asks instead what I intend to do with the free time. She cares, but my choice makes no difference to her. I can be honest without being hassled by the need to be realistic. I do not, I cannot, expect such objectivity from my wife.

The other woman in my life helps me test out feelings and ideas. Sometimes a man doesn't know how he feels until he talks to somebody else. Yet it seems as though everything talked about between a husband and wife must be acted on—if not now, later. With Sharon, I can experiment without having to act before I'm ready. She also is a safety valve, an outlet for some of the pressure that builds up in a marriage, someone I can react to without fearing retribution. Finally, with another woman as a best friend, I get that much more insight into the world of women. My friend helps me understand my wife.

Janet has finally understood—partially. As she said, "It's the same reason Tom needs me for his best friend. I can accept your relationship with Sharon. But what about our relationship? Why do you feel there are things you can't tell me?"

I have some more explaining to do.

MEN AT

WORK

MICHAEL KORDA

A Wardrobe for Starting Out

There are two male fashion worlds. One is what appears in the men's magazines and fashion sections—and all too often in the stores. The other is what people are wearing in business.

Just at the moment, for example, young people have taken up the fashionable 1920s WASP–Ivy League clothing as a look: narrow ties, tiny collars, baggy trousers, bulky tweed sports jackets. To most people over forty, this naturally represents an improvement over the era when young people wore torn blue jeans and Army-surplus combat jackets festooned with obligatory buttons announcing messages of peace or dire threats. However, and this is a big however, most of the people who have the power to give you a job or a raise in the business world still wear dark suits, shirts with conventional collars and sober, medium-width ties. The first lesson of business life is that you are dressing to please them, not yourself. Of course, this doesn't apply to every profession; these days, art directors and "creative people" in general can get away with a good deal, but even in the movie business I note that the dark suit has come into fashion.

I suspect that it's about three generations—two, anyway—since the question of what a young man should wear to start out on his career last came up as a problem for anyone. In the 1950s a whole culture existed whose sole purpose was to provide this information, either by example or instruction. Young men went to J. Press or Brooks Brothers, or their less expensive equivalents in cities all over the country, and were basically outfitted in what their fathers

163

had worn. In the 1960s and 1970s, all of this vanished, or went underground, under the weight of social change. As hair grew longer, clothes grew more eccentric and shabby, and even corporations bent with the wind, afraid that they might not be able to recruit anyone at all.

Now, in the 1980s, the tide has turned. There are more people looking for jobs than there are jobs; it's once again respectable to have conservative attitudes (including attitudes about clothing), and a great many young men entering business, in fact, would like to dress the way their fathers and grandfathers did, but aren't sure how to do it. Dressing for business has become a half-forgotten art, with a certain nostalgic quality, like blacksmithing or sailmaking.

There is no area in which it is easier to make a wrong impression or waste money more quickly than in buying clothes. Even the most knowledgeable people have closets full of clothes that were mistakes, so it's sensible for a young person starting out in business to cling to a few basic rules.

The first rule is simple: Put your money into suits, not accessories.

A "name brand" belt buckle or Gucci loafers won't help if the suit is badly fitted or made of cheap material. An expensive shirt is nice, if one can afford it, but it's not necessary. Ties, socks and underwear need not be expensive. Spend money on the basics. If you go up in the world, you can then add the accessories.

For any kind of business career, one needs, at minimum, three good suits. They do not have to be tailor-made, but you should go to some trouble to make sure they fit. If you can find a good custom tailor who will do alterations, it's worth the time and the effort.

These suits, which will provide a basic wardrobe for business success, should be of wool blend. All-wool is more expensive; all-synthetic material tends to look cheap and shiny, and wrinkles easily. Wool or wool blends have the advantage of keeping a crease; and if you hang the suit up in the bathroom while taking a shower, you can usually get a week's wear out of it before it needs pressing.

The material should also be medium-weight. Light-weight suits wrinkle the moment they are put on, while the heavier fabrics are too uncomfortable to wear for eight hours in a heated office.

As for color, my suggestion would be: one dark-blue single-breasted suit with a faint, narrow stripe; one plain dark-blue single-breasted suit; and one dark-gray suit, also single-breasted. The lapels should be medium width. There should be at least three buttons on the sleeves. And trousers with cuffs hang better.

If yours is the kind of office where people work in their shirt-sleeves (the main question is: Does your boss work in shirtsleeves?), then it makes sense to buy some good shirts, preferably fitted at the waist, since most shirts seem to be made with a hippo in mind. The shirts, in any case, should be white or a plain light blue; cotton is best. They should not have contrasting collars, oddly shaped collars or French cuffs, which are generally more appropriate for evening wear than business.

The Duchess of Windsor is said to have once remarked, "You can never be too rich or too thin." This is probably true, but you can add to this piece of wisdom that your ties can never be too dark or too simple. Buying a tie should be easy. It should be medium width, a dark color and a muted pattern, if any. Silk knit ties in navy blue, burgundy or dark green are easy to find and appropriate with any suit. Fancy ties make you look like someone starting out on a business career with Nathan Detroit as your role model.

Shoes should be simple, too. Plain black lace-up shoes, without fancy stitching or thick soles, are all one needs; and they should be meticulously polished. Since it's considered rude to look people too fixedly in the eyes, most of us unconsciously look down when we're talking to someone, and the first thing we see is their shoes. Hence, scruffy shoes make an immediate impression.

Overcoats are expensive. Here, I would suggest a lifetime invest-ment in one of those Burberry trench coats (or a good imitation) that has a button-in camel's hair lining. It's expensive, but less ex-pensive than buying both a raincoat and a topcoat, and it serves both functions rather elegantly. With the lining buttoned in and perhaps a camel's hair scarf, it should keep you warm until you reach the point where you'll be using the corporate limo.

And that, of course, is the point. If you want to get ahead, you should dress for success before you are a success. Different companies have different standards, and God knows, no subject produces more prejudices than men's clothes, but to my knowledge nobody objects to a dark-blue suit, a plain shirt and a dark tie, so why give yourself more trouble than you need?

What you don't need is: a bow tie (except in very WASPish law firms, with a senior partner who looks like John Houseman or is John Houseman); cuff links, unless you're going to be a show-biz agent; a tie clip; pens or pencils in your breast pocket; a shoulder bag or a man's purse—businessmen carry a briefcase, even if it contains only *Playboy* magazine; socks that fall down around your ankles—buy black stretch socks; double-breasted suits—unless they are tailor-made, the jackets tend to bulge and wrinkle when you sit down; hats, unless you really look good in them.

You may also want to consider the advantage of a gray suit with two pairs of trousers and a dark-blue blazer (with plain gold-plated buttons). This creates the equivalent of two suits, plus something that will do for more informal wear—sales conferences, conventions, etc.

And one final point: When in doubt, look at what the man who has the power to hire or fire you, or determine your raise or promotion, is wearing, and model yourself on that. And if he's a she, as may be the case, look at the nearest male authority figure you can find, if there still is one.

JOHN KENNETH GALBRAITH

Corporate Man

Any consideration of the life and larger social existence of the modern corporate man—the individual in the reasonably senior ranks of the thousand largest corporations—begins and also largely ends with the effect of one all-embracing force. That is organization—the highly structured assemblage of men (and some women) of which he is a part. It is to this, at the expense of family, friends, sex, recreation and sometimes health and effective control of alcoholic intake, that he devotes his energies. We are all in some measure the creatures of organization and its constraints. The college professor who prides himself on his utter independence of speech and manner gives careful thought in all but the most convenient or eccentric cases to the effect of his voice and behavior on his faculty position and, in more exceptional cases, on the reputation of his college or university. The business executive, however, is subject to a far more severe and comprehensive discipline. It may not, on the job, be quite that of an army officer, but it embraces a far larger part of his life. He is never off duty.

There are notable social rewards from this. It provides the larger community with the services of an exceptionally hard-working, even driven, body of men. Among the many charges that, justly or unjustly, have been brought against the modern corporate executive, one has been totally lacking. Not even his most relentless critic suggests that he is lazy.

The modern business executive is also a well-spoken man, tolerant of disagreement, disposed always to negotiate—for that is how he spends his time—and otherwise given to persuasion rather than command. In all respects, he is a far more agreeable figure than his predecessor, the great captain of industry, the prototypical entrepreneur.

The counterpart of the modern executive's disciplined commitment to the job at hand is, however, an extremely severe sacrifice of the right to personal thought and expression. And also of a wide range of personal enjoyments. It is, of course, axiomatic that no responsible corporate executive expresses himself publicly in opposition to the decisions, purposes, social effects, political activities or malfeasances of his organization. He can dissent in private. But if things get really insupportable, he can only resign and explain that, although all is amicable, he feels that the time has come in his career when he should look for new challenges elsewhere. This, one day no doubt, will be called the DeLorean Exit.

The ban on unlicensed expression is not quite the same as silence. The modern business executive does make speeches—to stockholders, financial analysts, business organizations, service clubs, church groups and, on occasion, still to the Boy Scouts. But there is no form of spoken literature, Sunday sermons possibly excepted, that invokes such a profound silence. The press and other media ignore entirely such executive communications or, if they say something about prospective earnings, subject them to a truly masterful condensation. Though often offered with no slight vehemence, executive views on public policy are also ignored. Nor should the aspiring corporate leader be in doubt as to the reason. What he says is required by the rules and ethics of organization to be both predictable and dull. He does not speak for himself; he speaks for the firm. Good policy is not what he wants but what the organization believes it needs. In the normal case, his speech will be written and vetted by his fellow organization men. In the process, it will drop to the lowest common denominator of novelty. Lindbergh, as has too often been told, could never have flown the Atlantic with a committee. It is equally certain that General Motors could never have written Shakespeare or even a column by Art Buchwald. Executive expression is ignored because, by the nature of organization, it must be at an exceptionally tedious level of organization stereotype and caution.

This is not the only constraint to which the executive is subject. There is a subjective effect that is far more comprehensive and that is very little noticed in our time. Every year, the Harvard Business School graduates some 750 students. They are an extremely bright and diverse convocation with, as students go, exceptionally high standards of dress and personal hygiene. Meeting with them on frequent occasion over the years has always been a pleasure. All, with the rarest exceptions, will enjoy extraordinarily ample incomes for the rest of their lives. None, with only the most eccentric exceptions, will ever make any personal contribution in music, painting, the theater, film, writing, serious learning or the lower art of politics. Once, a good income was thought to allow of such diversions; that was its purpose. From the modern business executive the most that can be expected is a check in support of someone else's achievements.

The income of the corporate executive in our time is a topic of much comment and some envy. (It owes something to the convenient circumstance that in the upper reaches of the modern corporation the executive has a more than modest role in setting his own perquisites.) More attention needs to be accorded to what the executive gives up in return.

This increasingly includes personal identity. Once we knew the names of the heads of great corporations—that Alfred P. Sloan, Jr., was the head of General Motors, Thomas J. Watson of IBM, Ford of Ford—and there is little doubt that John D. Rockefeller had total name identification, as it is called, as the founder and head of Standard Oil of New Jersey. Now a poll asking the name of the present heads of these corporations (or their successors) would draw a truly impressive number of blanks. The organization has taken over; the head is unknown. The point is emphasized by what happens when he leaves office: While there, he unquestionably commands a considerable measure of respect, even deference, from his fellow executives and when he shows up for high-level meetings in Washington. On the day he leaves office, he joins past Secretaries of Defense, also men who are made by the organization, in an oblivion that continues until the few touching lines appear in the obituary columns. I do not suggest that, given his sacrifices, the modern business executive is underpaid; there are some millions more in line worthy of that concern. I do note that it is worth something to give up so much—considering the present state of knowledge on the matter—of one's only certain life.

JIM FUSILLI

A Wall Street Rocker

"Who says you can't have it all?" asks the beer commercial. "Who says you can't have pinstripes and rock 'n' roll?"

Me. I say you can't have it all. I try, so I know. Five days a week I write and edit employee newsletters and do a variety of other corporate tasks. Two nights a week, I sing and play guitar in a rock 'n' roll band. The two aren't compatible. Not even close.

Other people with full-blown careers play instruments. Richard Nixon plays the piano, Johnny Carson the drums; Sherlock Holmes played the violin. But playing in the band is not like that. It's not a once-in-a-while thing. You don't sit at home and pluck the strings for yourself. That's fun. There's no pressure.

But with a band, especially one that's serious about its business, you have to put up with all the ancillary activity that goes with the turf. There's the interaction with group members—in my case, five other guys, three of whom are full-time music makers, all with artistic idiosyncrasies. There are endless rehearsals and conferences. If you write your own songs, as we do, there are musical and vocal arrangements to work out. Sometimes you have to defend your material, and sometimes you have to play a song you don't like.

That may sound like a typical day at the office to you. But for me, it comes *after* a day at the office, and there's a giant mindshift that has to take place. I take the E Train to an uptown New York rehearsal hall, and if I don't feel and think like a musician by the time I get there, I'm sunk. The practicality of business life doesn't apply. Progress comes slowly, if at all. There's little tangible evidence of achievement, except for the cassettes I make at each rehearsal. Frustration is acute. We practice the same number for a solid month. Not even accountants work on the same number every day.

And I think like a businessman now. I'm no longer interested in playing just for fun. I look at the bottom line; so far, I've lost time and money. I want schedules; I work best on deadline. I want the band's goals defined.

My goal is to get good tapes and send them out. It would be swell to get a song on the next album Quincy Jones produces and pull in a few million bucks in royalties. Accordingly, once we perform a song I've written and get a quality recording of it, I ask that we drop it from our repertory. Sometimes I ask the other guys what they want out of it. When they answer "I like to play," I don't understand.

And there are other problems: I'm the only guy who shows up at the rehearsal hall in a suit. Think of how you'd look if you showed up at the office with a sleeveless T-shirt, black studded jeans and leather gloves. My hair—standard Wall Street issue—looks fine at the office, ridiculous at rock clubs. I'm constantly dieting. Rockers are either thin or extremely fat, and I'm neither. I used to be able to jump from the piano top into a split. Now I have to sit to tie my shoes.

We are frequently the oldest band on the bill. We get booked in places designed for people trying to make it. People our age—I'm thirty-two—who haven't yet made it and have solid day jobs usually give up. At one gig, I sat in the dressing room and watched a kid I was certain was a girl change into costume. When the kid turned around, I saw he was just a very young boy. Then he said "Excuse me" as he walked by. I was thankful he didn't add "dad" to the sentence's end.

I recently asked Van Morrison if he ever felt too old to live the rock 'n' roll life. "No way," he said adamantly, but then described all the problems getting older in the rock world brings. Don't tell me Paul McCartney is forty-three, Dylan forty-four, Chuck Berry fifty-nine. Age isn't a dilemma if you've made it and can look back on the mayhem. If your troubles are before you, it's another thing altogether. Remember, Michael Jackson is twenty-seven, and he made some $70 million from his last album. And John Lennon's son is now a pop star.

The obvious question is "Why not walk away?" There's plenty of satisfaction in my Wall Street career, in writing and editing. I'm not leaving it. I certainly don't want to try to hustle a job as a guitarist or a singer in New York. There are more of those than newsletter editors.

When I was in high school, there were four reasons to form a rock band: to meet girls, have fun, show off in public while getting paid for it, and because we were crazy for the music. Reason 1 is definitely dead: the only ladies I'm interested in are my wife and our two-year-old daughter.

Number 2: Fun dribbles in, but sometimes not for weeks at a time. "Then you shouldn't do it if you feel that way," retorts our keyboard player. Two minutes later he says, "You aren't going to quit, are you?" "No," I say, "I'm not going to quit."

As for the in-public part, I truly enjoy performing. Leaving aside the pain of it—carting my own heavy equipment around, staying up until 4 A.M., arguing over who gets guest passes—it's still terrific to play in front of an audience, particularly a New York crowd that refuses to applaud unless you're good. We get a good reception. We're skilled technically and we maintain high energy, a rare combination, as far as I can tell. My material is well received, my voice is stronger than ever and, on guitar, I cut my parts with little difficulty. I do okay.

That leaves the music, which has something to do, I think, with a dream. In this case, it's the dream that I have something to say. It's cloaked in a four-minute song with maybe five chords and a pretty neat modulation. It's probably been said before, but this is how I say it, and I want it heard.

Bruce Springsteen—he's thirty-six—writes: "Talk about a dream, try to make it real." That sounds about right. I think you've got to go after it and give it your best shot until the dream is dead. When I complete a song and perform it, it's a wonderful feeling. I get butterflies and my skin tingles. It's actually thrilling. There's nothing like it. And that doesn't sound like a dead dream to me.

ALAN P. LIGHTMAN

Elapsed Expectations

The limber years for scientists, as for athletes, generally come at a young age. Isaac Newton was in his early twenties when he discovered the law of gravity. Albert Einstein was twenty-six when he formulated special relativity, and James Clerk Maxwell had polished off electromagnetic theory and retired to the country by thirty-five. When I hit thirty-five myself, some months ago, I went through the unpleasant but irresistible exercise of summing up my career in physics. By this age, or another few years, the most creative achievements are finished and visible. You've either got the stuff and used it or you haven't.

In my own case, as with the majority of my colleagues, I concluded that my work was respectable but not brilliant. Very well. Unfortunately, I now have to decide what to do with the rest of my life. My thirty-five-year-old friends who are attorneys and physicians and businessmen are still climbing toward their peeks, perhaps fifteen years up the road, and blissfully uncertain of how high they'll reach. It is an awful thing, at such an age, to fully grasp one's limitations.

Why do scientists peak sooner than most other professionals? No one knows for sure. I suspect it has something to do with the single focus and detachment of the subject. A handiness for visualizing in six dimensions or for abstracting the motion of a pendulum favors a nimble mind but apparently has little to do with anything else. In contrast, the arts and humanities require experience with life, expe-

175

rience that accumulates and deepens with age. In science, you're ultimately trying to connect with the clean logic of mathematics and the physical world; in the humanities, with people. Even within science itself, a telling trend is evident. Progressing from the more pure and self-contained of sciences to the less tidy, the seminal contributions spring forth later and later in life. The average age of election to England's Royal Society is lowest in mathematics. In physics, the average age at which Nobel Prize winners do their prize-winning work is thirty-six; in chemistry it is thirty-nine, and so on.

Another factor is the enormous pressure to take on administrative and advisory tasks descending on you in your mid-thirties and leaving time for little else. Such pressures also occur in other professions, of course, but it seems to me they arrive sooner in a discipline where talent flowers in relative youth. Although the politics of science demands its own brand of talent, the ultimate source of approval—and invitation to supervise—is your personal contribution to the subject itself. As in so many other professions, the administrative and political plums conferred in recognition of past achievements can suffocate future ones. These plums may be politely refused, but perhaps the temptation to accept beckons more strongly when you're not constantly galloping off into new research.

Some of my colleagues brood as I do over this passage, many are oblivious to it, and many sail happily ahead into administration and teaching, without looking back. Service on national advisory panels, for example, benefits the professional community and nation at large, allowing senior scientists to share with society their technical knowledge. Writing textbooks can be satisfying and provides the soil that allows new ideas to take root. Most people also try to keep their hands in research, in some form or another. A favorite way is to gradually surround oneself with a large group of disciples, nourishing the imaginative youngsters with wisdom and perhaps enjoying the authority. Scientists with charisma and leadership contribute a great deal in this manner. Another, more subtle tactic is to hold on to the reins, single-handedly, but find thinner and thinner horses to ride. (This can easily be done by narrowing one's field in order to remain "the world's expert.") Or simply plow ahead with research as in earlier years, aware or not that the light has dimmed. The 1 percent of scientists who have truly illuminated their subject can continue in this manner, to good effect, well beyond their prime.

For me, none of these activities offers an agreeable way out. I hold no illusions about my own achievements in science, but I've had my moments, and I know what it feels like to unravel a mystery no one has understood before, sitting alone at my desk with only pencil and paper and wondering how it happened. The magic cannot be replaced. When I directed an astrophysics conference last summer and realized that most of the exciting research was being reported by ambitious young people in their mid-twenties, waving their calculations and ideas in the air and scarcely slowing down to acknowledge their predecessors, I would have instantly traded my position for theirs. It is the creative element of my profession, not the exposition or administration, that sets me on fire. In this regard, I side with the great mathematician G. H. Hardy, who wrote (at age sixty-three) that "the function of a mathematician is to do something, to prove new theorems, to add to mathematics, and not to talk about what he or other mathematicians have done."

In childhood, I used to lie in bed at night and fantasize about different things I might do with my life, whether I would be this or that, and what was so delicious was the limitless potential, the years shimmering ahead in unpredictability. It is the loss of that I grieve. In a way, I have gotten an unwanted glimpse of my mortality. The private discoveries of new territory are not as frequent now. Knowing this, I might make myself useful in other ways. But another thirty-five years of supervising students, serving on committees, reviewing others' work, is somehow too social. Inevitably, we must all reach our personal limits in whatever professions we choose. In science, this happens at an unreasonably young age, with a lot of life remaining. Some of my older colleagues, having passed through this soul-searching period themselves, tell me I'll get over it in time. I wonder how. None of my fragile childhood dreams, my parents' ambitious encouragement, my education at all the best schools, prepared me for this early seniority, this stiffening at thirty-five.

ROBERT FARRAR CAPON

Being Let Go

The euphemism for it is "resigning in order to pursue a career change," but in plain English it usually amounts to being fired. A man spends years or even decades in a line of work, only to find himself abruptly—there is, in the end, no gradual way to exit from a window—on the street. Even if he knows that his defenestration is only one of the system's deadly whimsies, being let go, despite its overtones of freedom and opportunity, is not of itself a liberating experience. Some men are lucky and gain a certain wisdom from the experience, but change confounds before it comforts.

I know. Seven years ago, I went through just such an experience, turned out of a deanship and the parish I had served for twenty-seven years. It was an edgy four months before even the beginnings of a career as a freelance writer limped slowly into place. And it has been a mixed seven years since.

For a while, admittedly, the shock of being let go numbs a man, enabling him to function as if nothing life-threatening were happening. And often nothing is—at first. Money, from either severance pay or unemployment benefits, enables him at least to subsist; moreover, his lifelong conviction that he is a marketable commodity has not yet been contradicted by rejection. For a few days or weeks, he actually enjoys his leisure.

But then (assuming he is not snapped up at twice the salary), the bloom slowly begins to fade. Desired jobs are not offered; offered jobs turn out to be deeply undesirable. He still has time, of course; but even before financial urgency sinks its teeth into him, certain comparisons begin to nip at his heels. He jogs, let us say, at eight each morning and smiles inwardly at the wage slaves. The smile wanes, though. Despite his still-unshaken belief that they are going nowhere fast, he begins to envy them the dependability of their destinations.

Or perhaps he finds himself—by the necessity of interviews or the mere desire for a social lunch—in other men's outer offices. Sitting there on the sidelines, waiting for a personnel vice president to get around to him or for an old friend to disentangle himself from some corporate huddle, he feels a pang of powerlessness. Three-piece suits clutching manila folders go in and out of doors explaining fine points to each other. A pair of vests with rolled-up shirtsleeves emerge from a room with smiles on their faces and the word "kneecap" on their lips. Power, he recalls hearing, is the one thing in the world you can't fake. For the first time, it occurs to him to call his confidence of recent weeks bravado.

Predictably, anger comes next. Perhaps it is at some known and certifiable villain, perhaps only at the way the Establishment conditions men to the responsibility of working and then denies them any work to be responsible for. For a while he nurses the suspicion that some baleful word has been put out against him; but then the shock of unemployment becomes a pathology in its own right, and he slides inexorably from the irrelevancy of paranoia into the crippling ravages of self-doubt.

A hundred fears come together in the anguish of a man's being out of work: failing to be a provider, losing an outlet for his talents or his masculinity, being deserted by his friends, destroying his future . . . But every item in that mixed bag is, appropriately or inappropriately, tied to the grand, almost sacramental fear of being without money. To be sure, each of those several fears could be dealt with more or less independently of financial considerations. He could provide less, or even accept his failure to provide at all. He could express his talents gratis or his masculinity as a lark. He could take responsibility for his own interests, find himself new friends, or simply stop trying to ace out the future. But for as long as he allows his separate fears a common foothold in the fear of losing money, he will have them all standing on his back at once.

His problem is that he defines the value of his work and of himself strictly in terms of money, and he should not. For many men, the slow realization of this fact is some recompense for being let go.

There are only two classes of out-of-work men: those who can subsist without a job and those who can't. If you listen to the stories of men in career crises, however, it is as if that distinction did not exist. Those who know they will survive are as fearful as those who think they won't. Both are enslaved to a monetary definition of survival. The work that might have nourished their souls is ignored in favor of financial fretting that can only give them indigestion.

What neither sees is that the monetary connection between work and reward is arbitrary at best and wacky at worst, and that no sane man ought to give the power to define his true wealth or poverty to such a whimsical proposition. To *be* poor is one thing; but to bow down uncritically before a system that teaches even the employed to *think* poor—to make money the principal measure of their worth—well, it's almost worth being fired, if that's what it takes to learn the trick of thumbing one's nose at the remuneration ethic. A man out of work has only the style that's inside him; the money-grabbing world should not be allowed to cramp it. If he wants to spend his last dollar on butter, so what if everyone who's not paying him thinks he should die eating margarine? He's been *let go:* scariness and all, it really is a liberation.

There is one last trick, though, that he still has to learn: when and if someone finally does hire him again, he must never slip back into letting the money dictate his style. He has hung with his feet off the ground and survived; he should be permanently past his fear of short ropes.

MORLEY TORGOV

An Empty Desk

As is often the case with lawyers, when my partner died his desk died with him. Overnight, eighty cubic feet of mahogany with brass fittings that he had occupied for almost forty years became a ghostly territory waiting to be ransacked and sealed off, perhaps for all time. It fell to his longtime secretary, Evelyn, and me, as executors of his estate, to strip clean the stolid piece of furniture of all the files and papers and personal effects it held. We would then have to make a decision: Should our law firm, which owned the desk, sell it to a second-hand dealer? Should we keep it on the chance that some incoming junior partner might find it inspirational?

After the funeral, Evelyn and I vowed in all good faith to make an early start, but day after day we offered each other excuses about why the task would have to be put off. Moving in on Harold's desk was a bit like invading a shrine. This was the container of much that he had accomplished—or hoped to accomplish—before his time ran out. In the final months of his life, it was to this desk that he escaped every morning after another long night made sleepless by his chronic illness. It was here that his world, so flat and jagged-edged before dawn, once again resumed its global shape; here that his clients, pinning him to earth by the gravity of their troubles, sent the blood coursing once again through his drying arteries.

A full week later, all excuses exhausted, Evelyn and I found ourselves standing in silence before the desk, surveying the chaotic landscape Harold had left behind. On its borders stood small mountains of uncompleted files, unread law reports. The center of the desk was a sizable plain, thick with unanswered letters, memos of unanswered calls and the odd unopened envelope.

We began, without the slightest enthusiasm, to examine each file. A reply was needed urgently on this one, the next was ready for billing . . . What the hell was this third? God only knew.

By midmorning, a certain crankiness began to creep into the process. We had set out with appropriate reverence, but gradually reverence turned to impatience and, finally, to outright resentment on my part. By noon I was asking myself angry questions. How dare Harold die leaving all these matters unfinished? How dare he shackle me to this wasteland of cardboard folders, papers, corporate minute books, stock certificates? By what right did he impose on me the burden of transforming the disorderly residue of his professional life into neat squares and perfect circles?

I sensed that Evelyn's feelings were not unlike my own. "Enough for today," I said. "We'll venture into the lowlands tomorrow."

Days passed before Evelyn and I summoned the strength and patience to hack our way through the overgrowth and undergrowth of loose papers in the center of the desk. We decided to arrange these in categories. One pile became Personal Notes: "Max Ackerman owes me $500." "Ask Julius if my trip to Miami is deductible."

Another pile was designated Office Matters. All at once, it struck me that my partner—outwardly the office humorist, casual, sporting—maintained an extraordinary interest in the billings and drawings of his colleagues in the firm. We came across notes comparing our performances from year to year, going back more than a decade. Other notes indicated that, even in his sunny corner office, the sunniest spot in our entire suite, our partner had harbored shadowy thoughts: "Ask H. about all these low fees to his wife's relatives." "P's entertainment expenses for December are out of sight!" There were slips containing detailed comparisons of Christmas-party costs for the years 1979 through 1983. While some of us were humming "Silent Night" and smiling benignly, what was *he* doing?

Having at last created order on the surface, we faced the prospect of plunging into the bowels of Harold's desk with unconcealed ill temper. "A man ought to travel light in this world," I grumbled, after unlocking the shallow top drawer to find it stuffed. Here and there, offering pale relief to the sober memorabilia of financial affairs, were postcards, mostly from Florida, mostly the obligatory beach scenes.

"He really loved Florida," said Evelyn.

"That's funny, I thought he hated Florida," I said. "Whenever he came back all he'd say was: 'Rain, rain and more rain at three hundred bucks a day!'"

Evelyn smiled wisely. "You're not supposed to enjoy yourself in Florida while your younger partners are slaving up here in the ice and snow."

Finally, we encountered a bundle of letters and cracked snapshots bound with an elastic so ancient it broke on contact. The photographs were of girls unknown to us. By the cars they posed against, some of which had running boards, we judged them to be alumnae of Harold's bachelorhood. I flipped the edges of the letters. The stationery was feminine. The handwriting, several different kinds, was also feminine. I looked up at Evelyn. "I have no taste for this," I said.

"*Something* will have to be done with them," said Evelyn.

We restored the bundle to its resting place.

The desk top was now almost bare, for the first time in memory. "I think the worst is over," Evelyn said. "At least now we can see the cigarette burns and coffee stains."

I made no comment. I was preoccupied with Harold's numerous fingerprints, accumulated, I reckoned, from the very first day he acquired the desk. Staring at these vestiges of his tenancy, I realized how little I really knew the man I'd practiced law with, side by side, all these decades. In fact, I knew only this for certain about him: He had a desk, therefore he existed.

The desk sits in Harold's still-vacant office. Many of its ghosts have now been evicted, but some hang on. We must do something about the remaining ones, Evelyn and I. Maybe tomorrow. But not today. Today I'm busy cleaning out my own desk.

MEN AT

PLAY

EDWARD TIVNAN

Buying a Baseball Glove

I met my wife during the 1974 World Series. Her hair was long or maybe short, she was wearing clothes, and the Oakland A's sewed up the Series in the fifth game with the Dodgers when Joe Rudi belted one out to break a 2–2 tie. I recall that one of the things that impressed me so much about Marilyn was that she seemed to understand the poetry of the hook slide, the esthetics of spitting tobacco juice. Finally, I had fallen for a baseball fan. She even liked to drink Ballantine Ale. I was in love.

"I hate baseball," said Marilyn, the avid ale-drinking viewer of the '74 World Series, after we were married. "But I really do like to drink ale." Lucky for her.

That she would trick me so—and actually admit it—is just more evidence of how little those of the female persuasion know about men. Baseball, as I keep telling my wife, is indelibly marked on the male soul, a cornerstone of his personal identity, the conservator of the boy ever in the man. Proof is the fact that for almost every man I know, his fondest memory is not that first car or even that first love affair—it is that moment he slipped on his first baseball glove.

I remember little else from my fourth year but a dark brown, dizzyingly odoriferous hunk of cowhide in the shape of a first baseman's mitt, a present from my father. I also recall some disappointment as he unwrapped it before hopeful eyes because I had been expecting a catcher's glove. Quickly, my father explained that a catcher's mitt that could be lifted by a four-year-old was nowhere

189

to be found. Just as quickly, I recognized that the glove I now held in my baby hands was definitely no baby model.

Baseball, politics and religion formed a holy trinity in my family, and the high point of my adolescence was confirmation. I had chosen as my "sponsor" into Catholic manhood a second cousin who had been a legendary pitcher at a nearby college and was presently a revered high-school baseball coach in my hometown. Cousin John came through: my confirmation present was a Wilson A-2400 catcher's mitt, top of the line, the "professional model" that, back in 1958, retailed for the impressive sum of $40. God was good. That evening I crouched catcherlike before a full-length mirror for a pitcher's-eye view into the pocket of my new glove. It fit me perfectly, as did the sin of pride.

During the next decade, I must have worn out five more A-2400s, until I hung up my spikes convinced by a very expensive liberal arts education (albeit partly occasioned by a better-than-average expertise with those catcher's mitts) that there was more to life than playing baseball. Now I am not so sure, and, like a few million other adult men across the land, I look forward to summer as a time to prove that the onslaught of fiscal woes and career crises has not yet aged the boy in this man. Every summer Saturday morning I pound a fist into my glove and the sound vaporizes decades.

The game is now softball, but the devotion to it among my summer crowd is still fanatical. To ensure amusement and to decrease embarrassment, we play the slow-pitch version, and my only disappointment is that the role of catcher has become a refuge for players whose talent is not quite equal to their enthusiasm. And so I have become a third baseman. Although in our game the ball may be served to the batter quite slowly, it has been known to rocket into the field at terrific speeds. The only things standing between me and disfigurement, I quickly realized, were aging reflexes and a good glove. I went shopping for my first fielder's glove.

At Paragon, the sporting-goods store, I stared at a wall of cowhide and approximations thereof: six hundred gloves. Among them were the familiar brand names from my baseball days—Rawlings, MacGregor, Wilson. But there were some alien models, not to mention some gimcrackery: one had a plastic sunshield built into the webbing; another was covered with dimples ("to decrease the spin on the ball," said the salesman). There were black gloves, gloves made especially for women ("The Shady Lady") and "softball gloves" bigger than a Little Leaguer. I grabbed a glove off the hook—no one was looking—and put it to my nose. One sniff and I was a dizzy four-year-old again, hooked on cowhide. The prices brought me back to 1983. Some models listed for $150, though up to 40 percent discounts are the rule in large outlets such as Herman's and Paragon.

Money was no object. Yet I was forced to confront anew the ever-present philosophical question: What is a good glove? I am of course talking here of what philosophers, following Aristotle, call an "intrinsic good"—something that is valuable in and of itself, like health or happiness or a baseball glove. After extensive research and considerable reflection, I stand prepared to share my findings:

There is no reason, ever, to buy a black baseball glove. I hold that truth to be self-evident. And a good glove ought to cost more than a pair of designer jeans or lunch for two (no wine) at The Palm.

Alas, those industrious Japanese have invaded the baseball market, and with some very high-quality stuff. Mizuno, Japan's most successful glove maker, and SSK both sell gloves for up to $100. Nevertheless, I have found few experts (granted, none of them Japanese) who find them a match for a Wilson or Rawlings pro model, though, one must warn, because of their high-quality leather (Rawlings features deerskin), American-made gloves take some time to break in. As an excuse, "I'm still breaking it in" does have a statute of limitations.

Some major leaguers have been known to break in a new glove by placing it carefully on the ground—and then driving an expensive car over the poor thing, repeatedly. Bucky Dent claims rubbing shaving cream on a new model does the trick. Sporting-goods stores now sell something called "Glovolium," though any mixture with a name like that ought to be viewed with suspicion.

In my neighborhood, the surefire method to soften cowhide was massaging it with neat's-foot oil; periodic jets of spit added a more personal touch. Then one put a ball in the glove and wrapped it with a rawhide thong to form a pocket. (Placing it under one's pillow was optional.)

Traditionally, infielders have preferred a small glove: all the better to stop the ball, pluck it out of the pocket and fire it to first. Outfielders like them big; and pitchers bigger, in order to hide their magic from everyone in the stadium. For the aging weekend softballer who is likely to find himself in just about every position, I recommend medium-large, though always err on the side of big. There is only one thing more pleasurable in life than leaping into the air and then touching ground with the ball stuck in the webbing of your glove.

Any game in which players wear hats designed to protect their eyes from the sun, even though they play mostly at night, has nothing to do with reality. So buy a glove that is, literally, fantastic. A Little League teammate of mine was convinced that owning a Mickey Mantle glove meant he was destined to be the next Mantle; doubtless, like most fans, he still dreams of a phone call in the middle of the night—George Steinbrenner finally admitting the Yankees cannot win without his glove in center field. Keep dreaming, but try to find a glove that fits your hand as well as your fantasy because—I know it's not easy to admit—major leaguers are different from you and me.

"Dave Winfield uses this very glove," says the salesman, which is true (of the Rawlings HFG-12); what is also true is that Dave Winfield is six foot six, 220 pounds, and an extraordinarily gifted athlete, even among pros; his hand is also the size of a subcompact car. Chances are you and Dave have different preferences for a lot of things. So don't be afraid to try on a glove, get the feel of it, flex your wrist a bit, see where your fingers rub. Then tell the salesman to stand forty feet away and burn one in. Gloves ought to fit like, well, a glove.

ADAM LIPTAK

Playing Air Guitar

When I hear a song on the radio that I really like, or that used to be a favorite, I sometimes dance around a little bit and pretend to play guitar. I play air guitar. It probably looks dumb to an outsider, but to the man who plays, it is quite serious—a primal and private dance. Men identify with the great rock guitarists the way they do with sports legends, and we mimic their gestures and attitudes in an instinctive quest for grace.

What you do is: extend your left arm sort of crookedly, faking chord changes on the neck of an invisible electric guitar, rhythmically. Your right hand strums. Your head bobs. Your hips twitch. A nearby mirror reflects your grimaces. There is loud music on.

When I was a teenager, I used to play all the time. The impulse arose at odd moments. Just walking around, in an empty late-afternoon school hallway, say, I might be seized by the inner music, drop to a crouch and let loose a devastating solo, the whole thing over in ten seconds. A favorite song on the car radio, I am embarrassed to recount, could make me take my hands from the wheel and imitate a Stones riff—stopping only to keep my father's car from drifting into the next lane.

Certainly air guitar was handy at parties, where by stiffening and lowering the arms a little it passed for dancing. Countless men still dance this way.

But the true essence of air guitar is intensely personal and a little embarrassing, a strange conflation of fantasy and desire. I remember summer dusks in anticipation of parties—this at a time when a

party was a promise of wonder, of a life transformed—climbing out
of the shower, the evening's first beer lodged precariously on the
soap tray, and hearing the perfect song. Here was pleasure: a long
swig, a half-turn on the volume knob, the hallucinatory rush of
adrenaline, followed by mindless dancing around in front of the
fogged-up mirror.

As with anything, it is possible to play air guitar well or poorly,
but it has nothing at all to do with being able to play guitar, which
is in fact a drawback. One is after an image, a look; technical profi-
ciency is distracting. The choice of role model is important, but
what one copies is stance, attitude and character. Virtuosity is for
the most part irrelevant. Only the electric guitar counts; there is no
such thing as playing acoustic air guitar. Years of practice help,
and so does an appreciation for loud, dumb music.

I am certain that the success of the movie *Risky Business* had a
great deal to do with the scene in which Tom Cruise bounds about
the living room in a shirt, socks and underpants. His parents are
out of town, of course. He turns up the stereo and indulges in a
whole array of rock-star moves and prancing.

Talking with friends afterward, I discovered that our enjoyment
of the scene—of its celebratory tone—was tempered by an uneasy
feeling of having somehow been found out. A kind of reverse identification had taken place, and we saw ourselves not as guitar
heroes but as slightly absurd kids from the suburbs. This shock of
recognition was followed by a shudder.

In college, I played less often but more openly. Sometimes, at the
end of a beery night, my friends and I would put together a whole
band—it was always the Stones, and I always wanted to be Keith
Richards—and clamber up onto the furniture and play, each of us
with his eyes closed, in a way alone. It sounds like a silly and
slightly aggressive scene, and it was.

At the same time, this was a way men could dance with other
men without compromising their version of masculinity. At parties,
dancing with women, my best friend and I might step away and
take a moment to jam, leaning on each other this way and that,
falling over and playing incredible dual solos on our invisible

Fenders. The women we abandoned were generally not amused.

We joked about it, air guitar being a perfect subject for my generation's mode of discourse, which is a mix of the intimate and the ironic. Here we could say just what we meant, confessing to the odd habit in a deadpan way, so that no listener could be quite sure if we really meant it. Or we could go beyond our own experience—admit to playing naked on city rooftops, say—and then double back and make fun of anyone taken in or, worse, who admitted to doing the same thing.

I have noticed lately the attempt to institutionalize air guitar, in the form of "concerts" at colleges, "lip-sync" contests at certain nightclubs in the boroughs of New York and on television shows. There is something peculiarly American about making the intimate public and competitive, something reassuring at first but in the long run repulsive.

This is not to say that an air guitar contest is without humor. To see four or five people aping the movements of an entire band with the appropriate music in the background can be hilarious. An ensemble called Men Without Instruments, at Princeton University, is funny even to contemplate.

I don't know if teenagers today find in Prince and Bruce Springsteen adequate idols. I suspect they do. And I suppose they know the moves better than we ever did, thanks to music videos.

These days, I find myself at some emotional distance from most of the popular music I hear, and going to rock concerts has lost its appeal. I still put on loud music first thing in the morning, though, loud enough to hear in the shower, which is down the hall from my stereo. And sometimes, as I start to dress—barefoot, my shirt unbuttoned and my tie loose around my neck—I play a couple of notes if it feels right. And then, refreshed, I finish dressing and go to work.

FREDERIC MORTON

The Jogger's Code

Every day except Sunday I'm a multiple personality. (I don't jog on Sundays.) The change in roles starts around noon, with my stretching exercises. By the time I lace on my Nikes a protocol has taken hold of me which has no meaning to my leather-shod self. A certain signal will trigger one response when I amble along at 3 miles per hour; but when I'm running at 13 . . . well, here are a few examples:

Footsteps dog me while I am walking. They are persistent. They are gaining. I glance back. It's not a mugger but the mailman in a hurry. I smile at him, entirely unembarrassed. The look-behind-thee tic is just normal urban survival procedure. I'm walking on upper Broadway.

Similar footsteps dog me while I'm sneakered, footsteps emerging quite possibly from the underbrush. They are persistent. They are gaining. My face remains stalwartly turned forward. Those sounds at my back may be malevolence about to pounce. But they may also be a fellow sportsman's. I will not lapse into an unduly competitive gesture. I will show no nervousness about someone else being faster. I will not look back. I'm jogging in Riverside Park.

Or: a woman is walking toward me, a woman in her sumptuous thirties—without a bra. I indulge in an appreciative glance that might be mistaken for a crass stare. So what? We are all swingers, we *boulevardiers* of Broadway. Yet let that same woman run toward me while I'm running, and my eyes, as well as my smile, chastely focus on her forehead. I will not mar with lust the comradeship of athletes. I am jogging in Riverside Park.

Or: I'm taking a "work walk" up West 83rd Street, one of my neighborhood's quieter streets. I'm trying to think of a couple of transitions that will give the embryonic chaos of the chapter I'm writing a veneer of coherence. I pass the garage near Amsterdam Avenue and—blessed moment!—the transition comes to me. I pronounce it out loud, because the sound of the words will fix them in my memory. "All of which informed Edna that summer was here," I say to the driver of the Pontiac backing into the street. He nods from behind the wheel. What vibrant Upper West Sider doesn't talk to himself when out for a stroll?

An hour later, my brain lights up, unexpectedly, with a second and more difficult transition: "That was the month Edna discovered how good she was at cultivating people she didn't like." It's a serviceable phrase, but it must remain unspoken, because it was born during my jog in Riverside Park. Silently I lope on, obeying decorum—and a sense of civic duty. You see, the world will be out of joint once even runners start blathering into the thin air. Runners set up expectancies that have become rare and precious in our time.

The public contours of the jogger suggest someone disciplined, dedicated, responsible, quasi-heroic, a veritable emblem of muscular rectitude. He is very different from other high-profile characters of our street theater. How meritorious the contrast between him and the drug heads, winos and exhibitionists! The jogger looks undebauchable. Consider the steely steadiness of his stride, the elevated fanaticism tautening his features, the hardy skimpiness of his athletic shirt in the cold gusts. Like the aristocrat on horseback, he is more prominent in his locomotion, faster and nobler than the pedestrians in his wake. He looms on a pinnacle where machismo and morality meet.

Indeed, the jogger encompasses the hallmarks of two august models: Pilgrim Father (upright, admirably goal-directed, pleasure-deferring, ascetic) and Arthurian Knight (borne along by his mission, lonely and yet undeterred). True, the errand of this knight-errant is narcissistic. He pursues only the fitness of his own body. On the other hand, Sir Galahad wasn't so very different, being rather vain about his soul. Holy Grail or five-minute mile: both are targets of a perfectionism that will brook no indulgence before the end of the quest. Anyone worried that society is falling apart ought to find reassurance on the track around the Central Park Reservoir. Here the moral fibers of the Occident are regrouping from the rot, warming up and vibrating. Too bad William Butler Yeats did not live to see the spectacle. Would he still feel that "the center cannot hold"? Hundreds of joggers seem to be rushing in to steady the damn thing.

Of course, I stick to Riverside Park, where running addicts diffuse among jugglers, mothers on roller skates pushing prams, winter suntanners, and midgets tossing Frisbees to their Schnauzers. Amid all that, I attempt to do justice to the specialness of my habit, to the obligations of its noblesse oblige. In other words, I must live up to a code capable of admirable subtleties.

If I overtake a man, I will never rub in my superiority by looking at him or even looking haughtily ahead as I pass. No, I will glance up a tree, interested in the twitter of that blue jay and in nothing else. If I pass a woman, the ethics of the situation are a bit more arduous. I will make an elaborate detour around her, insuring that my higher speed gets lost in the space between us.

And if I'm the one who's overtaken? It happens, and it's always a little hairy. As long as the hustler is still behind me, I will not—as you know already—turn around to see who's doing all that huffing and stomping. When he passes me and turns out to be a gray-haired fellow who gives me hope for my own later years, I'll be a complacent sluggard. I'll let him pull away in glory. If he's young and brash, however, I'll whistle a few bars of "It's a Long Way to Tipperary" while the punk is still in earshot, just to let him know how much unused wind there's left in the old boy.

If he who overtakes me is a she . . . ah, then you'll find me severely tested. Then I'll try very hard not to try to stay ahead with my last reserves. I'll try very hard not to swerve down the side road to the 79th Street Marina that will take me away from the defeat.

I'll try very hard not to develop a suddenly sprained ankle, forcing me to stop and thus fudge the outcome of what should never have been a contest. And if I defy all these temptations, if I succeed in just simply, frankly falling behind her, why then I console myself with self-congratulation. I have paid my final dues to running gallantry. I am the jogger *sans peur et sans reproche*.

DAVID MAMET

The Things Poker Teaches

In twenty years of playing poker, I have seen very few poor losers. Poker is a game of skill and chance. Playing poker is also a masculine ritual, and, most times, losers feel either sufficiently chagrined or sufficiently reflective to retire, if not with grace, at least with alacrity.

I have seen many poor winners. They attribute their success to divine intervention and celebrate either God's good sense in sending them lucky cards or God's wisdom in making them technically superior to the others at the table. Most are eventually brought back to reality when the cards begin to even out.

Any poker player knows that, despite what mathematicians say, there are phenomenal runs of luck that defy explanation. The poker player learns that sometimes both science and common sense are wrong. There is such a thing as absolute premonition of cards, a rock-bottom *surety* of what will happen next. A good poker player knows that there is a time to push your luck and a time to retire gracefully, that all roads have a turning.

What do you do when you are pushing your luck beyond its limits? You must behave like a good philosopher and ask what axiom you must infer that you are acting under. Having determined that, you ask if this axiom, in the long run, will leave you a winner. For instance, you are drawing to a flush. You have a 1-in-4½ chance. The pot is offering you money odds of 5 to 1. It seems a close thing, but if you did it all day, you must receive a 10 percent return.

200

If the axiom you are acting under is not designed to make you money, you may discover that your real objective at the game is something else: you may be trying to prove yourself beloved of God. You *then* must ask yourself if—financially and emotionally—you can afford the potential rejection. For the first will certainly, and the second will most probably, ensue.

Poker is boring. If you sit down at the table to experience excitement, you will, consciously and subconsciously, do things to make the game exciting. You will take long-odds chances, you will create emergencies, and they will lose you money. The poker players I admire most are like that wise old owl who sat on the oak and kept his mouth shut and his eye on the action.

When you are proud of having made the correct decision (that is, the decision which, in the long run, *must* eventually make you a winner), you are inclined to look forward to the results of that decision with some degree of impassivity. When you are so resolved, you become less fearful and more calm. You are less interested in yourself and more naturally interested in the other players: now *they* begin to reveal themselves. Is their nervousness feigned? Is their hand made already? Are they bluffing? These elections are impossible to make when you are afraid, but they become easier the more content you are with your own actions.

Poker reveals to the frank observer something else of import—it will teach him about his own nature. Many bad players do not improve because they cannot bear self-knowledge. The bad player will not deign to determine what he thinks by watching what he does. To do so might, and frequently would, reveal a need to be abused (in calling what must be a superior hand); a need to be loved (in staying for "that one magic card"); a need to have Daddy relent (in trying to bluff out the obvious best hand), etc. It is painful to observe this sort of thing about oneself. Many times we'd rather suffer on than fix it.

The pain of losing is diverting. So is the thrill of winning. Winning, however, is lonelier, because those you've taken money from are not apt to commiserate with you. Winning takes some getting used to.

Many of us, and most of us from time to time, try to escape a blunt fact that may not tally with our self-image. When we are depressed, we recreate the world around us to rationalize our mood. We are then apt to overlook or misinterpret happy circumstances. At the poker table, this can be expensive, for opportunity may knock, but it seldom nags. Which brings us to a crass thought many genteel players cannot grasp: poker is about money.

The ability of a poker player is judged solely by the difference between his stack when he sits down and his stack when he gets up. The point is not to win the most hands, the point is not even to win the most games. The point is to win the most money. This probably means playing fewer hands than the guy who has just come for the action; it means not giving your fellow players a break because you value their feelings; it means not giving some back at the end of the night because you feel embarrassed by winning; it means taking those steps and creating those habits of thought and action that, in the long run, must prevail.

The long run for me—to date—has been those twenty years. One day in college I promoted myself from the dormitory game to the *big* poker game in town, up on the Hill. After graduation, I would occasionally come back for visits. I told myself my visits were to renew friendships, to use the library, to see the leaves. But I was really coming back to play in the Hill game.

Last September, one of the players pointed out that five of us at the table that night had been doing this for two decades. As a group, we have all improved. Some of us have improved drastically. Because the facts, the statistics, the tactics are known to us all, and because we are men of equal intelligence, that improvement can be due to only one thing: to character, which, as I finally begin to improve a bit myself, I see that the game of poker is all about.

A. ALVAREZ

A Test of Will

I started climbing in the summer of 1950, just before my twentieth birthday, hit my peak at the sport about fifteen years later, and have been on a gradually accelerating decline ever since. Yet I still try to get onto the rocks any Sunday when the weather is halfway decent, although my stamina and flexibility are sharply diminishing, and the rocks I usually go to—a little sandstone outcrop south of London—would fit comfortably into the foyer of the new AT&T Building. These days, I climb mostly with my son. At fifteen, he is too young to know any better. Yet the fact is, whenever work or rain deprives us of our weekly fix of climbing we exhibit identical withdrawal symptoms: restlessness, irritability, fretfulness, a glum conviction that our week has been spoiled. Climbing is an addictive sport that changes the psyche's chemistry as irredeemably as heroin changes the body's, and both of us are hooked.

When Mallory was asked why he wanted to climb Everest, he answered with a famous evasion: "Because it's there." I suspect that what he really meant was: "Because you're here"—"you" being not only his aggrieved and aggressive questioner but also the town, the noise, the involvements, the problems, the routine. You climb to get away from all that, to clear the head, to breathe free air. Yet most weekend sportsmen—the fishermen and yachtsmen, golfers, even Sunday painters—do what they do in order to get away, without risking their necks in the process. Why, then, does climbing exert such a curiously addictive power?

First, because it is one of the purest, least cluttered sports, re-

203

quiring a minimum of equipment: a pair of special boots, a rope, a safety helmet, a few carabiners (snap links), nylon slings and artificial steel chockstones or pitons for protection. The whole lot costs very little, lasts for years and hangs easily around your neck and from your waist. Unlike other sports, if something goes wrong, the fault is nearly always in you, not in your gear. Conversely, the reward, when a climb has gone well, is an intense sense of physical well-being. On those rare occasions when mood, fitness and rock all come together and everything goes perfectly, you experience an extraordinary combination of elation and calm—tension dissolves, movement becomes effortless, every risk is under control—a kind of inner silence like that of the mountains themselves. No doubt every athlete feels that on his best days, but in climbing that style of contentment is attainable long after you pass, as I have, your physical prime.

It is also not a competitive sport, however much the top climbers vie among themselves for first ascents or ascents in the best style. The competition is not even with the mountain or the rock face. You are competing, instead, with yourself—with your protesting body, your nerves and, when the going gets really tough, with your reserves of character.

In 1964, for example, a companion and I spent a night belayed to a small ledge—a couple of feet long and 18 inches wide—1,300 feet up an overhanging face in the Italian Dolomites. We had been benighted on it by a sudden snowstorm and were soaked to the skin; but because this was August in Italy, we were climbing light, which meant we had neither protective clothing nor food. The route finished up a thousand-foot vertical corner, down which a waterfall of melted snow was pouring. It froze solid during the night, and privately both of us assumed that we would do the same. But neither of us mentioned the possibility, because to have done so would not only have undermined our confidence to complete the last 500 icy feet the next morning—if there was a next morning for us—it would also have been a violation of privacy. Our survival depended, as much as anything else, on tact. It was not just a question of being young enough and fit enough to withstand the cold, we also had to behave well and respect each other's feelings. Melo-drama and self-pity would have done us in more surely than the freezing temperature.

I suspect that most men are secretly worried about how they will behave under pressure. Certainly, I emerged from that night on the bare mountain with frostbitten fingers and a good deal more self-confidence than I had had before—a confidence that was quite apart from the pleasure of having got up a difficult climb in bad conditions. I had learned that the ability to sit quiet in a crisis and not fuss was more valuable than physical strength. I also discovered in myself an unsuspected, obstinate ability to survive and that, in some devious way, seemed to absolve me from the youthful need continually to apologize and explain. As the poet Thom Gunn wrote, "I was myself: subject to no man's breath." Perhaps I should also add that I have not felt the need to repeat the experiment; the Via Comici on the north face of the Cima Grande di Lavaredo was the last serious climb I did without checking the weather forecast beforehand.

"Life loses in interest," wrote Freud, "when the highest stake in the game, life itself, may not be risked." Those who cultivate risk for its own sake, however, are probably emphasizing only their own inner torpor, just as the people who talk most fervently about the beautiful emotions induced by drugs are those who have most difficulty in feeling anything at all. The pleasure of risk is in the control needed to ride it with assurance so that what appears dangerous to the outsider is, to the participant, simply a matter of intelligence, skill, intuition, coordination—in a word, experience. Climbing, in particular, is a paradoxically intellectual pastime, but with this difference: you have to think with your body. Each pitch becomes a series of specific local problems: which holds to use, and in which combinations, in order to get up safely and with the least expenditure of energy. Every move has to be worked out by a kind of physical strategy, in terms of effort, balance and consequences. It is like playing chess with your body.

And that, for me, is the final satisfaction. To be a professional writer is, in the end, a sedentary, middle-class occupation, like accountancy or psychoanalysis, though more lonely. For five or six days each week, I sit at my desk and try to get sentences right. If I make a mistake, I can rewrite it the following day or the next, or catch it in proof. And if I fail to do so, who cares? Who even notices?

On a climb, my concentration is no less, but I am thinking with my body rather than my weary, addled head, and if I make a mistake, the consequences are immediate, obvious, embarrassing and possibly painful. For a brief period and on a small scale, I have to be directly responsible for my actions, without evasions, without excuses. In that beautiful, silent, useless world of the mountains, you can achieve at least a certain clarity, even seriousness of a wayward kind. It seems to me worth a little risk.

TERENCE SMITH

The Sailboat Addiction

———

There is a cliché about men and sailboats that, like most clichés, contains more than a little truth. The adage is that the two happiest days in a boat owner's life are the day he gets his boat and the day he gets rid of her. As a man who bought his first sailboat five years ago, fell obsessively in love with her and finally parted with her last summer, I am here to tell you that the second day is at least as satisfying as the first.

This is heresy, of course, among the nautical set. All boats, but especially sailboats, are an addiction, no less costly than cocaine and no less damaging to the system than alcohol. The Betty Ford Center should open a special wing for boat nuts. Carleton Mitchell, the author and veteran ocean racer, captured the essential insanity of boat nuts when he described his own particular passion, which is ocean racing, as the moral equivalent of standing under a cold shower tearing up $1,000 bills.

Even for the weekend sailor, the relationship between men and boats is a bit like a love affair. There's the same initial infatuation, the same preoccupying passion, the same pain of separation. For a married man, there's even the same kind of tension he has with his spouse. Not for nothing are boats so frequently named "Other Woman" or "Second Mistress." And so it follows that selling a boat is a bit like ending an affair: a mixture of pain and guilt and—let's admit it—relief.

I had sailed since I was twelve, but it was not until I was forty that I finally bought a boat of my own. She was a Pearson 26 One

Design, a sleek, fiberglass-hulled, 26-foot sloop that I sailed on Chesapeake Bay. I can still remember the excitement of the day I took commission of her at a yacht yard in Annapolis and the thrill when we got the sails up for the first time. There was a wonderful quiet as we turned off the motor, then a firm pull on the tiller as the sails filled. In a moment we were heeled over, knifing through the water, the wind whistling through the shrouds. It was glorious.

A lot of good times followed. There were Sunday races around the buoys, day sails with friends to the Eastern Shore and raucous nights in a dockside crab house in the lovely harbor at St. Michaels. During the week, I found myself possessed by the boat, calling the marina to see if she was all right, following the marine weather forecasts. Whenever a good breeze stiffened the flag atop the office building across the street, my thoughts drifted to the bay. I was a confirmed addict.

But by the second season, and certainly the third, conflicts had begun to develop. Weekends that I wanted to spend on the bay had to be devoted to long-overdue chores. The children even had the audacity to develop schedules and interests of their own. "Don't you want to go sailing this Saturday?" I would ask each of them. "No, Dad, I've got plans."

Beyond that—and this is the hard part to admit—there were weekends when I discovered that *I* really wanted to be elsewhere; on the tennis court, perhaps, or at a football game. The boat posed a continual dilemma: if I used her, other things were neglected and I felt guilty; if I didn't use her, I felt guilty about *that*.

When I didn't use the boat, the costs of maintaining her suddenly seemed like an extravagance. A 26-foot boat is hardly a yacht of the proportions J. P. Morgan had in mind, but the routine expenses were considerable nonetheless. The slip fees, the yard bill, the equipment—it all adds up. Nor do the costs stop when the sailing season is over. Everything from the teak brightwork to the bank loan has to be maintained through the winter. Even in the age of fiberglass, a sailboat is an astonishing amount of work.

I used the boat less and less in the fourth and fifth seasons, and finally even I had to admit that the rewards no longer justified the expenses. (You can ruin a boat owner's day by forcing him to calculate his per-sail costs.)

Finally, reluctantly, I put her on the block. I was depressed for weeks. When the yacht broker would call with an offer, I would make it my business to be out. On weekends, when most people go boat shopping, I would arrive at the brokerage dock early Saturday morning, gleefully strip off the For Sale sign and take her out for a forbidden sail. It was borrowed time, I knew it—and I loved it. Despite my dilatory tactics, the boat was finally sold to a bureaucrat in the Treasury Department. On a cold rainy Sunday, I removed my personal possessions from her, took a last, lingering look and drove away.

I frankly expected to be devastated. Instead, I felt strangely exhilarated. No more did I fret when a storm blew through, no longer did I have to worry about whether her lines were secure, no longer did I feel guilty about the fading teak and fraying jib sheets. That was someone else's worry now. I rediscovered tennis and became reacquainted with my children. They're really quite nice, and my son's tennis game had improved sharply while I was away.

To ease the withdrawal pains, I now occasionally charter boats for the weekend, usually sharing the costs with friends. The charters tend to be larger, more commodious boats than I could ever afford to buy, and a typical weekend charter is less than the monthly slip fee for my own boat. Best of all, I can walk away from the charter on Sunday evenings and leave the work and worry to someone else. It is liberation.

I consider myself a reformed case, free at last. Like a rescued drunk, however, I have to be careful. My mind is willing, but the spirit is weak. Old sailing magazines are especially dangerous for me. I leaf through the four-color ads that read "Imagine yourself the proud owner of this beauty" and there is a deliriously happy, carefree skipper heading his gleaming white yacht into the sunset. I know it isn't really like that, of course, and yet, when the breeze stiffens the flag atop the office building across the street . . .

MARK GOODSON

Lousy at Sports

I've decided to come out of the closet. It is not an easy decision to admit openly that I really don't like sports. There—I've said it.

Do you know what it's like to be a man who is not a sports fan? Who not only doesn't care who wins the World Series but who is never exactly sure which teams are playing? Who never, but never, reads the sports section?

I approach this subject with a light touch, but in truth it has been a problem that has plagued me for most of my life, particularly when I was a young boy. For to be a boy not interested in sports was, particularly back then, to run the risk of being thought a homosexual. As a matter of fact, at an early age, when I began to face the awful truth that I simply had no taste for the world of athletics either as participant or observer, I kept it very quiet. Could it be that, indeed, I was a "fairy" or reasonable facsimile thereof? (The euphemism "gay" came into the language later.)

When I married and my wife became pregnant, I kept my fingers crossed. "Please don't make it a boy." He'll insist that I play ball with him, take him to Yankee Stadium and engage in the sports rituals so necessary for healthy male bonding. It was a girl, and I was saved. But only for a while. Three and a half years later, Jonathan was born. When he was eight years old, I forced the poor kid to go to a park in New York, where I would lob softballs his way, demanding that he hit them back to me. I saw, almost at once, that Jonathan had inherited my disease. He was lousy at sports, too.

210

Even after three marriages, three children, and some in-between love affairs, plus the sure knowledge that I adore women, I still feel, from time to time, that, somehow, I must be lacking in the right male genes.

When I first came to New York in the 1940s, I had been a newscaster and announcer at a San Francisco radio station. Gotham was tough for a newcomer. I was hungry, anxious and in need of work. I auditioned for everything.

One day, I was called in by radio station WOR and told there was an opportunity to audition for the job of host of a panel game. "What sort of game?" I asked politely, although I knew that whatever it was, I would grab it if I could.

"It's a sports quiz," the executive explained.

I felt the blood leave my face.

"We were hoping to make Jack Dempsey the host," he went on, "but when we put a microphone in front of Jack's face, he froze. So what we want is for Dempsey to sit at your side to give the program authenticity, but you'll be the real moderator. We've lined up the best sportswriters in the country to be on the panel. Do you think you can handle it?"

I agonized. I saw the $150 fee (huge money back then) fade into the distance. I took a breath. "Absolutely," I said. "I can certainly handle a sports quiz." I looked the executive right in the eye.

Before the audition, I took care to find out that Jack Dempsey was a former heavyweight boxing champion. Then I tried out and—*mirabile dictu!*—got the job. For twenty-six weeks, every Monday night, I would bravely pitch sports questions at the experts arrayed at the panel desk in front of me. It was an excruciating experience. It made me remember boyhood nightmares in which I would be in a strange classroom about to take a final exam in a course I had never heard of.

Apparently, I got away with the bluff, because not one of the sports mavens ever seemed to doubt that I knew whereof I spoke. The proof came a few weeks after the demise of that quiz when I was called into my employer's office. He smiled benevolently. "You've done a good job, Goodson. Now I have a *real* opportunity

for you. We are looking for someone to help describe the Dodger
ball games from Ebbets Field. How does that strike you?"

I paused. I had never been to a major-league ball game. I knew
nothing, minus zero, about baseball. He responded to my hesitation, "This is a big deal, guaranteed $25,000 a year." I swallowed.
"I'll do it." "Good," he replied, looking at his calendar. "We will
give you an on-the-air test in about two weeks." "Terrific," I
said—and dashed to the nearest bookstore.

There, I bought *Baseball: The Official Rules*. If it wasn't a hundred pages thick, it seemed to be. I began on page 1, where the
precise measurements of the "diamond" were diagramed, then
went on to the functions and duties of each player in the infield and
outfield, the definition of a strike, a foul, an infield fly, and on and
on through the fine print. As I got to the tenth page, I collapsed.
Much as I needed the money, I knew there was no way that I could
manage this bluff! I can't remember the alibi I gave the executive,
but certainly it wasn't anything as shameful as "I've really never
seen a baseball game." But I did bow out.

Twenty years later, long after I had given up performing and was
running a television production company specializing in game
shows (quite an irony for a non-sports-fan to earn a living at
games), I was invited by my banker to have dinner on the company
yacht while cruising around Manhattan Island. It was a "men
only" party, and the talk centered on business and, of course,
sports.

After dinner, I stood on the deck in a group that included Gene
Tunney, another former heavyweight champion and by then a successful Wall Street investor. I thought I was doing an acceptable
job of being responsive to the sports chatter, when Tunney suddenly broke off from the conversation, turned and gazed down at
me suspiciously from his enormous height. "Goodson," he asked,
"tell me about you. What do you do for a living?"

Because "What's My Line?" was my show at that time, it seemed
natural for me to respond, "What do you think I do?" He looked at
me thoughtfully. "Goodson, I'd say you are a poet."

I blushed. I knew what he meant. He'd found me out.

MEN AT

WAR

RICHARD F. SHEPARD

In Enemy Waters

We went, my son and I, to see the movie *Das Boot,* and when it ended, with the German submariners being machine-gunned by an Allied plane on an Italian pier, I burst into applause. My son, in his twenties and very tolerant of his father's eccentricities, was amused by my predictable reaction, but others in the theater threw looks that could only be construed as hostile to my insensitivity. Here were young men—on the wrong side, to be sure—who were cut off at the start of their manhood, and here was this old guy, a man in his sixties, who was clapping his hands in satisfaction. What could the death of these unfortunate lads possibly mean to this New York type?

The problem was that *Das Boot* was a persuasive, realistic film, one that gave me a look at an enemy I had never met but had dreaded. As a merchant mariner in World War II, I had been wakened in the small hours of the night to the deep, shaking thud of depth charges loosed by Navy escort ships as they tried to kill U-boats that were trying to kill us in the North Atlantic. More than once I had come on deck to see a neighboring merchant ship lift out of the water and plunge into the sea, gone forever, or to see another transformed into a pillar of flame and smoke, with her crew leaping over the side into burning water.

I feared das Boot and therefore I hated it and all of its breed. When I saw the film, those feelings flooded back into my mind, and those young men on the screen became, once again, the villains out to destroy the young man that was me at that time. It was all very

215

difficult to explain to an audience to many of whom even Vietnam was fast receding into ancient history.

When we emerged into the hard light of an East Side afternoon, I thought about my reactions, and I was shocked to realize that we are now further from World War II than I was from the Spanish-American War when Hitler sent his troops crashing into Poland. It was a thought full of relativity, one that gave me, for a moment, some comprehension of the reaction to my passionate response to the movie.

Back in the 1930s, American Legion conventions brought throngs of high-spirited World War I veterans to New York for conventions and parades that my friends and I thought were the height of irrelevance in a period when we were worried about the spread of racism. Those men seemed old, smug and far too jovial about an ancient event. The Great War was then not quite twenty years in the past, but it had happened before we were born, and therefore it was one with the Civil War, the American Revolution, Caesar's Gallic Wars. Small wonder that younger generations should disapprove of a sixty-year-old troglodyte getting emotionally agitated over events that hark back to the ages!

I have, like everyone else, met the enemy of those war years, Germans and Japanese, former fighters now in their late middle years. Once I shared a box seat with a one-armed gentleman about my age during a holiday in Vienna at a performance of *The Merry Widow*. He was a polite and gentle person, solicitous of our comfort and enjoyment, yet even the lively, whipped-cream waltz could not stop me from wondering, somewhat wickedly, "What did you do during the war and how did you lose that arm?"

Mostly, though, these former enemies do not recall the war to me. They come across as ordinary folk relishing the things that we relish, fearing the things that we fear. This is what the crew of das Boot would be today, I suppose, and I would not have the feeling of enmity that welled up within me when I saw them reconstructed in their wartime youth on film. Time does not heal all wounds and absence does not always make the heart grow fonder, but one goes into later years linked by a certain sharing of enmity with old foes, a curiosity about whatever became of them. More so, perhaps, with the personal enemies from one's own private life than with national enemies.

Much has been made of generation-gap enemies—don't trust anyone over/under thirty. But, as age will eventually reveal, this is not true enmity. It falls more in the zone of exasperated misunderstanding. Enmity runs much deeper. Although it can be handed down generation to generation, like a family heirloom, I suspect that each generation has to make its own enemies, enemies that may make little sense to another layer of age. Can I understand my son's wrangles, personal conflicts that seem as incomprehensible to me as they did when he was a little boy wrestling with some other kid who seemed to be not much different than he was? There is nothing more inane than the enmities of others, hostilities that obviously could be ironed out more easily than one's own run-ins. Younger people have not learned from history, meaning that they have not studied us closely enough. It is probably more true that they have studied us too well and persist in the tradition of confrontation.

Yet younger generations, on the large scale, not only inherit hand-me-down enmities (the Middle East, Northern Ireland, India, all will suffice as models), but they have found themselves immersed in new, more intangible battles that have come up in their own times. There are sides taken on issues of environment, health, nuclear energy, economy, controversies even more difficult to comprehend because they are rooted in cool, scientific fact of the rational civilization. But they arouse no less passion than the old schisms did.

Each generation believes that somehow it is more open-minded than the one just going out, that it is more reasonable and more susceptible to settling things fairly. This may, sadly, be an illusion, and one fears that the human being is still programmed in old formats. Not long ago, I saw two men pummeling each other in the gutter, where each had a car half-parked, one frontward, one

backward, in a parking space. It was an appallingly violent erup-
tion of mankind's ancient scourge, territoriality, and I walked away
with mixed emotions. The irrationality of it all was emphasized by
a sign that said No Parking. In a world that believes it has radically
changed, the scene was most depressingly reassuring.

NELSON BRYANT

The Sorcery of War

We sat facing each other in two long rows as the C-47 flew low over the farms, woodlands and hedgerows of Normandy. It was the night before D-day, and I was embarked on an endeavor that has, I am troubled to say, overshadowed all that has happened to me in the years since the war.

I felt more eagerness than fear that night. I had not yet been in combat, and long, hard weeks of training in the blazing, dusty Georgia summer had convinced me that paratroopers were a breed apart. Had we not, our qualifying jumps completed, been allowed to tuck our trousers into our shiny boots and to wear the emblem that was, we were told, "the silver badge of courage"?

Consuming fear came later, weeks after one bullet from the machine-gun burst that killed my fellow scout tore through my chest and hurled me on my back in a pasture in whose far corner milk cows grazed. At the moment of being hit, I felt only sadness—and astonishment that my plan to emerge a hero had so quickly gone awry.

The week before, my comrades and I had waited day after day at an aerodrome in England for the launching of what General Eisenhower called the "great crusade." I was so ready for the effort that it was a relief when we were finally ordered to climb aboard our aircraft. And I was horrified when the harness of the parachute they handed me was so small I couldn't buckle it on. Engines were warming up, and I imagined myself standing alone on the tarmac, all the planes and gliders gone. I was finally given a parachute

219

that—with help, and by expelling most of the air from my lungs—I could don.

My memories of the Normandy and Holland jumps and the snow and bitter cold of the Battle of the Bulge both possess and sustain me.

The baptismal entry was violent, a leap from the left flank of the jouncing aircraft into a rush of wind. From the earth, perhaps five hundred feet below, came the snarl of automatic weapons firing with a rapidity I hadn't known was possible, the tracers from them looping up in graceful arcs, then hurtling past. An apple orchard appeared beneath and I knew I would be an easy target hanging from a tree, but the branches broke and I landed standing up and cut my constricting harness loose. For a few minutes there was no gunfire, just a night and country silence that was followed by the droning approach of more planes, parachutes blossoming in the moonlight and the gliders—like giant birds with wings fixed in death—crashing into the trees with their cargoes of screaming men.

Why does that night and the few months of actual combat in Normandy and the other campaigns mean more to me than the ensuing years of college and work, happiness, sorrow and love, marriage and children?

Part of the answer is clear. Man craves simplistic solutions to life's multitudinous riddles. For me and many others, World War II was the only time when the enemy and the course to take to defeat him were clearly defined. We had yet to mount an assault on the enemy within.

For some of us, civilian life is a series of unending choices in which almost nothing is black or white, in which there is usually something to be said for whatever move is made. Because of this, we often wallow in enervating indecision and descend to meanness born of frustration. I recall telling a buddy, as we stumbled through the snow-filled forests of the Ardennes, that if I lived to see the war's end I would never, in the years that remained, indulge in whimpering or petty acts or hurt another human being. And now, having violated that promise scores of times, I sometimes announce—always seeking the easy solution—that my only wish is to go out with a bang, not a whimper, not drooling from slack mouth in a hospital bed, but assaulting some flaming hill, as if there were a final heroic act which would atone for a performance I regard as mediocre.

It has been said that battle forges boys into men. That can happen, but war can also blind one to the unending courage needed to live the years that follow with unswerving decency and integrity. To some combat veterans, seeking security and comfort is a pale, flaccid substitute for entering an obvious hell with no hesitation. Yet many veterans, and I am one of them, fear and detest war.

It is both bizarre and sad that we gain sustenance from something so hated and so feared. In recent months I have taken to wearing a red beret adorned with my paratrooper's wings to which two stars—standing for the Normandy and Holland drops—are affixed. Am I asking to be measured by once being carried, shoulder-high, through the marketplace of history, not by what I am today?

There have been long periods when the war was not with me, but something always brings it back: a truck tire exploding on a superhighway or the metallic shriek—it sounded like a passing round from a dreaded German 88 artillery piece—of a gale-blown sign on a deserted November street.

And sometimes the connection is more direct: the telephone call I received a few years ago on Christmas Eve. The caller had been drinking. His speech was slurred and the background chatter seemed to come from a bar.

He said, "You won't remember me, but I wanted to thank you for saving my life."

I pleaded with him to identify himself and the incident, but he refused.

"I just wanted to tell you," he said, and hung up.

I would like him to be the man I cradled in my arms in a hillside cave in Belgium for two days, sometimes getting him to swallow a little of the soup I had heated in my helmet, and telling him over and over that I had also been hit in the chest and lived. It wasn't an honest comparison, for his shell-caused wound was not a clean hole fore and aft but a ragged, pulsating orifice in his back nearly as big as my fist. He was taken to the rear. I heard no more of him, and have forgotten his name.

He probably will not call again, but there will be other messages, whether actual or induced by memory, and I know that the sorcery will not cease.

EDWARD TICK

Apocalypse Continued

Like seventeen million other men who came of age during Vietnam, I did not serve in the armed forces. It was a blessing, then, to have escaped; it is a burden now. I find there is something missing in me. I have unwanted feelings that nag me in unexpected ways and at unexpected times.

Although a number of other nonveterans years ago began expressing similar problems in print and on television, I did not know that the problems applied to me. Perhaps I blocked out my feelings. In any case, I first became aware of these feelings when a man named Fred sought my psychotherapeutic services. Exactly my age, Fred wanted help for anxiety attacks and recurring nightmares. In his dreams, he was pursued by a galloping horseman determined to cut out his heart.

Through psychotherapy, we searched his past for reasons for his present suffering. Nothing proved promising until, because he could bear it no longer, Fred confessed: he had fulfilled his military obligation by spending two years stateside unloading and processing body bags from Vietnam.

We had found the horseman. Fred had handled the bodies of other men like so much supermarket ware, listing names and numbers and arranging transportation. He had never been in danger himself until much later, when the deaths he processed and his profound guilt returned to haunt him.

But I, also, changed with Fred's admission. I felt uneasy, incomplete. If Fred was one step removed from the war, I was too. If he was haunted, what was I?

I searched for clues to my discomfort. The work of the psychiatrist Robert J. Lifton and others on combat veterans suffering posttraumatic stress told me what I had not experienced. Another small body of writing, on an elusive subject known as "Vietnam guilt," told me that I was not the only man who had been happy to escape service in my teens only to feel angry, confused and incomplete years later.

In high school, during the mid-1960s, I had considered enlisting as a medic, not because I believed in the war, but because many of my neighbors and classmates were fighting it. Later, my objections to the war overrode my desire to be counted among those serving. I was prepared, during my junior year in college, to apply for conscientious-objector status. If it were not granted, I would then decide whether I would go to jail, flee the country or take some other course. I was unsure what I would do.

In the end, Lottery No. 244 rescued me from that dilemma. But it plunged me into a state of permanent moral ambiguity, because part of our heritage insists that, if there is a war to be fought, young men are expected to fight it. War, if it exists, is a required course, and a course with a final examination. I was, I came to feel, among those men of my generation who had never been tested.

After learning of Fred's horseman, I began to seek out psychotherapeutic work with Vietnam veterans. They had a need to tell their stories, and I could join them in the jungle in this way.

Ron was the first veteran of jungle combat with whom I worked. "*Apocalypse Now*," he chuckled during one session. "A picnic compared to the real thing." Ron was emotionally disabled by his combat experiences and his reception when he came back to America. He had been spat on, jailed and hospitalized. In the hospital, he had been drugged into a stupor. "Why get better?" he asked. "The government pays me more for being disabled than I could ever make working."

Ron wanted my help to find meaning in a life whose usefulness had officially ended at age twenty-two. But, sitting across from him, I felt weak, inadequate, physically smaller, although we were the same size. I had to fight the urge to look at the floor instead of directly into the eyes that were avoiding mine.

This was because I felt Ron had something over me. He had survived a long tour in the demilitarized zone and the decimation of his battalion. The closest I had come to physical danger was being chased down a deserted Washington street on the night of the first Moratorium Against the War. The guardsman who had chased me was my age, spoke my language and, though he prodded me with his bayonet, ordered me to move with a "please."

It is not because I protested the war that I felt guilty before Ron. In fact, I am even more convinced now that the war was a mistake. I think it hurt all of us in ways that linger long into adulthood. The warriors, honorable men like Ron who served in Vietnam, suffer, unlike veterans of other wars, because the correctness of what our nation did will forever be in question. Those like me who, for one reason or another, did not serve, suffer because we chose not to perform a primary and expected rite of passage. We were never inducted, not merely into the Army, but into manhood. Recently, I was contacted by Sam, a former draft resister who fled to Canada to avoid prison. He told me: "I think about Vietnam every day. I can't join in with others. Can a resister also suffer post-traumatic stress?"

I have had some of the usual rites—marriage, educational and professional recognition. But no matter how many passages or accomplishments I garner, I never quite feel complete. Nor do I think that, had I served in Vietnam, I would now be enjoying the contentment I seek. A nonveteran I know says, "I cannot recall any winners at all."

I think that none of us escaped, that not one of us feels whole. All our choices—service in Vietnam, service at home, freedom from service altogether—failed to provide the rite of passage that every man needs. I want to feel my own strength, worth and wholeness, and I want to belong to my country and my generation. But history got in the way. I wonder if I will forever be seeking something that cannot be.

ROGER HOFFMANN

Nicknames

I won't answer to Rosebeak anymore. Or Karate Joe. Those were youthful nicknames; Friday-night sock-hop bruises that hurt when applied but faded away by the last slow dance. The nicknames that haunt me now were born during my brief military career, which included three tours in Vietnam.

Sergeant Major Lucas slapped Half-Man on me in basic training during an evening mail call. With a look, he silenced the company clerk's song of names midway through the *H*'s. He glared deep into the cardboard box of mail, scanned the entire formation, focused on my platoon, then squeezed off a look at me and spat. My heart thudded.

He held aloft a ragged manila envelope. A nylon stocking dripped from one torn corner. I felt sick. The sergeant major's bark brought me to the platform front and center, my eyes level with his name tag. "Hoffmann," he purred as he leaned down and got into my face. "What *have* we here?" Ever so slowly he drew out the— yes, perfumed—stocking, I watching the envelope fall to the floor. I couldn't recognize the handwriting. Who had done this to me? The troops let loose a chorus of hoots.

On command, I removed helmet and glasses. Two giant hands hauled the stocking down over my head. It bent the tops of my ears and flattened my nose. My lips felt stapled together. Everything looked underwater. I wondered how people wearing stocking masks robbed banks. Lucas loaded the glasses back on my noseball

226

and earstumps and thwocked my helmet to eyebrow level. "You smell goooood, HALF-Man. Real good. Now drop on down and low-crawl over to the Pit and do some laps for that Big Ranger in the Sky."

I spent the night squinting through beige mesh and perfecting my low-crawl technique in the huge, log-rimmed sandbox. Sporadic cries of "Half-Man in the Pit! All's well!" kept me company. At dawn my platoon sergeant pulled me out and removed the stocking. Exhausted, I crab-walked to the barracks. The envelope rested on my bunk. I stumbled into the latrine and shook the one-page letter out onto my lap. A former girlfriend with a sense of humor was acting out a rerun 1940s war movie she'd just seen: Flyboy Hero clutched Best Girl's scented stocking as he scoured the unfriendly skies.

Fortunately, few witnesses to the stocking incident shared my next training cycle and so Half-Man fell from use. I joined a new crew for the progressively harder schools. We gave one another fresh nicknames. Being skinny, I caught Rib Cage. A miserable card player drew Ace. Like us, the nicknames stayed relatively harmless—loose-fitting clothes we had time to grow into, or so we thought.

I had enlisted in the Army, as had most of the others in my unit, and I *wanted* to go to Vietnam. The more I trained, the more impatient I became to get there. Each nickname awarded me by my buddies brought me a step closer. The first uneasiness hit me on the long flight over. Everyone on the plane got quieter and quieter. I felt as if I were shrinking in my seat. By the time we landed, my eagerness had evaporated. Then the plane doors swung open and the lung-sucking heat swept through. End of the line, boys, everybody off. No more bayonet courses with little straw-stuffed men in cone hats and black pajamas. Here you could die. We climbed down the steps and double-timed to the olive-drab buses. Grenade screens covered the windows.

"In-country," nicknames flourished. In a high-casualty unit you might last an entire tour without using anybody's real name. The nicknames offered us structure and sanctuary—a pecking order and a hiding place. Replacement troops came in one or two at a time. They were simply Cherries at first. Inexperienced, they were dangerous to be around, foolish to get close to in any way. This generic labeling isolated them. When a Cherry died, we didn't blink.

A Cherry who survived long enough earned the right to harass the next rookie. He moved up a notch, perhaps with a sweet rite of passage: acceptance, a nickname, maybe one that glued him to the pack, maybe one that ran a wall around him. Smoke and Blade and Sly—GI's won their nicknames like prizes, wore them like tattoos.

I shared a nineteenth birthday with a helicopter door gunner from Ohio who had six weeks left before he went home. I knew him only as the Iceman. He was shot down the next week. By the time I had turned twenty, I was working with small teams of indigenous Montagnards. Hindered by our different languages and customs, our nicknames communicated acceptance, trust and, eventually, deep affection. We operated together for months before my team named me Birdchester. I was gawky as a bird and favored a Winchester shotgun. I felt christened. Over time, I dubbed them with nicknames easier on my tongue than their given names—frequently ones to remind me of home. Slick, Marshal Dillon, Bogart. We gave, and accepted, nicknames as gifts.

A few years ago, I joined two regularly held poker games. One is mostly social; it's work to win or lose forty dollars in a night. The other gets more serious. You can drop a couple of hundred dollars in an hour. Common to both are a certain small-team camaraderie and a give-and-take of verbal abuse. The banter sometimes tags a player with a short-lived nickname. Mr. Excitement. Woman Warrior. Hero. I laugh as much as anyone else.

But on one early-morning ride home, I had to pull off to the shoulder of the highway. I cut my lights. I heard their voices before I saw them. Walking point was that red-haired Cherry with the limp, then Marshal Dillon and Slick, followed by the Iceman, No Bones, Snake. All wrapped in a soft, gauzelike glow. They looked straight ahead as they shuffled by, ignoring me completely. I twisted toward the low, uneven hum of their conversation and ached to catch a stray Birdchester, or even Half-Man. Nothing. I waited for them to pass, for the light to disappear. It took a long time.

MIKE MALLOWE

Among Warriors

I always considered 322 the luckiest set of digits in history. That was my draft lottery number in the late 1960s, a time when the higher the number, the better. The numbers stopped at 366, and 322 kept me out of the military and in St. Joseph's University, the Jesuit school in Philadelphia. The one instinctive thing I knew about the military was that I wanted no part of it. It denied life.

A rugby player from a little town outside Boston, who sat next to me in a math class, had a lottery number in the low 50's. I said goodbye to him one Friday in autumn. He was going home for the weekend. The following Monday he didn't show up for class. By the Monday after that, we realized he wasn't coming back. The war was devouring bodies fast. For the rest of that semester and into the next, no one would sit at his desk. He was our first casualty.

I started thinking about him again when, on a magazine assignment, I recently visited another school, the United States Army War College at Carlisle, in the fertile green farmland of central Pennsylvania, just a short forced march from Gettysburg.

I was going there to meet what might be called our professional warriors, a class of men that traces its lineage back to the misty time warp of feudal Prussia.

America being America, we aren't supposed to have a class like this; or at least not admit to it. But the War College glories in the concept. Here, for the first time, I had the opportunity to observe career soldiers pursuing their vocations on the highest level, pre-

230

paring for the kind of massive, conventional land war—a world war—that some modern skeptics have facilely dismissed as the stuff of textbooks. Not so the men who are gearing up to wage it, men like the hard-eyed ranger with five tours in Vietnam who confided to me sincerely: "If the Russians really knew what was going on here, they'd be plenty worried."

Physically, the War College is a splendid collection of very old buildings and very up-to-date equipment. In its wainscotted libraries and musty archive rooms, there's the hush of a museum—long, carpeted corridors are lined with glass cases that exhibit uniforms. The walls are hung with captured battle flags and pictures of decorated heroes. Young sentries in greatcoats stand gazing across the expanse of the parade ground, where once, a century ago, the cavalry practiced drills. Horsemanship is still considered a personal virtue here and a priceless talisman of command. The place is all about valor, honor, country. Even the mannequins in their stiff blue uniforms seem animated with pride.

At the same time, the War College is a functioning military installation—just another base. The stifling dreariness of Pentagon bureaucracy constantly intrudes. The chatter and clatter of secretaries and typewriters drifts from the open doors of fluorescent-lighted offices. There is nothing dashing in the simulated wars the men train to fight. Ponderous columns of armor are massed and remassed, theoretically, at the border of some unsuspecting nation. Reality has sucked every drop of romance out of war, yet the good, gray colonels who sit at their personal computers here, tinkering with troop movements and force projections, carry on just the same, attempting to temper the technology with what one critic has called the need for "traditional warrior values." "War is what this place is all about," one husky infantry officer told me, reflecting that very attitude. "We don't call it the Peace College."

They spend ten months here, about 250 in a class, mostly colonels and lieutenant colonels in their mid-forties, usually twenty-year men (there are a few civilians each year and usually several women). They live on campus or in the town, recuperating from the burnout and the petty politics of the peacetime Army as they study the great conflicts of the past, discuss the imperatives of the present and prepare for all manner of future Armageddons.

Most are known as "dirty boots officers." That's because they are still young enough to have been low-level commanders in Vietnam, where they watched the kids in their outfits get blown away. They know what it's like to see dying men pay for other people's mistakes. That wasn't always the case here. Once, armchair generals predominated, teaching the theory of battles they had never faced to a generation of unbloodied officers too young for Korea and too old for Vietnam. Not anymore. Now, it's quick minds in hard bodies with the scars to prove it. Plenty of scars. Especially the kind that don't show.

These new officers are poised to take over. Whatever the war, they mean to win it. They are going about it very deliberately. No one has to remind them that the United States hasn't had a single significant land victory since the invasion of Inchon in 1950. Merciless revisionists that they are, they fall asleep most nights worrying about the appalling absence of right stuff.

Their heroes are Matt Ridgway, Omar Bradley, Mark Clark. Their ideal is the spirit of Normandy's Operation Overlord. What they'd probably like is a very conventional war—winnable and inevitable and of very human scale. In the day of the MX, that's asking a lot, but at the War College they have the gift of faith. They have also seen enough of war to try to prevent it, even as they prepare to wage it.

"We don't have one now," a colonel told me with a deep sense of satisfaction. "That means we're doing our job. It's working."

I came away liking these men enormously, wanting them desperately to succeed. My talks with them showed me how they have wrestled with the ethics of their vocation and considered their ramifications. They seem as passionate about life, as contradictory, as capable of glorious excess and sobering sacrifice as the rest of us— as the best of us.

Someday we may need such men. I, for one, take great comfort now in knowing that they are there, perfecting their arcane arts, ancient as Spartans.

THE

MEANING

OF

MANHOOD

PAUL THEROUX

The Male Myth

There is a pathetic sentence in the chapter "Fetishism" in Dr. Norman Cameron's book *Personality Development and Psychopathology*. It goes: "Fetishists are nearly always men; and their commonest fetish is a woman's shoe." I cannot read that sentence without thinking that it is just one more awful thing about being a man—and perhaps it is the most important thing to know about us.

I have always disliked being a man. The whole idea of manhood in America is pitiful, a little like having to wear an ill-fitting coat for one's entire life. (By contrast, I imagine femininity to be an oppressive sense of nakedness.) Even the expression "Be a man!" strikes me as insulting and abusive. It means: Be stupid, be unfeeling, obedient and soldierly, and stop thinking. Man means "manly"—how can one think "about men" without considering the terrible ambition of manliness? And yet it is part of every man's life. It is a hideous and crippling lie; it not only insists on difference and connives at superiority, it is also by its very nature destructive—emotionally damaging and socially harmful.

The youth who is subverted, as most are, into believing in the masculine ideal is effectively separated from women—it is the most savage tribal logic—and he spends the rest of his life finding women a riddle and a nuisance. Of course, there is a female version of this male affliction. It begins with mothers encouraging little girls to say (to other adults), "Do you like my new dress?" In a sense, girls are traditionally urged to please adults with a kind of coquettishness, while boys are enjoined to behave like monkeys toward each other. The nine-year-old coquette proceeds to become womanish in a subtle power game in which she learns to be sexually indispensable, socially decorative and always alert to a man's sense of inadequacy.

Femininity—being ladylike—implies needing a man as witness and seducer; but masculinity celebrates the exclusive company of men. That is why it is so grotesque; and that is also why there is no manliness without inadequacy—because it denies men the natural friendship of women.

It is very hard to imagine any concept of manliness that does not belittle women, and it begins very early. At an age when I wanted to meet girls—let's say the treacherous years of thirteen to sixteen—I was told to take up a sport, get more fresh air, join the Boy Scouts, and I was urged not to read so much. It was the 1950s and, if you asked too many questions about sex, you were sent to camp—boys' camp, of course: the nightmare. Nothing is more unnatural or prisonlike than a boys' camp, but if it were not for them, we would have no Elks Lodges, no poolrooms, no boxing matches, no marines.

And perhaps no sports as we know them. Everyone is aware of how few in number are the athletes who behave like gentlemen. Just as high school basketball teaches you how to be a poor loser, the manly attitude toward sports seems to be little more than a recipe for creating bad marriages, social misfits, moral degenerates, sadists, latent rapists and just plain louts. I regard high school sports as a drug far worse than marijuana, and it is the reason that the average tennis champion, say, is a pathetic oaf.

Any objective study would find the quest for manliness essentially right-wing, puritanical, cowardly, neurotic and fueled largely by a fear of women. It is also certainly philistine. There is no book hater like a Little League coach. But, indeed, all the creative arts are obnoxious to the manly ideal, because at their best the arts are pursued by uncompetitive and essentially solitary people. It makes it very hard for a creative youngster, for any boy who expresses the desire to be alone seems to be saying that there is something wrong with him.

It ought to be clear by now that I have an objection to the way we turn boys into men. It does not surprise me that when the President of the United States has his customary weekend off, he dresses like a cowboy—it is both a measure of his insecurity and his willingness to please. In many ways, American culture does little more for a man than prepare him for modeling clothes for the L. L. Bean catalog. I take this as a personal insult because for many years I found it impossible to admit to myself that I wanted to be a writer. It was my guilty secret, because being a writer was incompatible with being a man.

There are people who might deny this, but that is because the American writer, typically, has been so at pains to prove his manliness. But first there was a fear that writing was not a manly profession—indeed, not a profession at all. (The paradox in American letters is that it has always been easier for a woman to write and for a man to be published.) Growing up, I had thought of sports as wasteful and humiliating, and the idea of manliness as a bore. My wanting to become a writer was not a flight from that oppressive role playing, but I quickly saw that it was at odds with it. Everything in stereotyped manliness goes against the life of the mind. The Hemingway personality is too tedious to go into here, but certainly it was not until this aberrant behavior was examined by feminists in the 1960s that any male writer dared question the pugnacity in Hemingway's fiction. All that bullfighting and arm wrestling and elephant shooting diminished Hemingway as a writer: one cannot be a male writer without first proving that one is a man.

It is normal in America for a man to be dismissive or even somewhat apologetic about being a writer. Various factors make it easier. There is a heartiness about journalism that makes it acceptable—journalism is the manliest form of American writing and, therefore, the profession the most independent-minded women seek (yes, it is an illusion, but that is my point). Fiction writing is equated with a kind of dispirited failure and is only manly when it produces wealth. Money is masculinity. So is drinking. Being a drunkard is another assertion, if misplaced, of manliness. The American male writer is traditionally proud of his heavy drinking. But we are also very literal-minded people. A man proves his manhood in America in old-fashioned ways. He kills lions, like Hemingway; or he hunts ducks, like Nathanael West; or he makes pronouncements like "A man should carry enough knife to defend himself with," as James Jones is said to have once told an interviewer. And we are familiar with the lengths to which Norman Mailer is prepared, in his endearing way, to go to prove that he is just as much a monster as the next man.

When the novelist John Irving was revealed as a wrestler, people took him to be a very serious writer. But what interests me is that it is inconceivable that any woman writer would be shown in such a posture. How surprised we would be if Joyce Carol Oates were revealed as a sumo wrestler or Joan Didion enjoyed pumping iron. "Lives in New York City with her three children" is the typical woman-writer's biographical note, for just as the male writer must prove he has achieved a sort of muscular manhood, the woman writer—or rather her publicists—must prove her motherhood.

There would be no point in saying any of this if it were not generally accepted that to be a man is somehow—even now in feminist-influenced America—a privilege. It is on the contrary an unmerciful and punishing burden. Being a man is bad enough; being manly is appalling. It is the sinister silliness of men's fashions that inspires the so-called dress code of the Ritz-Carlton Hotel in Boston. It is the institutionalized cheating in college sports. It is pathetic and primitive insecurity.

And this is also why men often object to feminism, but are afraid to explain why: of course women have a justified grievance, but most men believe—and with reason—that their lives are much worse.

THOMAS FLANAGAN

The Ways of a Wimp

The word "wimp" has, in the last few years, achieved a baleful centrality in our political and cultural discourse. He is an indecisive sort of fellow, burdened by an extravagant sense of complexities and difficulties, disinclined to act with fierce, swift and unreflecting resolve. Like many of a culture's controlling terms, however, it neither possesses nor requires precise definition. We know what a wimp is, and why it is awful to be one, and awful for a nation that it should contain many of them. But no wimp has presented himself for close inspection, presumably because wimps, almost by definition, lack the necessary courage.

I suspect that I myself am one. I cannot drive a car, and am bored by sports. When my wife drives us to a dinner party during a World Series, she coaches me in the names of the contending teams. By midnight I have forgotten them. The novelists who have meant most to me are Jane Austen, Proust, and Henry James. I cherish the music of Schumann and Ravel, and the paintings of Watteau and Monet. Such a list of accusing preferences could be extended endlessly, but would not speak to the immediate point. At the moment, the real charge against the wimp is political, and here, too, I stand condemned.

Specific affiliation is not here at issue. I am a liberal Democrat, but there are also many Republican wimps, although they are not admired by the current stridently victorious wing of their party. Political habits of mind, the moral sentiments of politics, are at issue. Thus, I believe that no national priority is higher than that of attending to those who have been damaged or neglected by our society—the poor, the ill, the old, those maimed both by our present racism and by the consequences of our history of racism. I detest capital punishment, which I regard as a compact of violence made by our society with its murderers. I am uneasy about abortion, but believe that the matter should be entrusted to the consciences of pregnant women rather than to the remorseless dogmatism of celibate archbishops.

The "new" patriotism seems to me a shrill and vulgar hysteria when contrasted with the old patriotism of Jefferson and Madison. Dr. Johnson notwithstanding, I believe that patriotism is not the last, but the first refuge of a scoundrel—first because it is easy and can assert itself in the confidence of mob support. There is indeed a deep malaise in our society, and the "new" patriotism is not its cure but, rather, one of its symptoms.

I am also what the self-proclaimed moral majority calls a "humanist." My college readings in Erasmus and Montaigne long ago instructed me to regard that word as an honorable one, but then, I was also instructed by Thucydides that words lose their meanings in times of cultural crisis. In religious matters, however, I am indeed what the moral majority intends by that term—I am an agnostic, and assume that whatever value human life possesses is that with which human beings are able to endow it.

What I have said may seem confident and poised, even arrogant, and therefore not wimplike. But, in fact, I lack such confidence. Like most wimps, I regard matters of the spirit, and questions of morality, art and political choice, as complex and contradictory, ambiguous and shaded. As might be inferred, if not from what I have said, then from my Irish surname, I am no admirer of Oliver Cromwell, but I greatly admire his letter of 1650 to the Church of Scotland: "I beseech you, in the bowels of Christ, think it possible you may be mistaken."

Literature and teaching, the two crafts that I profess, have nurtured this indecisiveness. Literature grants us access to diverse modes of being and feeling, alternative ways of thinking and doing. And teaching is, in part, the task of repeating year after year to class after class the injunction of Cromwell to the Church of Scotland.

With the perverse courtesy of my breed, I acknowledge that an impatience with the wimp is not a whim of the moment but, rather, lies deep within the grain of our national culture. But not deeper than the doubts and hesitations, the heresies and recessions, of the wimp. Hawthorne and Melville are to be numbered among the great American wimps, and the voice of the wimp can be heard murmuring beneath the manly assurances of Whitman and Twain and Frost. Perhaps, and I put forward the idea with an appropriate tentativeness, a dash of the wimp is necessary if one is to come to a full consciousness of the powers and paradoxes of the American experience.

I am puzzled, however, by the assumption that the wimp can easily be thrust aside, or can be derided with impunity. Both art and history argue to the contrary.

Hamlet is literature's supreme example of the wimp. The native hue of his resolution is sicklied o'er with the pale cast of thought. He is hesitant, indecisive, oppressed by an awareness of alternative possibilities. He is skeptical, invents and reinvents his world, and the play in which he appears is so ambiguous that scholars argue as to whether its prevailing spiritual tone is Protestant or Roman Catholic. He displays an unmanly love of language. Worse yet, he is a wit: sarcastic, sardonic, playful—the very quality that revealed to American eyes the wimpiness of Adlai Stevenson and Eugene McCarthy.

But when his world and his being goad him into action, he litters Denmark with corpses—stabbing one man to death through an arras, sending to their deaths two others, and killing a final two by his sword. And with his dying breath, he names his successor and sets in order the affairs of his kingdom.

An extreme example. It requires translation into the native and the immediate idiom. America seems to have decided for the moment that it is unhealthy to question too closely our national purposes and intentions, that it is effete and debilitating to nourish scruples and reservations, that it is unmanly to perceive our circumstances as complex and infinitely delicate. But it requires a sinewy and muscular strength of spirit to live within uncertainties and complexities. The true American wimp may not be the intellectual but, rather, to borrow a phase from Yeats, "one that ruffles in a manly pose for all his timid heart."

NOEL PERRIN

The Androgynous Man

The summer I was sixteen, I took a train from New York to Steamboat Springs, Colorado, where I was going to be assistant horse wrangler at a camp. The trip took three days, and since I was much too shy to talk to strangers, I had quite a lot of time for reading. I read all of *Gone With the Wind*. I read all the interesting articles in a couple of magazines I had, and then I went back and read all the dull stuff. I also took all the quizzes, a thing of which magazines were even fuller then than now.

The one that held my undivided attention was called "How Masculine/Feminine Are You?" It consisted of a large number of ink-blots. The reader was supposed to decide which of four objects each blot most resembled. The choices might be a cloud, a steam engine, a caterpillar and a sofa.

When I finished the test, I was shocked to find that I was barely masculine at all. On a scale of 1 to 10, I was about 1.2. Me, the horse wrangler? (And not just wrangler, either. That summer, I had to skin a couple of horses that died—the camp owner wanted the hides.)

The results of that test were so terrifying to me that for the first time in my life I did a piece of original analysis. Having unlimited time on the train, I looked at the "masculine" answers over and over, trying to find what it was that distinguished real men from people like me—and eventually I discovered two very simple patterns. It was "masculine" to think the blots looked like man-made objects, and "feminine" to think they looked like natural objects. It

243

was masculine to think they looked like things capable of causing harm, and feminine to think of innocent things.

Even at sixteen, I had the sense to see that the compilers of the test were using rather limited criteria—maleness and femaleness are both more complicated than *that*—and I breathed a huge sigh of relief. I wasn't necessarily a wimp, after all.

That the test did reveal something other than the superficiality of its makers I realized only many years later. What it revealed was that there is a large class of men and women both, to which I belong, who are essentially androgynous. That doesn't mean we're gay, or low in the appropriate hormones, or uncomfortable performing the jobs traditionally assigned our sexes. (A few years after that summer, I was leading troops in combat and, unfashionable as it now is to admit this, having a very good time. War is exciting. What a pity the twentieth century went and spoiled it with high-tech weapons.)

What it does mean to be spiritually androgynous is a kind of freedom. Men who are all-male, or he-man, or 100 percent red-blooded Americans, have a little biological set that causes them to be attracted to physical power, and probably also to dominance. Maybe even to watching football. I don't say this to criticize them. Completely masculine men are quite often wonderful people: good husbands, good (though sometimes overwhelming) fathers, good members of society. Furthermore, they are often so unselfconsciously at ease in the world that other men seek to imitate them. They just aren't as free as us androgynes. They pretty nearly have to be what they are; we have a range of choices open.

The sad part is that many of us never discover that. Men who are not 100 percent red-blooded Americans—say, those who are only 75 percent red-blooded—often fail to notice their freedom. They are too busy trying to copy the he-men ever to realize that men, like women, come in a wide variety of acceptable types. Why this frantic imitation? My answer is mere speculation, but not casual. I have speculated on this for a long time.

Partly they're just envious of the he-man's unconscious ease. Mostly they're terrified of finding that there may be something wrong with them deep down, some weakness at the heart. To avoid discovering that, they spend their lives acting out the role that the he-man naturally lives. Sad.

One thing that men owe to the women's movement is that this kind of failure is less common than it used to be. In releasing themselves from the single ideal of the dependent woman, women have more or less incidentally released a lot of men from the single ideal of the dominant male. The one mistake the feminists have made, I think, is in supposing that *all* men need this release, or that the world would be a better place if all men achieved it. It wouldn't. It would just be duller.

So far I have been pretty vague about just what the freedom of the androgynous man is. Obviously it varies with the case. In the case I know best, my own, I can be quite specific. It has freed me most as a parent. I am, among other things, a fairly good natural mother. I like the nurturing role. It makes me feel good to see a child eat—and it turns me to mush to see a four-year-old holding a glass with both small hands, in order to drink. I even enjoyed sewing patches on the knees of my daughter Amy's Dr. Dentons when she was at the crawling stage. All that pleasure I would have lost if I had made myself stick to the notion of the paternal role that I started with.

Or take a smaller and rather ridiculous example. I feel free to kiss cats. Until recently it never occurred to me that I would want to, though my daughters have been doing it all their lives. But my elder daughter is now twenty-two, and in London. Of course, I get to look after her cat while she is gone. He's a big, handsome farm cat named Petrushka, very unsentimental, though used from kittenhood to being kissed on the top of the head by Elizabeth. I've gotten very fond of him (he's the adventurous kind of cat who likes to climb hills with you), and one night I simply felt like kissing him on the top of his head, and did. Why did no one tell me sooner how silky cat fur is?

Then there's my relation to cars. I am completely unembarrassed by my inability to diagnose even minor problems in whatever object I happen to be driving, and don't have to make some insider's remark to mechanics to try to establish that I, too, am a "Man with His Machine."

The same ease extends to household maintenance. I do it, of course. Service people are expensive. But for the last decade my house has functioned better than it used to because I've had the aid of a volume called *Home Repairs Any Woman Can Do,* which is pitched just right for people at my technical level. As a youth, I'd as soon have touched such a book as I would have become a trans-vestite. Even though common sense says there is really nothing sexual whatsoever about fixing sinks.

Or take public emotion. All my life I have easily been moved by certain kinds of voices. The actress Siobhan McKenna's, to take a notable case. Give her an emotional scene in a play, and within ten words my eyes are full of tears. In boyhood, my great dread was that someone might notice. I struggled manfully, you might say, to suppress this weakness. Now, of course, I don't see it as a weakness at all, but as a kind of fulfillment. I even suspect that the true he-men feel the same way, or one kind of them does, at least, and it's only the poor imitators who have to struggle to repress themselves.

Let me come back to the inkblots, with their assumption that masculine equates with machinery and science, and feminine with art and nature. I have no idea whether the right pronoun for God is He, She or It. But this I'm pretty sure of. If God could somehow be induced to take that test, God would not come out macho, and not feminismo, either, but right in the middle. Fellow androgynes, it's a nice thought.

ROGER HOFFMANN

The Dare

The secret to diving under a moving freight train and rolling out the other side with all your parts attached lies in picking the right spot between the tracks to hit with your back. Ideally, you want soft dirt or pea gravel, clear of glass shards and railroad spikes that could cause you instinctively, and fatally, to sit up. Today, at thirty-eight, I couldn't be threatened or baited enough to attempt that dive. But as a seventh grader struggling to make the cut in a tough Atlanta grammar school, all it took was a dare.

I coasted through my first years of school as a fussed-over smart kid, the teacher's pet who finished his work first and then strutted around the room tutoring other students. By the seventh grade, I had more A's than friends. Even my old cronies, Dwayne and O.T., made it clear I'd never be one of the guys in junior high if I didn't dirty up my act. They challenged me to break the rules, and I did. The I-dare-you's escalated: shoplifting, sugaring teachers' gas tanks, dropping lighted matches into public mailboxes. Each guerrilla act won me the approval I never got for just being smart.

Walking home by the railroad tracks after school, we started playing chicken with oncoming trains. O.T., who was failing that year, always won. One afternoon he charged a boxcar from the side, stopping just short of throwing himself between the wheels. I was stunned. After the train disappeared, we debated whether someone could dive under a moving car, stay put for a 10-count, then scramble out the other side. I thought it could be done and said so. O.T. immediately stepped in front of me and smiled. Not

247

by me, I added quickly, I certainly didn't mean that I could do it. "A smart guy like you," he said, his smile evaporating, "you could figure it out easy." And then, squeezing each word for effect, "I . . . DARE . . . you." I'd just turned twelve. The monkey clawing my back was Teacher's Pet. And I'd been dared.

As an adult, I've been on both ends of life's implicit business and social I-dare-you's, although adults don't use those words. We provoke with body language, tone of voice, ambiguous phrases. I dare you to: argue with the boss, tell Fred what you think of him, send the wine back. Only rarely are the risks physical. How we respond to dares when we are young may have something to do with which of the truly hazardous male inner dares—attacking mountains, tempting bulls at Pamplona—we embrace or ignore as men.

For two weeks, I scouted trains and tracks. I studied moving boxcars close up, memorizing how they squatted on their axles, never getting used to the squeal or the way the air fell hot from the sides. I created an imaginary, friendly train and ran next to it. I mastered a shallow, head-first dive with a simple half-twist. I'd land on my back, count to ten, imagine wheels and, locking both hands on the rail to my left, heave myself over and out. Even under pure sky, though, I had to fight to keep my eyes open and my shoulders between the rails.

The next Saturday, O.T., Dwayne and three eighth graders met me below the hill that backed up to the lumberyard. The track followed a slow bend there and opened to a straight, slightly uphill climb for a solid third of a mile. My run started two hundred yards after the bend. The train would have its tongue hanging out.

The other boys huddled off to one side, a circle on another planet, and watched quietly as I double-knotted my shoelaces. My hands trembled. O.T. broke the circle and came over to me. He kept his hands hidden in the pockets of his jacket. We looked at each other. BB's of sweat appeared beneath his nose. I stuffed my wallet in one of his pockets, rubbing it against his knuckles on the way in, and slid my house key, wired to a red-and-white fishing bobber, into the other. We backed away from each other, and he turned and ran to join the four already climbing up the hill.

I watched them all the way to the top. They clustered together as if I were taking their picture. Their silhouette resembled a round-shouldered tombstone. They waved down to me, and I dropped them from my mind and sat down on the rail. Immediately, I jumped back. The steel was vibrating.

The train sounded like a cow going short of breath. I pulled my shirttail out and looked down at my spot, then up the incline of track ahead of me. Suddenly the air went hot, and the engine was by me. I hadn't pictured it moving that fast. A man's bare head leaned out and stared at me. I waved to him with my left hand and turned into the train, burying my face in the incredible noise. When I looked up, the head was gone.

I started running alongside the boxcars. Quickly, I found their pace, held it, and then eased off, concentrating on each thick wheel that cut past me. I slowed another notch. Over my shoulder, I picked my car as it came off the bend, locking in the image of the white mountain goat painted on its side. I waited, leaning forward like the anchor in a 440-relay, wishing the baton up the track behind me. Then the big goat fired by me, and I was flying and then tucking my shoulder as I dipped under the train.

A heavy blanket of red dust settled over me. I felt bolted to the earth. Sheet-metal bellies thundered and shook above my face. Count to ten, a voice said, watch the axles and look to your left for daylight. But I couldn't count, and I couldn't find left if my life depended on it, which it did. The colors overhead went from brown to red to black to red again. Finally, I ripped my hands free, forced them to the rail, and, in one convulsive jerk, threw myself into the blue light.

I lay there face down until there was no more noise, and I could feel the sun against the back of my neck. I sat up. The last ribbon of train was slipping away in the distance. Across the tracks, O.T. was leading a cavalry charge down the hill, five very small, galloping boys, their fists whirling above them. I pulled my knees to my chest. My corduroy pants puckered wet across my thighs. I didn't care.

LEONARD KRIEGEL

Taking It

In 1944, at the age of eleven, I had polio. I spent the next two years of my life in an orthopedic hospital, appropriately called a reconstruction home. By 1946, when I returned to my native Bronx, polio had reconstructed me to the point that I walked very haltingly on steel braces and crutches.

But polio also taught me that, if I were to survive, I would have to become a man—and become a man quickly. "Be a man!" my immigrant father urged, by which he meant "become an American." For, in 1946, this country had very specific expectations about how a man faced adversity. Endurance, courage, determination, stoicism—these might right the balance with fate.

"I couldn't take it, and I took it," says the wheelchair-doomed poolroom entrepreneur William Einhorn in Saul Bellow's *The Adventures of Augie March*. "And I *can't* take it, yet I do take it." In 1953, when I first read these words, I knew that Einhorn spoke for me—as he spoke for scores of other men who had confronted the legacy of a maiming disease by risking whatever they possessed of substance in a country that believed that such risks were a man's wagers against his fate.

How one faced adversity was, like most of American life, in part a question of gender. Simply put, a woman endured, but a man fought back. You were better off struggling against the effects of polio as a man than as a woman, for polio was a disease that one confronted by being tough, aggressive, decisive, by assuming that all limitations could be overcome, beaten, conquered. In short, by being "a man." Even the vocabulary of rehabilitation was masculine. One "beat" polio by outmuscling the disease. At the age of eighteen, I felt that I was "a better man" than my friends because I had "overcome a handicap." And I had, in the process, showed that I could "take it." In the world of American men, to take it was a sign that you were among the elect. An assumption my "normal" friends shared. "You're lucky," my closest friend said to me during an intensely painful crisis in his own life. "You had polio." He meant it. We both believed it.

Obviously, I wasn't lucky. By nineteen, I was already beginning to understand—slowly, painfully, but inexorably—that disease is never "conquered" or "overcome." Still, I looked upon resistance to polio as the essence of my manhood. As an American, I was self-reliant. I could create my own possibilities from life. And so I walked mile after mile on braces and crutches. I did hundreds of push-ups every day to build my arms, chest, and shoulders. I lifted weights to the point that I would collapse, exhausted but strengthened, on the floor. And through it all, my desire to create a "normal" life for myself was transformed into a desire to become the man my disease had decreed I should be.

I took my heroes where I found them—a strange, disparate company of men: Hemingway, whom I would write of years later as "my nurse"; Peter Reiser, whom I dreamed of replacing in Ebbets Field's pastures and whose penchant for crashing into outfield walls fused in my mind with my own war against the virus; Franklin Delano Roosevelt, who had scornfully faced polio with aristocratic disdain and patrician distance (a historian acquaintance recently disabused me of that myth, a myth perpetrated, let me add, by almost all of Roosevelt's biographers); Henry Fonda and Gary Cooper, in whose resolute Anglo-Saxon faces Hollywood blended the simplicity, strength and courage a man needed if he was going to survive as a man; any number of boxers in whom heart, discipline and training combined to stave off defeats the boy's limitations made inevitable. These were the "manly" images I conjured up as I walked those miles of Bronx streets, as I did those relentless push-ups, as I moved up and down one subway staircase after another by turning each concrete step into a personal insult. And they were still the images when, fifteen years later, married, the father of two sons of my own, a Fulbright professor in the Netherlands, I would grab hold of vertical poles in a train in The Hague and swing my brace-bound body across the dead space between platform and carriage, filled with self-congratulatory vanity as amazement spread over the features of the Dutch conductor.

It is easy to dismiss such images as adolescent. Undoubtedly they were. But they helped remind me, time and time again, of how men handled their diseases and their pain. Of course, I realized even then that it was not the idea of manhood alone that had helped me fashion a life out of polio. I might write of Hemingway as "my nurse," but it was an immigrant Jewish mother—already transformed into a cliché by scores of male Jewish writers—who serviced my crippled body's needs and who fed me love, patience and care even as I fed her the rhetoric of my rage.

But it was the need to prove myself an American man—tough, resilient, independent, able to take it—that pulled me through the war with the virus. I have, of course, been reminded again and again of the price extracted for such ideas about manhood. And I am willing to admit that my sons may be better off in a country in which "manhood" will mean little more than, say, the name for an after-shave lotion. It is forty years since my war with the virus began. At fifty-one, even an American man knows that mortality is the only legacy and defeat the only guarantee. At fifty-one, my legs still encased in braces and crutches still beneath my shoulders, my elbows are increasingly arthritic from all those streets walked and weights lifted and stairs climbed. At fifty-one, my shoulders burn with pain from all those push-ups done so relentlessly. And at fifty-one, pain merely bores—and hurts.

Still, I remain an American man. If I know where I'm going, I know, too, where I have been. Best of all, I know the price I have paid. A man endures his diseases until he recognizes in them his vanity. He can't take it, but he takes it. Once, I relished my ability to take it. Now I find myself wishing that taking it were easier. In such quiet surrenders do we American men call it quits with our diseases.

CHRISTOPHER S. WREN

Midlife Macho

When my fifteen-year-old son pulled the faded green beret out of a trunk stashed away in our Vermont summer house, it was hard for him to reconcile this military artifact with the graying, slightly paunchy father who had to grope before breakfast for his spectacles.

Since he was a child, Chris had put up with my yarns about jumping out of airplanes and other derring-do, which he eventually wrote off to parental hyperbole until he confronted the evidence— a green beret and a bleached-out uniform shirt with its Airborne tab and arrow-shaped shoulder patch. Chris has pumped enough iron to deck me in a flash, but for the briefest moment he seemed impressed, though my pectorals didn't bulge enough to put me up there with Sylvester Stallone.

No, I explained, the Special Forces weren't really like that. We would have been out of uniform if we had run around wearing sweatbands and no shirts, like Rambo. Anyhow, I was never that clever at blowing things up or shooting things down, for all the money the Army wasted in trying to turn me lethal.

I wanted my son to understand that I had, in fact, distinguished myself by knowing how to spell better than anyone else in my airborne unit, which is why eventually I was asked—was handpicked—to write up citations about other men who did heroic feats. Sometimes these deeds were done so clandestinely that I was constrained from divulging quite how the men earned their honors.

Yet, I knew how my son felt. I remember I could never imagine my own cheerfully sedentary father in the cockpit of his trainer that had crashed, slamming the aircraft engine nearly into his chest but sparing his life. His service as an Army flier seemed just as improbable to me as my sojourn as a paratrooper was to my son.

My father took some of the glamour out of his military career by confessing that he had volunteered to fly because he thought it preferable to being killed in a trench. In my case, I went airborne not because I liked to jump but because I liked to be with people who liked to jump. I was as cocky after my first night jump as I had been terrified before it, and wearing the silver wings and trousers bloused into polished black boots made me feel tougher than I knew I was, with my myopic vision safely concealed behind contact lenses.

Yet, what dazzled me in youthful years no longer does so. I have changed. A woman now looks most attractive to me only after she turns forty, and I have revised some notions about what matters in masculine style.

Machismo, celebrating as it does the marvelous difference between the sexes, is still important for men, however they may try to disparage it. But the forms it takes mellow with age. For me, machismo now means driving more slowly, as if to prove that my libido is not attached to the accelerator. I do not think gold neck chains macho at all; they make the wearer look like an off-duty exotic dancer. But donning an apron to wash the dinner dishes seems highly macho, for the dishwasher doesn't care what kind of image his apron projects. So does having the guts to say "Sorry" if you bump into someone.

Hunting for sport does not strike me as macho, unless the animal is given the opportunity to shoot back. Though I discharged sundry firearms in the service of my country, and sometimes hit the target, I don't own a gun now. My trips to Lebanon as a journalist confirmed suspicions that arms don't make a man. To the contrary, they evoke a question posed at a Palestine Liberation Organization news conference by a journalist friend who pluckishly asked the spokesman if the pistol worn by his leader compensated for some kind of sexual inadequacy.

Real machismo does not need to advertise, and those who make a fuss about it are only telling me that they don't have much to flaunt. The most conspicuous display of machismo that I witnessed in Special Forces came from a sergeant who fell asleep leaning against my reserve parachute as we were circling over Fort Bragg on a moonless night. He roused himself in time to hook up his static line to the overhead cable and plunge out the door into the darkness ahead of me when the signal light flashed green. When I next saw him on the drop zone, he had dozed off again in the back of a truck sent to collect us.

From the perspective of middle age, the litmus test of machismo is what you overcome, not merely accomplish—doing the hard things that need doing without posturing. Fortunately, war never had a monopoly on heroes. Doug Scott, a British mountaineer of my acquaintance, broke both his legs in a fall high on a Himalayan peak called the Ogre. He crawled on his hands and knees down the mountain for three days until he reached help. As his ropemate, Chris Bonington, recounted it later, the most remarkable thing in their slow descent was that Doug never murmured one word about the pain. Finally out of the hospital, he went back to climbing in the Himalayas with metal pins in his legs.

I was born into a generation that believes real men wear undershirts. The heroes of my childhood have changed only physically. I recently scrutinized their worn faces in the photographs taken when they turned out to celebrate the fortieth anniversary of the end of World War II. They were young when they jumped into hostile drop zones at Normandy or Arnhem, when they waded ashore under fire at Guadalcanal or Iwo Jima. A few wars later, they don't look that tough. They wear bifocals, hearing aids and pacemakers. They may be grizzled or bald and hostage to arthritis, arteriosclerosis or more dreadful diseases. But when the courage was desperately needed, they delivered it, and afterward, like the veterans who followed them into Korea and Vietnam, they got on with less remarkable lives. My son, Chris, would call that cool. To me, that's macho.

WILLIAM F. BUCKLEY, JR.

The Clubhouse

I begin with a reminiscence. The scene was an all-male private club. It was late in the afternoon, cocktail time, and I was talking with Bart Giamatti, the freshly elected president of Yale University who was at the club as guest of a classmate of mine who, the year before, had invited Giamatti's predecessor as president of Yale, Kingman Brewster. "A difference between King and me," said Giamatti, "is that if King had come into this enclosure, he'd have made a beeline"—Giamatti pointed to the densest cluster of guests a few yards away—"for over there. I come in and I look for the loneliest sector of the congregation."

Male clubs have, probably need to have, the two kinds, and it blurs the question to assume that all clubmen are of the same social character. Those who are hypergregarious are absolutely necessary. On the other hand, if everyone were so, circumstances would be pretty hectic.

All-male voluntary associations tend to figure strongly in American life, and as usual it was Tocqueville who first pointed this out. Why? Here is one of three "Dreams" quoted by Richard E. McLean, about whom I know nothing more than that he attended our club in the summer of 1982. "Dream No. 1: 'Someday, damn it, we'll have a treehouse of our own. We'll build it out in the woods where Mother can't find us. And we'll eat when we want, what we want. We'll bring our friends. Have a secret club. And no girls.' —Little boy called home to dinner."

All right. And just who *are* "our friends"? In answer to this I think of the French sociologist-historian Anton Rossi, who in attempting to elucidate on one aspect of French individualism recited an encounter roughly (I render it from memory) as follows:

There are two strangers taking wine at a café in a city in the French provinces. After a while, one addresses the other, who is reading a newspaper, and asks, "Do you like Americans?" "No," is the curt answer. "Well, then, do you like Frenchmen?" Again, "No." "Well, do you like Jews?" "No." "Catholics?" "No." Finally, with some exasperation, "Well, whom *do* you like?" Without looking up from his newspaper: "I like my friends."

Now, I find this story very useful primarily because of what the protagonist refuses to say. In this case, just *why,* why did the little boy's dream contain the phrase "And no girls"? As with the big boy, with the same fancy, though of course differently phrased.

Here is Mr. McLean's Dream No. 2: " 'I mean, it's a damn shame it's got to end. The fraternity and everything. Someday we should build us all a fraternity house that wouldn't end. And we could initiate our friends and go off and drink like freshmen and never graduate. Hell! Why build a fraternity house? Let's build a gigantic fraternity system!' —Graduating senior, age twenty-one."

I am by no means complacent that the women's movement will not, even in its excesses, prevail. It appears to me to have become an ideology—moreover, one that comes up with socio-political programs which addicts of victimology will predictably kill for. The weakness of the movement lies, surely, in its unstated insistence that men should come forward with rational reasons why, in some situations, they prefer the company of their own gender, whether they are aggressively gregarious, or only passively so.

I am outraged at the planted axiom that one needs to account for every inclination. A cranky painter of great talent was asked in his studio by a woman examining his canvases, "Why do you use so much blue?" To which the painter replied icily, "Because it's cheaper." I know it is true that in a psychological examination a while back one of the questions asked was: "State your position on the color blue." But I cannot vouch for the accuracy of the story I heard a few years ago about a young man congenitally blind who, after his operation, awoke with eyesight restored, and from his hospital bed was able correctly to identify the principal colors. Suggesting? Well, suggesting at least a metaphysical, mysterious absorption of biases and attributes, and perhaps one of these is a bias for occasional segregation by sex. Then, of course, there is the legend of the Chinese man, born blind, miraculously cured by a faith healer to whom, after a few days, he returned to say that having seen the world, he would rather not continue to do so, and might the healer give him back his blindness?

As a nonaggressive, semigregarious male who belongs quite incidentally to three all-male clubs, I do wish that the creeping philosophical postulate were reexamined. Namely that one need explain "And no girls." And explain exactly what is meant by "I like my friends." I believe in the presumptive reluctance to abandon tradition. At the Century Club in New York, there has been great publicized activity on the matter of abandoning tradition and accepting women; indeed, a numerical majority (that is my impression) have come out in favor of the change. If that majority were motivated by an evolution in social taste, I should think that the only remaining obstacle to constitutional reform would be the question of the inchoate rights of the minority who joined a club on an understanding of its composition, now proposed to be transformed. But if it should turn out that the majority are voting to change tradition not so much because they really desire to do so, but because they feel they should, then the plebiscite is illegitimate, relying as it does on the false premise that that which we cannot explain we ought not to engage in.

I give here Mr. McLean's Dream No. 3: " 'I'd like to chuck it all. The business, the pressure, the family obligations. All of it. I'd like to go off alone where I wasn't president-of-this or in-charge-of-that. Just get away. Relax. Be myself. My real self. Do foolish things that nobody would remember. Maybe find guys like myself whom I could *really* talk to. Maybe someday.' —Company president, age forty-plus." For some folks, there ought to be a little supply-side activism, the all-male club.

ISAAC ASIMOV

Male Humor

Most of us, if we are male, have gathered in groups that happened to be exclusively masculine. On those occasions, at least according to my experience, it is extremely common to have conversation turn to an exchange of off-color jokes.

Such is the glee with which such jokes are told, and such the delight with which they are received, that one of the most serious objections to admitting women to the gatherings is that the presence of the female of the species would inhibit these exchanges and destroy much of the joy of the occasion.

But think about it. Why should jokes of this sort be told at all? Why should they be considered funny, and why *are* they (when told well) unfailingly funny at that? Why do even the most respectable and well-mannered men tell them and listen to others tell them? We might almost paraphrase Shakespeare and say, "One touch of smut makes the whole male world kin."

But is it really a mystery? Sex and elimination—the two staples of such jokes—are unmentionable in polite society (in theory) and yet are always with us. They are simply unavoidable, though the rules of the etiquette books tell us they don't exist.

What a horror is introduced into life by refusing to mention what we cannot escape. What a torture of roundabouts we are plunged into as a result.

Have you ever watched television commercials push laxatives and talk about the dread disease of "irregularity"? Irregularity of what? In fact, even irregularity has become suspect, and no abnor-

mal condition at all is mentioned by name. It has all sunk into a
tight-lipped look of gentle concern. The tight lips give it away, I
think.

When you dash for the washroom, is it a wild desire to wash
your hands that fills you? Is it for a nice rest that you go to the rest
room, for a chance to lounge about that you retreat to the lounge, a
last-minute adjustment to the top hat that makes it necessary to retire to the little room austerely marked "Gentlemen"? No civilized
man from Mars could possibly guess the function of such rooms
from the names we give them.

And is there a married couple (or an unmarried one, for that
matter) that doesn't invent some coy and innocuous phrase to serve
as a signal that indicates a desire for sex? What's yours? A mean-
ingful clearing of the throat?

What relief it is, then—what sheer release of tension—to tell
some story that involves the open admission that such things exist.
Add that release of tension to the natural humor such a joke might
contain and the laugh can be explosive. It might even be argued
that, given the distortions introduced by our social hypocrisy, the
dirty joke is an important contributor to the mental health of
males.

But don't women suffer from the same social hypocrisy as men
do? Aren't women repressed even more than men, since women are
supposed to be "ladylike" and "pure"? Of course! And it is my experience that women laugh as hard at dirty jokes as men do, and
show even greater tolerance for those that are not really very funny
but *are* very dirty.

Why, then, do men persist in believing that the presence of
women will spoil their fun? Partly, I suppose, it is because they are
victims of the myth of feminine purity, but partly it is because one
of the important components of the dirty joke is unabashed male
chauvinism. Women are almost always the butts and victims of
such jokes, and, indeed, a male chauvinist joke can be extremely
successful even when there is no hint of any element of either sex
or scatology.

Again, it's no mystery. Men are tyrannized by women from birth (or feel themselves to be—which comes to the same thing, of course). The young boy is hounded unmercifully and continually by his mother, who is perpetually at him to do what he does not want to do, and to *not* do what he *does* want to do. (The father is inevitably a more distant creature and, unless he is a monster, is more easily handled.)

The young man in love is constantly tantalized by the young woman he desires, and the young groom is harried to fulfill his campaign promises to his young bride. And, eventually, as married life settles down, the husband is hounded unmercifully and continually by his wife, who is perpetually at him to do what he does not want to do, and to *not* do what he *does* want to do. (At least, this is how it seems to him to be.)

Naturally, then, the male gathering is the one place (it seems to the man) where he can escape from this unending, lifelong feminine domination, and where he can retaliate, in safety, by telling jokes in which women get what they deserve.

You might argue that there's no harm in it. When all the jokes are done, he goes back home, having undergone a useful catharsis, and says his "Yes, dear" with far greater efficiency than he would have otherwise. Here again, such jokes may be essential to male mental health.

Do I approve?

No, I don't like male chauvinism—but let's not repress the jokes that serve a useful psychological purpose. I would, instead, prefer to invite women into the charmed circle and have them tell their jokes, too, which perhaps will help remove some of *their* hang-ups.

The trouble is that they leave the jokes to the men. Women by the hundreds have said to me, after having laughed fiendishly at some joke I have told: "Oh, I wish I could repeat it, but I never seem to be able to remember jokes, and when I do, I can't tell them."

Haven't we all heard that line?

Well, *why* can't women remember jokes? Have they poor memories?

Nonsense! They remember the price of every garment they have ever bought, and the exact place they bought it. They know where everything in the kitchen is, including the mustard jar that any husband will swear, after a thorough search, is nowhere in the house.

They're just defaulting on their responsibilities, and, as long as they do, they encourage us men to put our heads together and tell our chauvinist jokes after a nervous glance hither and thither assures us that no woman can hear us.

DAVID BINDER

Brotherhood of the Inept

Probably it runs in the family, this clumsiness, not as a river but at
least as a stream enveloping one of us each generation. My father
held on to a garage door handle after he had pulled it down. It
slammed on his thumb. He fell off a bicycle and broke his arm.
Once, when my mother threw a dress-up luncheon party in our
backyard for his business colleagues, a tablecloth concealed a large
irregularity on the edge of our rustic table. It was at this spot that
my father, wearing a white suit, placed his plate of spaghetti with
tomato sauce. It toppled into his lap. He changed into another
white suit, sat down at the same place and spilled a second plate.
Changing again upstairs, he dropped his pocket watch on the tile
floor of the bathroom. It stopped.

One wet and icy February, the roof above our living room began
to leak. In a business suit, my father mounted a ladder carrying a
claw hammer. Losing his footing, he desperately pounded the claw
through the asphalt shingles the way an Alpine climber uses an ice
ax. He broke through the ceiling, and the leak increased.

These incidents amused the members of our family and gave me
a brief and dangerous sense of superiority. Had I not recognized, at
the relatively late age of twelve, that I was heir to the clumsy
streak? Had the significance of my inability to throw a basketball
through a hoop, much less dribble it, escaped me?

One day a friend took me along to a country club to work for
him as a caddy. Golf was more alien to me than Albania. My first
and last golfer asked for "a wood." I handed him a 5-iron. We

reached the first green and he prepared to putt. I held the flag stick firmly in the hole. The ball hit the pole and bounced off. He cursed. "Clumsy!" I have kept my distance from the game these forty-three years.

At this distance, I can observe that what distinguishes the clumsy from the graceful is our total inability to recognize the functions at which we will surely fail—dancing, fancy diving, sanding wood, catching a fly ball or carrying a glass safely to a table. In high school, where sports were compulsory, I volunteered to dive for the swimming team, knowing, at least, that I would be a poor racer. I could never sufficiently coordinate two arm movements with two leg movements. I can still hear the voice through the loudspeaker announcing: "Binder will attempt a one-and-a-half gainer with a half twist." I lifted off the board, went into wild contortions and landed on my back, splashing the onlookers. I stayed for a time at the bottom of the pool, but when I finally surfaced they were still laughing. I retreated to the cross-country team.

In retrospect, it is the not-knowing that is so galling to the clumsy: not knowing when and where we are going to lumber. A modest facility at playing the clarinet or typing or even getting down a hill on skis is liable to seduce us into feeling that we may have overcome terminal awkwardness. Down this path, and not very far down it, lies a branch over which we will trip.

After years of summers paddling canoes and portaging them on narrow trails, I fancied myself handy with this mode of transportation. Not so. With my father in a canoe, I tipped over on a placid stretch of the upper Wisconsin River, prompting him, of all persons, to brand me: "Clumsy!" Recently I capsized a canoe while trying to retrieve a fishing lure that was snagged on a tree limb, dumping an old friend into the drink. Soon after, my friend lost his glasses. He, too, may belong to the brotherhood of the inept, but it is a mark of the clumsy not to be able to discern the trait readily in others.

When two clumsy persons get together, cataclysm is not far away. Once I was teasing my father in the presence of two of my friends. He playfully threw a short, clumsy punch that caught me in the stomach, sending me reeling across the room and slumping to the floor. My father and I were quite surprised at this sudden confluence of our mutual incoordination. My friends thought it was hilarious.

There is a blitheness that attends being clumsy. My father, for instance, floored the brake pedal of the family car at a crossroads where there was a conspicuous amount of loose gravel on the asphalt. The car spun completely around and ended up facing in the direction my father wished to go. His passenger, on leave after being wounded in the Africa campaign of World War II, was frightened more, he said, than by anything he had experienced in the desert fighting. Father only smiled and remarked: "Didn't I do that nicely?"

With the passage of much time, a degree of awareness may accumulate for the clumsy. Thus, I watched with a kind of eerie contentment as a recent house guest walked straight into our glass porch door twice within ten minutes. I was also able to appreciate the story of Vasil Bilak, the Czechoslovak Communist Politburo member whose proof of proletarian genuineness was displayed a few years ago at an exhibition commemorating the sixtieth anniversary of the founding of his ruling party in Prague. It was his certificate as a journeyman tailor from a town in Moravia, dated 1926. For ten crowns, a museum guard slipped the parchment out of its frame and displayed the reverse side. On it, the master tailor who examined young Bilak had written: "He is all right on the trousers, but don't let him at the jackets."

But awareness has its limits. So I go on determinedly felling trees on power lines, painting windows shut, bumping people on dance floors, sawing crookedly and spilling sugar. Those, at least, are the clumsinesses I remember, but there may be thousands I never even noticed. My wife is plainly sympathetic, maybe even empathetic. After I sharpen the kitchen knives, invariably nicking them, she usually cuts herself.

Perhaps recognition of clumsiness is at the root of my occasional dream of having only to take a deep breath to be able to rise unaided toward the heavens and, with a few deft hand movements, to fly to an altitude of about five hundred feet. No one else is up there with me, and those graceful tennis players, golfers and fly fishermen I can still see below are in awe of my gracefulness. In that dream I am never clumsy.

BRIAN MANNING

The Thirsty Animal

I was very young, but I still vividly remember how my father fascinated my brothers and me at the dinner table by running his finger around the rim of his wineglass. He sent a wonderful, crystal tone wafting through the room, and we loved it. When we laughed too raucously, he would stop, swirl the red liquid in his glass and take a sip.

There was a wine cellar in the basement of the house we moved into when I was eleven. My father put a few cases of Bordeaux down there in the dark. We played there with other boys in the neighborhood, hid there, made a secret place. It was musty and cool and private. We wrote things and stuck them in among the bottles and imagined someone way in the future baffled by our messages from the past.

Many years later, the very first time I drank, I had far too much. But I found I was suddenly able to tell a girl at my high school that I was mad about her.

When I drank in college with the men in my class, I was trying to define a self-image I could feel comfortable with. I wanted to be "an Irishman," I decided, a man who could drink a lot of liquor and hold it. My favorite play was Eugene O'Neill's *Long Day's Journey into Night,* my model the drunken Jamie Tyrone.

I got out of college, into the real world, and the drunk on weekends started to slip into the weekdays. Often I didn't know when one drunk ended and another began. The years were measured in hangovers. It took a long time to accept, and then to let the idea sink in, that I was an alcoholic.

It took even longer to do anything about it. I didn't want to believe it, and I didn't want to deny myself the exciting, brotherly feeling I had whenever I went boozing with my friends. For a long time, in my relationships with women, I could only feel comfortable with a woman who drank as much as I did. So I didn't meet many women and spent my time with men in dark barrooms, trying to be like them and hoping I'd be accepted.

It is now two years since I quit drinking, and that, as all alcoholics know who have come to grips with their problem, is not long ago at all. The urge to have "just one" includes a genuine longing for all the accouterments of drink: the popping of a cork, the color of Scotch through a glass, the warmth creeping over my shoulders with the third glass of stout. Those were joys. Ever since I gave them up I remember them as delicious.

I go to parties now and start off fine, but I have difficulty dealing with the changing rhythms as the night wears on. Everyone around me seems to be having a better time the more they drink, and I, not they, become awkward. I feel like the kid with a broken chain when everyone else has bicycled around the corner out of sight. I fight against feeling sorry for myself.

What were the things I was looking for and needed when I drank? I often find that what I am longing for when I want a drink is not really the alcohol, but the memories and laughter that seemed possible only with a glass in my hand. In a restaurant, I see the bottle of vintage port on the shelf, and imagine lolling in my chair, swirling the liquid around in the glass, inhaling those marvelous fumes. I think of my neighbor, Eileen, the funniest woman I ever got smashed with, and I want to get up on a bar stool next to her to hear again the wonderful stories she told. She could drink any man under the table, she claimed, and I wanted to be one of those men who tried. She always won, but it made me feel I belonged when I staggered out of the bar, her delighted laughter following me.

I had found a world to cling to, a way of belonging, and it still attracts me. I pass by the gin mills and pubs now and glance in at the men lined up inside, and I don't see them as suckers or fools. I remember how I felt sitting there after work, or watching a Sunday afternoon ball game, and I long for the smell of the barroom and that ease—toasts and songs, jokes and equality. I have to keep reminding myself of the wasting hangovers, the lost money, the days down the drain.

I imagine my problem as an animal living inside me, demanding a drink before it dies of thirst. That's what it says, but it will never die of thirst. The fact an alcoholic faces is that this animal breathes and waits. It is incapable of death and will spring back to lustful, consuming life with even one drop of sustenance.

When I was eighteen and my drinking began in earnest, I didn't play in the wine cellar at home anymore; I stole there. I sneaked bottles to my room, sat in the window and drank alone while my parents were away. I hated the taste of it, but I kept drinking it, without the kids from the neighborhood, without any thought that I was feeding the animal. And one day, I found one of those old notes we had hidden down there years before. It fell to the ground when I pulled a bottle from its cubbyhole. I read it with bleary eyes, then put the paper back into the rack. "Beware," it said, above a childish skull and crossbones, "all ye who enter here." A child, wiser than I was that day, had written that note.

I did a lot of stupid, disastrous, sometimes mean things in the years that followed, and remembering them is enough to snap me out of the memories and back to the reality that I quit just in time. I've done something I had to do, something difficult and necessary, and that gives me satisfaction and the strength to stay on the wagon. I'm very lucky so far. I don't get mad that I can't drink anymore; I can handle the self-pity that overwhelmed me in my early days of sobriety. From time to time, I daydream about summer afternoons and cold beer. I know such dreams will never go away. The thirsty animal is there, getting a little fainter every day. It will never die. A lot of my life now is all about keeping it in a very lonely cage.

MARSHALL SCHUON

Cars and Self-Image

I once had a fistfight with a kid named Alan. I think I won, although both Alan and my nose may dispute it. What we were fighting about was electric trains, specifically my insistence on the superior realism of American Flyer when compared to those clunky, three-rail Lionels. We were always arguing about something like that. We identified with *stuff*, and if it wasn't trains, it was comic strips, or the contention that the P-38 was a better fighter plane than the P-47. Later, in the early 1950s, it was cars, and the argument extended to all of our friends.

Back then, a sports car was an MG-TC with spindly wheels, wooden floorboards and a body made of old chewing-gum wrappers, nothing a real seventeen-year-old man would own. You were either a Ford guy or a Chevy guy. Plymouths didn't count, and we didn't even *talk* to the guy who bought a '41 Packard. Shows how much we knew. It also shows how rapt we were at the idea of a package to suit our image.

Ford had a V-8 engine. You could put dual exhausts on it. You could top it off with a whole gaggle of carburetors. You could throw in a hot cam and have something that was truly the terror of the streets. Or you could take a Jimmy truck engine, stuff it into a Chevy sedan and make a mohair monster that ate Fords for lunch. It all depended.

It still does, of course. A car says a lot about a man, and that is the real reason that dealers don't have generic automobiles on their shelves. No sensibly priced, plain-white, three-sizes-fit-all vehicles for us. What we want, whether we admit it or not, are rolling advertisements for ourselves, and the chief difficulty is in choosing the right billboard.

For myself, and for a long time after I gave up the hot-rod Fords, it was a successive line of vans and funny cars like Corvairs. And, finally, it was a Cadillac. I was wearing a cowboy hat then and, night after night, I would arrive at the newspaper I worked for, Stetson on my head, blonde on my arm and goblet of brandy in my hand. The guards in the lobby thought I was a real character. I know that because one of them told me about this bozo who was a real character. We were in the men's room and he didn't recognize me without my hat and blonde and brandy, which is what happens when you shuck the trappings.

The problem with the Cadillac, of course, was that it had to stay outside. It was just right for a man in a cowboy hat—powerful, lush and big to the point of being a crime against nature. But it wasn't any good out there in the parking lot with me in the office. I solved that by carrying the owner's manual and leaving it discreetly on the desk.

Since then, I've worked a bit on my profile, and these days I've got it down to a small Buick. I tell myself I'm more mature, less flamboyant. And I like to think it says something about increasing self-confidence. Those are nice things to think, even though I know it's only the recession.

Subtlety does have its place, however, and Mercedes-Benz has capitalized nicely on a slice of the market that demands quiet flair. "What it is," a smugly happy owner once told me, "is quality and engineering. You drive that car and it says something about you, about being smart enough to know it—and, second, being rich enough to afford it."

If money is no object, naturally, you can suit your image in the same disgusting way you can do anything when money is no object. I have a friend in the automobile business whose name is Fred. He did it by going on a diet and then buying a white Jaguar for days and a blue Ferrari for nights. He had to go on a diet because a Ferrari is a *thin* car. When you drive a Ferrari, you don't have room for an extra pack of king-size cigarettes, let alone your very own spare tire.

"The Jag is an open car, that's why it's for days," Fred says. "The Ferrari's a coupe and that's why it's for nights. But you talk about this image thing—you can pretty much typecast who will own that kind of car. If you're a pilot, for instance, you buy a Saab. Guys who are into mechanical weirdness always buy Saabs."

You can look at a guy, says Fred, and know he's an old Fiat or he's American Motors. "Take a Porsche guy," he says. "A Porsche owner is very image-conscious. He wants to be daring on the outside, but he'd never own a Ferrari because a Porsche is more practical. With a Ferrari, if you run into a repair problem, you can be in for as much as $2,000 or $3,000."

Another thing, says Fred, is the kind of man who owns a Corvette or a Pontiac Trans Am. "Those are cars people move out of," he says. "You'll see an ad that says 'Must sell my Corvette—getting married,' but you don't see it the other way, you don't see that ad for a Ferrari or a Mercedes 450 SL."

It is not just drivers who think about image, though; the men who make the cars think about it, too, and there have been some spectacular changes over the years in what a car is meant to say. When I was a kid, the Dodge was gray and grandfatherly. Stodgy. Nothing at all like the Dodges that were the hot ticket on the racing circuits of the late 1960s and early 1970s. And John Z. DeLorean, before garnering all his other celebrity, made a name for himself at General Motors by changing Pontiac from a dull and middle-aged widget into a wide-track screamer that was panted over by a nation's entire zit set.

It must be admitted, however, that power and pizazz are not all things to all men. There are those, a relative few in the scheme of things, who see a positive advantage in projecting a negative image. they delight in their perversity. They don't want flashy performance or Italian good looks or a car that drips gold instead of brake fluid. They are the people who made the Volkswagen Beetle a hit, and today they are the people who joyfully fling their arms and leap into the air when they see a Toyota Tercel.

Rolls-Royce is the ultimate image car, of course, but the company has only recently tried to find out who buys its product. "You know, we've always been a sort of cottage industry," says Reginald Abbiss, a former BBC reporter who now employs his dulcet British tones as the Rolls spokesman in the colonies. "We only make sixty cars a week, but we have to look ahead, and we are adopting a more aggressive approach in promotion and advertising."

What the company is finding, he said, is that—particularly in America—a Rolls customer is saying "I've worked damned hard for my money, and this is a tangible result."

Image, too, is the real reason the company continues to make the Bentley, which differs from the Rolls only in its radiator shell and costs $530 less than the $93,000 bottom-of-the-line Rolls. "With that sort of tariff," says Reg Abbiss, "the $530 obviously doesn't make any difference. What we like to believe is that the Bentley is for the man who has won the race but declines to wear the laurel."

AS A MAN

GROWS

OLDER

DAVID UPDIKE

The Little House

A few years ago, not long after I had gotten out of college, yet before I figured out how I was going to make my way in the world, I came upon the idea of building a small, one-room house for myself in the woods. I had recently returned from a tumultuous trip through Italy with my girlfriend and returned home penniless, homeless, unemployed and certainly more confused than I had been when I left, a month or two before.

For the time being, I stayed at my mother's house in the country, and during this hiatus I started reading *Walden*. I was filled with happy notions of self-sufficiency and independence, and I felt that if only I could make a little place for myself, a room to which I could always return, I would be safe, somehow, protected from future hardships.

Having received rather vague, disbelieving permission from my mother, I went out into the woods in search of a place to build. I soon found a treeless rectangle of land, roughly sixteen feet by twelve, in a deep thicket of woods halfway between the field and the marsh. I returned with a mattock and a hoe and began to clear away the undergrowth, hacking down through the roots and rotting branches, clearing the topsoil until I came to the sandy undersoil on which I would build my footing. It was late fall, almost winter, and it was not until the third day of excavation that I discovered that the plant I had been unearthing was poison ivy. I went to our hospital's emergency room for treatment, and, after several days, I

returned to the woods wearing a ski mask and sunglasses and resumed my work undaunted.

At the library, I found several books on house construction and
carpentry. Then, with a shovel, I dug foundation holes, filled them
with rocks and cinder blocks, and I began to forage around the
house for lumber. Because I was broke at the time, part of my aspi-
ration was to prove that, if one were clever and resourceful enough,
money was a necessity that could be done without.

In the barn, I found some old 4 by 4's that had once held up the
backboard on the tennis court and some heavy boards that had
once been the railing of a bridge. My greatest find was an enormous beam, 8 inches by 10 inches by 18 feet long, that had washed
up in the marsh. It must once have been part of a ship or a dock. I
sawed off its one pulpy end and, using a long pole as a lever, raised
it a few inches off the marsh so it could dry out. A few days later, I
used boards, rollers and a skateboard turned on its back (so the
beam rolled on its upturned wheels) and, in the style of the ancient
Egyptians, I managed with enormous difficulty and satisfaction to
roll the beam through the woods to the site. I then raised it up on
cinder blocks and made it level. It was to form the structural center,
the backbone, of the little house.

Not far from my mother's home, developers had begun to gut
my old elementary school in order to turn it into condominiums.
After receiving permission from the foreman, I drove up in our
family car and began to load it with 2 by 4's and old, bent floorboards that I had trod two decades before.

By this time, my project had begun to interest and amuse my
family. "So how's Walden Two?" my stepfather would inquire
when I came in from a long day in the woods.

"It's not Walden Two," I would say indignantly. "If I thought I
was Thoreau, I wouldn't build it in my mother's backyard."

"Well, that's true," he said. "How is it, anyway?"

"Fine," I said, but offered little else.

I soon moved back to the city, found an apartment and a job and
began to run my life in a reasonably orderly way. But my mind was
steadily working, turning, as I contemplated the next phase of con-

struction. And on my visits home, I continued to build. I used the old bridge railing as joists, and built the frame for the floor. I bought some rough pine floorboards from an old man who ran a small sawmill in a nearby town.

On one of my visits to my grandmother's farm in Pennsylvania, I studied the construction of her nineteenth-century barn and spent an afternoon carving oak pegs with which, I plotted, my house would be held together. On my mother's lawn I laid out pieces of the frame, and, using a dull drill and chisels, I began to cut mortise and tenon joints and then peg them together. With my brother's help, I raised the frames for the walls, braced them and made rafters from the boards from my old school. I found some beautiful old windows in the barn. My mother pilfered a small blue door from someone's trash. Last summer, I tar-papered the roof and boarded up the last of the walls.

During the winter, with the help of my stepfather, I installed an old wood stove, which, if the day is not too cold, brings the temperature to a reasonable level of warmth. On my visits home, I continued to work—shingling the sides, covering the roof, wondering how better to keep out the cold.

Now that it is finished, after two years of sporadic, though persistent, labor, I sometimes wonder what exact purpose I had imagined the house would serve when I began. My mother sometimes paints there, and when I visit I use it as a kind of retreat, a refuge from the familial throng. I light a fire, listen to the sound of wind in the trees, the shouts of the clammers out on the flats, the crunch of a visitor's approaching footsteps.

But the function of the little house, I now realize, was less in its finished form than in the making, and its construction served as a kind of catharsis, an agent of transformation. In the very act of scavenging lumber for my creation—from the barn, the house, the marsh, my old school—I assembled the artifacts of a receding past into a cohesive, functional whole. Strangely, all that time I was working alone in the woods, banging nails and sawing boards and wrestling with enormous pieces of wood, something was silently shifting, and when I finally looked up, it was only to discover that the world had changed in my absence, shifted beneath me, and the place where I was building was no longer my home. In the end, what I constructed, really, was a monument to the past, to child-hood—an empty room, absorbing the nights and the days and the seasons, sitting by itself in the trees.

EDWARD TIVNAN

A Touch of Vanity

And there I am in my third-grade class picture, the girls in white blouses and skirts, the boys in striped jerseys and cotton chinos—except for the curly-haired kid in the gabardines, white shirt, bow tie and (oh my God!) suspenders. "You look like a little twit," announced my dear wife, Marilyn. I guess I do, but I recall feeling quite dashing at the time. Those other boys would have fought that outfit to the death. I had picked out the suspenders.

"Gabardine Pants" is what they called me, the girls at the park where I played baseball as a child. When a friend informed me of the nickname, even I was surprised that I felt neither anger nor humiliation. What came over me was the same delicious feeling I got when I belted one out of that same park. I learned the emotion's name soon afterward in Sunday school—vanity, the one "deadly sin" I have cultivated for a lifetime.

It has not been easy. Spiritual mentors preached against excessive pride, though I soon noticed our bishop had a taste for ermine robes. At prep school, we were taught the virtues of moderation, charity and humility, though we seemed to spend most of our adolescence in search of the perfect haircut. In college, my friends and I shared contempt for "phonies," though even the dimmest of us got A's in intellectual pretension. One of the difficulties of surviving the 1960s was that to look good one had to look awful. Of course, we were as vain in our hippie gear as any Beau Brummell.

Historically, women have been more partial to vanity than men,

281

mainly because it was the only interesting thing they could get away with in public. A woman's appearance was her major achievement, her success. Today still, "real men" are expected to drink, chase women and rob their fellows in business, but for them to go public with a taste for fine clothes (or worse, for interior decor) causes eyebrows to be raised all around. Actors and rock stars may play the peacock, but what father or mother dreams of a daughter bringing home a chap sporting one silver glove or an earring? Europeans appreciate foulards, brocade vests and delicate leather shoes on the male animal, but in America the "best dressed" man is, simply, neat.

I came by my vanity quite naturally. When my father was a young man, or so the legend goes, he once skied in a camel's-hair coat and a snap-brim, thus scoring a double vanity, as a skier and a fashion plate. During World War II, my mother spent her entire Rosie-the-Riveter salary one year for an elegant Persian-lamb coat and matching pillbox hat. The favorite sports in my family were baseball and shopping. I became expert at both, and for the same reason: the results made me feel terrific about myself.

But by the end of the crazy sixties, I was ambivalent about my taste for good clothes. My ambitions were then thoroughly academic, and I was bright enough to deduce that dapper dressing was hardly a ticket to tenure and, more than likely, an obstacle. ("No elbow patches on that jacket—surely a second-rate mind" was the comment I imagined among the wise men at whose feet I was eager to sit, in spite of the horrid Hush Puppies on them.) I once mistook the great Thomistic philosopher Etienne Gilson for a college janitor, until I realized that no self-respecting workingman would dress so badly.

Was I too taken with appearances? Too distracted from the noumena by phenomena? I thought I was until, in graduate school, I learned what I had already understood in the third grade: "The animals do not admire one another," declared Pascal.

Of course, it is vulgar and self-absorbed to care solely about one's appearance or reputation. Yet what is the value of wealth and health, even life, if one is not held in the good opinion of others? I discovered that vanity can be the front line of defense against criticism and failure; it can also be a starting point to feeling good about oneself, and then about one's world. I think this is why the coolest kid on the block in any poor neighborhood is usually the best-dressed. It's a quick way to recognition and self-esteem—and possibilities. Recognizing the pleasures of vanity, one is more likely to strive for something else to be vain about.

I will not claim vanity is without its risks. Several years ago I was a guest at a small Thanksgiving dinner attended also by a beautiful young actress. "Stunning," said a fellow guest as she made her entrance. I could hardly disagree—we were wearing the same elegant English tweed suit. "Where did you get your suit?" she asked me. In the same shop she had, it turned out. My consolation was that it was a man's suit. Her consolation was that she looked a lot better in it than I. My only regret: I still wear the thing, while she, now a major star, was wearing something a bit frillier at the last Academy Awards.

But as sins go, vanity, I have found, has little downside: no hangovers, no jealous husbands, no threat of jail. On the other hand, the main virtue of my favorite sin is that vanity offers comfort when things are going bad. One wants to be great, but one stands small. One is eager to be rich, but checks rebound around town. One wants to be loved, but critics are everywhere, pointing out one's faults. Like every good man, I strive for perfection, and, like every ordinary man, I have found that perfection is out of reach—but not the perfect suit.

JEFF SHEAR

Going Bald Gracelessly

I talked with Edd Byrnes on the telephone the other day. You remember Edd: he played Kookie, the parking lot attendant in the
television series "77 Sunset Strip," which ran from 1958 to 1964. As
a pop icon, he was, in the breathy superlatives of the day, "the
maximum upmost!" And what was it that made Kookie uppermost
in most girls' minds? His hair.

"Kookie, Kookie, Lend Me Your Comb" was the name of the
hit tune Edd Byrnes recorded with Connie Stevens. And that's why
I was calling him at his home in Los Angeles. I wanted to know if,
after more than twenty years, the real-life Edd Byrnes had anything left of the "maximum upmost." His reply was a good-natured
chuckle. "There's your answer," he said, and laughed again.

To many men, the subject of hair—or, more correctly, the lack of
it—is not fit for discussion, and the reasons should be obvious.
Balding is the hammerlock that mortality holds on a man's conceits. Cumulatively, along with the extra notch in the belt, the soft-
ening around the middle, a nevus or two, a bleeding gum, it is the
final takedown in the fight to stay youthful. From our teens
through our middle years, signs of aging accumulate so gradually
they go unnoticed. And though balding, too, often occurs gradually, the recognition of it is sudden. No other change in a man's
life, I think, takes place so quickly or is so evident—with the single
exception of puberty.

The first time I noticed my scalp creeping through my hairline
was in a men's room at a movie theater. My immediate reaction

was denial. And sure enough, with the proper combing, my scalp disappeared. The problem wasn't my hair, I convinced myself, it was the bright lighting over the mirror.

Soon, however, I began to discover certain irrefutable signs of encroaching baldness. Short, thin hairs began appearing in the sink after I used the dryer. Seen against the gleaming porcelain, they had the appearance of a spidery script, an augury. Now, on closer inspection, I detected a mere runt crop of tiny hairs stunted by the spreading pink desert of my scalp. I was going bald.

The thought of losing my hair made me self-conscious. I squirmed in restaurants when the waitress stood over me to take my order. Surely she would notice my bald spot; my vanity was at stake. Then, too, when I made trips to the barber I would feel exposed and vulnerable, cringing at his suggestion for styling my "thinning hair." My dignity was at stake.

To my alarm, I began taking notice of advertisements for retro-fitters who would weave, plug or implant new hair into me. I was alarmed, because I've always felt ill at ease with men who wear hairpieces or comb their hair to hide their bald spots. But now I was gaining new insight. Where else do you put what hair you have left if not over your bald spot? Still, I wondered what I would do when parting my hair called attention to the problem rather than concealed it. Would I get in line for snake oil?

I saw my vanity posed against my dignity. It was one or the other. Yet, stated in such a way, the choice seemed clear. Dignity would win: no hairpiece.

I was reminded recently that women frequently find bald men attractive. That may be true. But wherever I look, I see our culture offering up evidence to the contrary. The ideal image of masculine good looks is seldom a bald one. Look at the male models appearing in advertisements, the movie stars with their hair transplants. Or what about a line from a story that appeared recently in a magazine; it spoke of a rock star and "his famous blond hair." The Edd Byrnes idea lives: famed for his hair! Given the choice, would any man go bald? And why do you suppose that is?

All this discomfiture at the prospect of approaching baldness has come as a surprise to me. I am a relatively modest man who imagined himself reacting to signs of thinning hair with resignation; even, perhaps, relief, the way I took the passage from my twenties into my thirties. But instead, I feel diminished. Cheated. It is an effort to maintain a proper perspective. It's the luck of the draw, I tell myself, the role of the genes. After all, I am losing my hair, not my head. So I try to accept that growing bald tells me I am growing older; I try to accept that baldness releases me from certain conceits; that baldness, after all, is something I am powerless to reverse. It is this last that gnaws at me: that I am powerless to reverse it. My sister, who hadn't visited me in some time, noting my receding hairline, asked, "What happened?" What happened indeed?

All this upset no doubt has its origins in the deep identification my generation has had with hair. Perhaps it was Elvis and his D.A. that started it all. I recall the regular efforts I once made to maneuver opposing sets of my mother's mirrors into position so I could see the rump feathers I preened back of my ears. In those days, hair was your passport to your peer group. Our hairstyles changed with our pop idols. All I had to do at one point was to hop into the barber chair, say "Gimme a Peter Gunn," and my hair was cut "cool" and combed to one side.

More important, perhaps, was the moment on television when Jack Kennedy paused, as he watched his inaugural parade, to take a discreet swipe at his hair with a concealed pocket comb. For me, that gesture symbolized an end to the hairless Eisenhower years and heralded the beginning of the New Frontier: wild, woolly . . . hirsute.

The year Kennedy was killed, the Beatles had their first big hit. Shaggy hair became the style, then a fetish, an Off Broadway show and, finally, an emblem symbolizing our youthful rejection of all that was pin-striped and narrow-ruled. Young men who wore a ponytail, as I did, called it a "freak flag." Today, the iconoclasm of the punks reflects the idealism of the Hair Generation. Hair remains a form of personal expression, a social declaration that my bald spot recalls, then renders mute.

CAREY WINFREY

Taming Ambition

Now, in retrospect, I trace the first glimmerings to the source of the Nile.

There, on the shores of Uganda's Lake Victoria of an April dawn in 1979, I found myself with the Tanzanian Army in hot pursuit of a rapidly retreating Idi Amin.

The past few days had been heady ones, filled with enough adventure, excitement and challenge to satisfy even those intrepid British explorers who first beheld these vistas a century before. As a foreign correspondent, I was living out fantasies I'd nurtured since childhood.

Then why, I kept asking myself, am I so discontented?

The obvious answer was that I was lonely. Recently divorced, I had come to Africa alone, and alone I had more or less remained. With fifty-five countries to cover, there had not been time to make many new friends. I'd hook up with this reporter or that one in Lagos or Lusaka and share a beer, a taxi or a source or two. But then we'd go our separate ways.

So you're lonely, I told myself. Give it time. It'll pass.

But now, with the Tanzanians on the heels of Amin, and with an army of reporters on the heels of the Tanzanians, I began to feel the pull of strange, new tides.

Amin's retreat made good copy, my stories were making page one, and the abundant camaraderie made me realize that loneliness was not my only problem. A force more powerful than the Tanzanian Army was tugging at my psyche. Closing in fast on forty, I was having intimations of mortality.

Suddenly, the things I needed most to do—roots to put down; a new marriage to make; in time, I hoped, children to father—seemed impossible in Africa.

Until then, I had lived by a fairly simple rule: If it advanced my journalistic career, do it. Social concerns had always been secondary. To ask the paper to let me come back to the United States after less than a year as a foreign correspondent would mark my first clear violation of that credo.

Though puzzled by my request, the editors granted it without recrimination, and, for a time, just to be home again was enough. Then, after only a few months, my midlife passage prompted yet another change of course.

On impulse, a few days before my thirty-ninth birthday, I made up my mind to leave the paper. I wanted, I explained, to try my hand at fiction, to find out if I had the talent for it before it was too late. "Taking my shot," I called it. Again, the editors acquiesced to my wishes.

One of the last stories I wrote for the *Times* was based on an interview with the writer Robert Penn Warren. While preparing for it, a passage in one of his poems had caught my eye:

Can the heart's meditation wake us from life's long sleep,
And instruct us how foolish and fond was all labor spent?—
Us who now know that only at death of ambition does the deep
Energy crack crust, spurt forth, leap
From grottoes, dark—and from the caverned enchainment.

In the interview, I asked the poet when his own ambition had died.

It happened on vacation in Italy, he said, in the mid-1950s, in a fortress built by Philip II of Spain.

"It was the most incredibly beautiful place," Mr. Warren explained, "with the sea on three sides, and we had our beautiful little

daughter with golden hair, this innocent child on blood-soaked
stones. . . . I was so wrapped up in the thing itself—the moment—
that I had no sense of career."

He went on: "A young man's ambition to get along in the world
and make a place for himself, half your life goes that way. . . .
Then, if you're lucky, you make terms with life, you get released."

I thought about his words as I drove back to the city from the
Warren home in Connecticut. As much as I envied him his equa-
nimity, I had to admit that I had yet to experience the release he
spoke of.

In the year that followed, I wrote one respectable screenplay and
half of a not very good novel before returning to the workaday
world with the questions I had left the paper to answer still largely
unresolved.

I had not learned whether I could, with more time and greater
application, make a "success" of writing fiction. Though there was
much I had liked about the quiet life at the typewriter, I hadn't
even found out for certain if I was cut out for such solitude. By almost any professional assessment, the year had been pretty much
of a washout.

Then why did I feel so good about it?

In the years that have passed since then, I've given that question
more than a little thought. I've come to realize that I am grateful
simply to have taken the chance. Risk, in measured proportions, I
now believe, is life-enhancing, and at least that year silenced—if
only for a while—the little voice in the back of my head that used
to ask, "What if?"

Of course, falling in love with a woman more concerned with
what I am than with anything I might accomplish has helped enormously to reduce the importance of my own small strivings to a
more appropriate scale.

But no event has so reordered my priorities as the birth of our
twin sons. In the rare moments they allow for reflection between
feedings and changing of diapers, I realize that they have added a
dimension to my life I only dimly sensed had been lacking. Home

after a day filled with the frustrations of the get-ahead world, I respond to their bright eyes and toothless grins with feelings of wonder and gratitude.

If those moments are as close as I have yet come to an epiphany of the kind Robert Penn Warren experienced in the fortress, I nonetheless feel I am making progress in understanding what he was talking about.

I don't want to mislead; my ambition has not died. I continue to jockey for a place for myself. The energy has yet to spurt from grottoes.

But if there is satisfaction to be taken from my midlife passage—and I believe there is—it comes from a new awareness that these are vanities to be tamed; someday, even conquered. Such knowledge, I assure myself, puts me at least at the beginning of the path the poet discovered that summer day in the Mediterranean sunshine.

RICHARD REEVES

Breaking Down

My left arm had been hurting a bit. The upper arm. Not too bad. I imagined it felt something like the way a left-handed pitcher's arm must feel after ten or fifteen years in the big time. Warren Spahn, maybe. Thinking of Spahn took me back. Say, 1954. Grass and sunshine, the feeling when your left arm straightens with the bat at the perfect instant you hit a baseball well. The pain took me back to being seventeen, and I was smiling.

But this was 1978. I was forty-one. I was on the road, in a hotel room, and I was dropping to the floor to do some push-ups. I'd do forty in the morning. But, this morning, I did none. There was no strength in that tingling left arm.

I didn't realize it then, but that was the first sign of what I've come to think of as the machinery breaking down. The body, my body, the machine that I control and that controls me, is wearing out. The loose perpetual-motion machine to which they used to give trophies for hitting baseballs and medals for moving through the water while people clicked stopwatches and cheered and cheered—it's breaking down.

I had trouble believing it at first. Then I found myself thinking about my first car. A 1947 Chevy Fleetline. Black. Vacuum shift. $100. I bought it in Union City, New Jersey, and kept it running for two years, somehow. Those were the days I knew junkyards and Pep Boys stores the way I now know airports and hotels. Something went every week. The generator. The muffler. A tire. The water pump. The points . . .

Now, it's my turn. I'm not as mad at my machine as I used to get at the car. I am shocked. Amused. Bemused. Determined. Frustrated. Frightened. And careful. Careful is the worst of all. Lower-back problems have popped up—literally—since that day, and I circle around boxes before I pick them up, if I pick them up. I slide over to windows to read papers or bills. I suck at candy or nuts that I used to delight in cracking between my teeth, because my teeth seem to be wobbling a bit.

I also have to spend almost an hour a day to get through a day. Like the old Chevy, I don't start easily, so I have to plod through the exercises and routines prescribed by various doctors who have become the Pep Boys of my middle age.

And I remember well that there came a day when all the wonders sold at Pep Boys couldn't keep the Chevy running. It ended up in a junkyard in Jersey City. And so will I.

The pinched nerve, the pain in my left arm, was the beginning of . . . of the end. As the pain approached something like unbearable over the next few days, I went to my doctor, who in turn sent me to a back doctor, my first. "Like a stiff neck? Pain down the outside of your arm? A tingling at the ends of your fingers? Classic symptoms. Fourth and fifth vertebrae . . . ," said the back doctor. He showed me the X rays, and, indeed, there did seem to be very little room for nerves, or anything else, between the fourth and fifth knobs of my spine. I was assured that it would get worse.

He sent me off with cheerful words about aging, taking it easy, not driving too much and avoiding typing. Terrific! We compromised; I promised faithfully to use the soft neck brace I am wearing at the moment.

The next reminder of pending mortality came to me at dusk in a car on Long Island. My wife and I were looking for a road that we knew was marked on the map. She was driving. I was looking—for what seemed to her a long time. "Why can't you find it?" she said. "Because," I said between gritted teeth, "I can't read the small letters." And I haven't been able to since, even though I've managed to avoid the inevitable trip to one of my new Pep Boys for reading glasses.

The gritted teeth were next. I was reading (under strong light) and, as usual, tapping the bit of my pipe against my lower teeth. Which were moving. Which had never moved before. My teeth were loose. It was not enough that they were hardly real teeth anymore after an expensive, painful and long round of root canals; now they were falling out. Giving up the pipe was the first step, leaving me forever with the problem of what to do with my hands.

I was given, then, the choice between periodontia involving a lot of slicing up of my rubbery, failing gums or a relatively new procedure involving a lot of gold and salt in my mouth. I chose gold and salt. My dentist artfully, but not quickly, built a bridge of gold behind my lower teeth, bonding the four loose ones in the middle to sturdier ones on either side. But, to keep that contraption clean and to prevent erosion or something of my gums, I am supposed, every night for the rest of my life, to go through a ritual of: (1) cleaning my teeth using a salt solution and a Water Pik; (2) brushing them with an electric toothbrush and a solution of bicarbonate of soda and hydrogen peroxide; (3) repeating the Water Pik treatment with fresh water.

Great fun. You're tired. Maybe you've had a little too much to drink. Maybe there's something else you'd like to do before going to sleep. But you begin mixing and plugging in everything to play with your new little chemistry set.

It takes time. Keeping the machine going clips the day at both ends. My morning routine, which used to be just push-ups and sit-ups—I now know they were the worst things I could have been doing—begins with stretching exercises. I have to wake up my back—my lower back this time—before I can use anything else. That began only recently, when I bent over to pick up an electric typewriter.

We're going to need another room in the house one of these days to hold the tools and spare parts that come with lower-back trouble: The weights I strap to my ankles for the exercises to strengthen my left leg, which seems to be the cause of my curvy back. The heating pad. The steel-ribbed brace I wear to the frustration of security guards at metal-detector stations in airports around the world.

I spend a lot of time in airports, which happen to be very bad places to be when the machinery begins breaking down. Lifting baggage is about the riskiest chore for people with back problems, especially after they've spent hours in the same cramped position on a cross-country or intercontinental flight. But I'm caught in this vicious cycle: the tools and the parts I seem to need to keep going continue to increase the weight of the one bag I usually carry. The ankle weights, alone, are seventeen pounds.

Or, I should say, used to carry. I'm easy to spot in an airport. I'm the one walking alongside a staggering five-foot-five brunette, my wife, who is loaded with bags, hers and mine. I carry only a newspaper.

They never told us about this. There's manhood at stake here. How would you feel about pretending not to speak English when someone's grandmother asks for help picking up a suitcase or a pencil?

"I'm sorry, madam," I could say. "I look better than I am. In fact, I'm breaking down. Think of me as a '47 Chevy with a good paint job. Good day."

KENNETH H. BROWN

The Bright Side of 50

Nothing worked out the way I thought it would; as if anything ever does. I figured that when I got to be fifty, if I ever did, I'd be firmly ensconced in some insignificant niche with a wife and kids and maybe a few grandchildren. The idea came to me, as such ideas often do, while I was a student at a good prep school, and it hung on doggedly through a hitch in the Marine Corps and a year at Columbia, but then things started to go haywire.

I had always been a good student interested in pursuing a professional career. Law seemed to be my field, but my hobby, ever since I could remember, had been writing. I wrote poems and short stories in my spare time. I must have been about twenty-two when my hobby became an obsession. I stopped going to school and got a job as a bartender at night. That freed me to write all day, but I didn't consider myself a writer. Somewhere in the back of my mind, I was still a law student, or at least some kind of student. I was sowing my wild oats. Someday soon I would return to the classroom and take myself more seriously.

Four years later, one of my plays found its way to the stage and created quite a stir. *The Brig* won awards, was translated into nine languages, went on a European tour and was getting produced in cities all over the world. I was off and running, with grants and fellowships, teaching jobs and jaunts to faraway places. Perhaps I *was* a writer. Maybe I could make a go of it in the rarefied atmosphere of literature. I applied myself to it.

By the time the smoke cleared, eight years had passed. I had written a dozen plays, all of which had been produced, two books, one of which had been published, and scores of poems, articles and essays, most of which had found their way into print. And I was broke. I was thirty-five, recently married and very much in love. I took my wife with me to the only place I knew to make a living, the saloons. We worked side by side, she as a waitress and bookkeeper and I as a bartender and manager. We looked on the jobs as temporary things, much the same way as I had regarded my writing in the early days. Her true vocation had to do with horses. She was an Iowa farm girl and knew a lot about them, and somebody was certain to pick up one of my literary efforts and get us out of the dawn patrol of drunks and ne'er-do-wells. We would get our house in the country and a better life. It was just a matter of time.

That time never came. One of my plays was produced in Hartford, but it never came to New York. My wife became a jockey and then a trainer of thoroughbreds, but she wasn't able to overcome the prejudice against women then prevalent in the sport. Our schedules conflicted. I was coming home from the bar at the same time she was leaving for the track. We became strangers living under the same roof, and eventually, after eight years of marriage, we were divorced. She has returned to Iowa, and I have continued writing and exchanging empty glasses for full ones.

Because I have always considered self-pity, like self-justification, among the most futile of all pursuits, I have managed to remain relatively cheerful through most of my misadventures and to learn something from them. The lesson, in a nutshell, is that disappointments, like achievements, are temporary, and the unexpected occurs frequently enough to keep the journey interesting and worth the effort.

As my fiftieth birthday draws near, I discover more and more men who, like myself, are living alone with dashed dreams and unrealized ambitions. What makes me different from them, almost to a man, is that they are depressed by their circumstances and in despair about what they consider a dim future. There seems to be an emotional and psychological cancer abroad in the land that attacks the endless possibilities of each new day and kills energy. The concentration on and adoration of youth in our popular culture appears to be part of a conspiratorial preachment that lectures us all: "If you're not comfortable and secure in your position by fifty, it's all over. You might as well roll over and give up the struggle."

One day as I was getting ready to roll over, I realized that I had too much to do. There was the shopping and the laundry. Somebody had to wash the window in the living room, and there was nobody to do it but me. There are definitely some advantages to a solitary existence. For one thing, it leaves me very few hours to stew in my own juices. For another, it affords no spouse to remind me to be unhappy, and there are no children around to become agonizing symbols of my inadequate income.

So here comes John Doe, a full-blown portrait of failure in middle age. He has been beaten to his knees by the television image of youngsters frolicking in the sunlight. He pulls up a stool and orders a vodka and tonic. I've known this guy a long time. "Hello, John," I say. "How's the lawyer business?"

"The firm has got me on this child-custody case," he replies. "I wish they'd given it to somebody else. It reminds me of my own problems. How's the writing coming?"

"All right," I say. "I've started working on a book about getting older. Someone told me that if my first play hadn't been such a success, I might have been a better writer sooner. You'd probably have become a better lawyer if you hadn't been so intent on proving to the world that you were Oliver Wendell Holmes at the age of twenty-eight."

John laughs. "I *was* Oliver Wendell Holmes when I was twenty-eight."

"No, you weren't," I say. "You're a much better lawyer now than you were when you were a kid. All you have to do is give yourself a chance."

"I'm too tired to think about that now," John says. And without so much as a backward glance, he makes his way out the door.

At 4 A.M., I wash the last of my glasses and wipe the bar down. It's time to go home and get some sleep. After I've awakened in the noon sunlight and lingered over hot coffee, I'll put in a good three hours on the new book. I know it's the best thing I've ever done. I'm a better writer now than I ever was. I'm sure I'll be able to sell this one and get out of the saloon business. And then there's the woman in my life, the one that doesn't exist at the moment. She is going to turn the corner when I least expect it. I'm convinced.

MELVIN L. MARKS

When a Nightingale Sang

It is 6 A.M. and I am at the airport on my way to Philadelphia. I have not slept well. Around midnight last night I turned on the radio. Ray Eberle was singing Glenn Miller's arrangement of "A Nightingale Sang in Berkeley Square," and it made me think of London in 1944 and of Rainbow Corner and the drone of buzz bombs coming from across the Channel. In those days, life had an immediacy about it. The future was that day, that moment, in the shy glances and warm smiles of the girls in Piccadilly.

There is ample time to catch my plane. I walk into the airport coffee shop and order a small tomato juice and coffee. The waitress, an attractive young woman, returns in a few minutes. "Was that a large or small tomato?" she asks. "Small," I tell her.

I am tired and impatient for coffee. Last night Eberle had sung: "That certain night, the night we met, there was magic abroad in the air. There were angels dining at the Ritz, and a nightingale . . ."

The waitress returns with orange juice.

"I asked for tomato."

"Make up your mind."

I get my seat assignment and walk through the gate. I think about the war and about Anita, whom I met at the Hollywood Canteen. I was then stationed at Camp Irwin, in the Mojave Desert, training for North Africa. I would write to her during the week and hitchhike to Los Angeles to see her when I had a weekend pass. For those occasions, I would scrub my khakis with G.I. soap and, before rinsing them, spread them to dry in the desert sun. It

299

made them fade evenly and take on a salty appearance so that I looked like an old trooper who had served at Pearl. It was a trick I had picked up from the Regular Army guys who had been stationed at Schofield Barracks.

Anita and I would walk together down Hollywood Boulevard or stand in front of the Brown Derby on Vine, watching for movie stars. But most of the time, I just waited for her to get off duty at the canteen. "Won't you tell me when we will meet again, Sunday, Monday, or always?" Nan Wynn would sing on the jukeboxes. It was 1943, and I was only eighteen. The song was played so often it became part of Anita. She was tall, older than I, and far wiser. She had sharp features and soft blond hair, and was very kind to me. Later, she wrote to me regularly in England, France and Germany. Throughout Europe, I wept at night at the thought of her.

In the plane, I place my hat and coat in the overhead rack and sit down. I start to think about what happened the day before. I was walking toward my office on Michigan Avenue. It was a clear morning, and I was in good spirits. As I moved toward the entrance of the building, I accidentally cut in front of a young woman. No physical contact was made, and at worst I momentarily threw her off stride. She was very pretty, cool and crisp, smartly dressed.

"I'm sorry," I said.

She looked at me with contempt.

"I am really very sorry."

"Get lost."

Once you're in your sixties, time becomes important. Back in 1944, when I was in England, there was either plenty of time or else so little time that you could not afford to let yourself think about it. We were stationed outside of Folkestone, in Buzz Bomb Alley. Our antiaircraft guns, pointed toward the Channel, waited for the robots targeted for London to come within range. One evening, in a pub, I met Diane, a girl in the Women's Land Army. She was short and heavyset, her brown woolen uniform was not becoming to her, but she was pretty and had a sweet smile. We held hands as we walked through the back roads of Kent and down the cobblestone streets of Hythe. I left for Southampton late that spring, on my way to Normandy. "Take good care of yourself," she said, as I kissed her goodbye. We were both nineteen.

The plane is aloft. I feel tired. I find myself thinking that I have suddenly awakened to a world that has changed in ways I do not quite understand. All I know is that innocence and civility seem to have disappeared, and I don't like what is left. I recall a time, a few weeks ago, when I was running on the concrete promenade along the Chicago lakefront. It was a bright morning, and the sun felt good on my face. I was running close to the concrete retaining wall on my right, leaving a good fifteen feet or more for bicyclists to pass on my left. Lately, a number of runners have been sideswiped by cyclists, so I occasionally glanced back over my left shoulder to make sure no one was approaching me too closely.

Suddenly, a cyclist, riding at high speed, knifed through on my right, between the retaining wall and my shoulder, nearly knocking me over. The rider had long, tanned legs and was pumping hard, her hair, bleached from the sun, flowing over her backpack.

"Hey, bicycle rider," I yelled, "how about a little warning next time."

She was at least twenty-five yards beyond me when she told me what I could do with myself.

I gaze out the airplane window. I suddenly realize that my memories of the war years—supposedly cruel and terrible years—are warm and still vivid, as vivid as the white clouds drifting by. Where have they gone, all those years? What happened to Josephine? By now she is surely a fat Dutch housewife. When we first met she was living with her parents on a small farm near Maastricht, close to my observation post. It was late in 1944, and in another six months the war in Europe would be over. I had stayed for a time with her family. She wrote to me through the cold winter of 1945, first in Dutch, later in English. Her last letter came as our battalion approached Hanover, near the Elbe. I know it by heart.

"Lieve Melvin," she wrote. "It is already long time since we heard anything of you. We have had much soldier boys in our house but I didn't meet such a nice boy as you. I have always thought of you and I hope you didn't forget me. I forget you never."

But, dear Josephine, do you still think of me now as I think of you?

Wherever you are today, do you sometimes wonder, as I do, whether your view of the world is merely a matter of getting old? Or has the world changed that much for you, too?

CHARLES SIMMONS

The Age of Maturity

When I was young and miserable and pretty
And poor, I'd wish
What all girls wish: to have a husband,
A house and children. Now that I'm old, my wish
Is womanish;
That the boy putting groceries in my car
See me. It bewilders me that he doesn't see me.

For so many years, the woman in this poem by Randall Jarrell explains, "I was good enough to eat: the world looked at me / And its mouth watered. . . . Now the boy pats my dog / And we start home. Now I am good." This is what women are taught to expect from the world after a certain age. When I was forty, a woman friend of forty-three, speaking of the short female life of women, added, "But for men it's different." And that is what men are taught—that, given health, good looks and enthusiasm, a man remains male till old age.

My friend was right and wrong. It is a commonplace that an older man with a young woman is an easier sight than the reverse; but she was wrong if she thought the checkout girl at the supermarket flirts with a man forever. There comes a time when, like the boy putting groceries into the car, she doesn't see you. She sees the cold cuts and beer, the half loaf of bread, and that's all. A few years before she might have said "Bachelor dinner?" and you might have taken it from there.

But I'm not talking now about making out, just about the little consoling flirtations of everyday life. The compliment on her dress to the strange woman in the elevator. The hand held out on impulse, which on impulse she takes, to help her across the puddle. Or as you leave your cab and hold the door for her to enter, that three-second dance of gallantry in which you are Tyrone Power playing Count Fersen to her Norma Shearer playing Marie Antoinette. That doesn't happen after a certain age. After a certain age you are Robert Morley playing Louis XVI, and she is taking the cab to *meet* Tyrone Power and add an inch to your horns.

Now when the girl stops you on the street to ask directions, she does it because you are safe, not because you are beautiful. So which men do I mean, and when in their lives? I mean only men who are used to being attractive to women. The men who don't know what that feels like are only too glad for the change. And when does it occur? If you've kept your smile and that quality mentioned above, enthusiasm, maybe it begins at fifty. It begins when you catch sight of yourself in the store window and wonder who that . . . *mature* man is. You look around, there is no one else, it is you.

You don't see yourself in the morning mirror. To see yourself you have to be taken by surprise. I used to watch my eighty-year-old mother pass a mirror. She would present a profile, chin up, forehead relaxed, eyes wide observing to the side. The you the world sees is the you in the middle of the night under the sudden bathroom light, less color in your face than in your dreams, hair in disarray, eyes not entirely symmetrical.

What about you at your best? Tall (which you'll always be), dressed in casual good taste, walking on Broadway in the Seventies, the Upper West Side, where strangers talk to one another, men sport cunning hats and girls don't own brassieres, where everyone appreciates a sunny day and understands mortality. If in this enclave of humanness you cannot catch a woman's eye for the sake of a smile, where can you?

This bewilders you, and then you realize that all your life you have screened women out. Too tall, too short, too fat, too thin, ill-dressed, disturbed. And, of course, too . . . mature. The gray hair, the dowager's hump, the stringy arms. You didn't have to *look,* actually, not to be interested. A hint in the eye's corner kept the eye moving for the fresh face, the springy hair, the youthful waist between firm hips and bust. Negative efficiency. When you're looking for an object, the eye in an instant discards a thousand that are not it.

You are being screened out. You have not applied to sunlamps, hairpieces, facelifts. You have trusted to nature, even to your pride in reaching this age with all your teeth and buttons. You can still change a tire, turn a sonnet, drink a pint and face the day. If your shoulder twinges when you lift your arm into a sweater and without your glasses the Westchester highway sign says "Coney Island," this is undiscernible to others.

Still you are screened out. Even under special circumstances. Let's say you have achieved something, and someone throws a party for you. Everybody has come. More than everybody has come. There are people here you hardly know. There was a time when the strangers watched you. You controlled their attention. You might eventually count in their world. They might have to deal with the idea of you someday. But now you see as many backs as faces. You hear some kid ask who this party's for. The young are intent on themselves. They will be here forever, and you will soon be gone. No etiquette or charity contravenes that.

Or let's say you are asked to read at a college. Afterward, the youngsters gather around. You answer questions and sign books; but they go home and you go home. They haven't *seen* you, except in a way you don't care about. You have suffered changes, and one of them is that for the first time you see the woman in the Jarrell poem. Not with the kind of seeing she wants, of course.

MALCOLM COWLEY

Being Old Old

Some years ago I published a little book, *The View from 80,* that has been pretty widely read by my coevals. Many of them said in letters, "We're waiting for you to produce a sequel, 'The View from 90.'" I can't do that yet and perhaps never can, but I might offer some observations from the intervening vantage point of eighty-six.

Men of my age group—or "cohort," as social observers call it—are by now more numerous than one would think. We seem to be the subject of more and more studies and reports which call us the "old old." Most of them, I note, are written by younger scholars looking from the outside. It is time for more testimony—and advice—direct from the old horse's mouth. How does a man *feel* when he enters the second half of his ninth decade?

Sometimes he feels terrible, as had better be admitted. "After seventy," a friend told me, "if you wake without any pains at all, you're dead." Infirmities accumulate, as they have a habit of doing in spite of gerontologists. Little daily routines are harder to carry out and take more time. The old old man can no longer depend on his instinctive reflexes. He has to learn new methods of doing everything, as if he were starting over in early childhood. How to get into bed and out again, how to stand up, how to sit in what sort of chair, how to walk and even how to crawl, if he has to. Each of these becomes a problem to be solved if he is trying—as he should—to remain an independent person.

Women seem able to live for years without companions (except, too often, the bottle), but an old man is more fragile. If he has a wife of his own age, he is very lucky; having a daughter is the next best thing, but any woman in the house is better than none if she can cook and make beds. As a matter of fact, the offer of help from any quarter should be gratefully accepted—an arm across the street, a place on a crowded bus, a served plate at a dinner eaten in the living room. No matter if it conflicts with a man's desire to be independent. Accept, accept is the rule. Let younger persons exult in their strong arms and their confident stride or in their eagerness to be helpful. An old old man has other reasons for self-esteem, including simple pride in survival.

I always make a mental survey of any room, noting the location of chairs, tables and light switches. I keep a light burning all night in the bathroom. That is the room where most falls occur, and falls are the greatest hazard of the old old. I have found that shower stalls and bathtubs never have enough handgrips within easy reach, especially if the bather is bending over (another hazard) to wash his feet.

Another good idea is a physical therapist, who will usually be a woman. She won't make an old old man strong again even if he follows her instructions, but at least she will retard the process of muscular deterioration.

A friend says, "The best part of your day is over when the alarm clock rings." Getting up becomes chiefly a moral problem, but my advice is to place both feet firmly on the floor, bend forward from the hips, rise to an erect posture, and take one sideward step to keep your balance. That sideward step is useful in many situations; practice it.

For a man of uncertain balance, the big problem is pulling on his pants. It is something that can't be done in the middle of a room without danger of falling. Years ago the aged Senator Alben Barkley of Kentucky brought the problem to the White House physician, who was a woman. "Sit down in a chair," she advised him, and her succinct answer was reported in the press. But she had no experience in such matters, and her advice was impractical. If the aged Senator had pulled on his pants while sitting in a chair, they would have tumbled around his ankles as soon as he tried to rise. No, the safe procedure is to stand next to a wall, or better still, in the angle formed by a wall and a bureau so you can steady yourself with an elbow while standing on one foot. Be content if you don't put both of your own legs into one leg of the pants.

I avoid basement stairs, which are always perilous. For other stairs, I grasp the railing firmly, take one step up or down, then pause to survey what is ahead. I take the other steps more quickly, but I count them as I go. Remembering the number of steps is an interesting game and it can prevent stumbling in the darkness.

Deep, comfortable overstuffed chairs or sofas may become prison cells for the old old man, but still he can escape from incarceration if they have at least one firm arm. Grasping the arm, he inches forward, then pushes himself to his feet, always adding that sideward step to keep his balance. Solidly made hard-bottom chairs are the safest.

Walking is the crowning achievement, besides being the best form of exercise. Keep your feet wide apart, raise each of them in turn to avoid stumbling (don't shuffle), and move forward in a sort of duck waddle; it isn't elegant, but it is relatively secure. Avoid sudden stops and be deliberate in changing direction, always leaning on your cane. Have the cane in your hand even when you aren't using it. Pause often.

Then there is the matter, less everyday than the others, of finding a purpose in continued living that is beyond simple instinct for survival. Always, there is something to be done or something to be said that nobody else seems willing to do or say. It could offer a man a purpose of his own among the multitude of human possibilities. Cases occur, and I have seen them, in which having such a purpose has transformed and prolonged an otherwise commonplace existence.

Old men have to be endlessly ingenious; it is one of the circumstances that keep them fully alive. There is truly a reward for following such self-imposed rules, tedious as they may seem to be. The old old man can wake without apprehension, prepared for whatever the day might bring. He has earned for himself the privilege of surviving in this miraculous world as a free agent, not as a patient subject to regulations imposed by others. He can say to himself on going to bed, "Some of my sills have rotted, but there are no leaks in the attic."

WILLIAM D. ZABEL

Last Will and Testament

Few men, if any, love their wills. Many seem not to want one at all.

Jacob, the father of Joseph, is thought by scholars to have made the first will (see Genesis 48, especially verse 22). Some say Noah had a will, but, as one doubter asked, "Who were the disinterested witnesses?" The oldest will of which there is a known copy is that of Uah, an Egyptian, made in 2548 B.C. Ever since, millions of men have made wills, but even more should have and did not.

Presidents Lincoln, Andrew Johnson, Grant and Garfield died without wills. So did Chief Justice Fred Vinson of the United States Supreme Court, who also died broke. Thomas Jarman, considered by many to have been the world's greatest legal expert on wills, died without one. When Pablo Picasso died at age ninety-one after a night of painting in his studio, he died intestate (without a will) and with approximately $260 million to leave. Howard Hughes had even more, but he at least appears at one time or other to have made a will, or wills.

Why do so many men refuse? After drawing wills for over twenty years, I think it is because they are unable to resolve their true feelings about their death, their property and their families. I tell clients the obvious—that making a good will does not advance the date of death. But some seem to doubt it. One of Picasso's lawyers told me he urged the artist many times to make a will but that "he never did because of superstition. A way of avoiding death, one might say."

Refusing to make a will—or to sign it, once done—is often a way a man refuses to confront his fear of death. In many cases, it leads to a kind of intellectual paralysis, even in normally efficient, rational adults.

A will expresses a relationship between the people a man loves and the property he owns, delineating it immutably if the will is indeed his last. Many men, consciously or unconsciously, do not want to quantify their relationships. They would rather not decide whether to protect a child with a trust or to give the property outright to him; whether to divide the estate between the children or to make sure each grandchild gets an equal amount (providing for grandchildren *per stirpes* or *per capita* in legal lingo); whether to apportion property among sets of children from different marriages or among such children and a second spouse.

Many men rationalize and say they do not have enough property to need a will. But the lack of one, even with modest estates, usually causes pain to the surviving members of the family and costs them money. Intestacy means that state laws determine the estate's distribution, often with results contrary to what any thoughtful person would want. Children may inherit more than the spouse, the mother of the children; the heirs incur needless legal expenses, death taxes, premiums for a fiduciary's bond, and the like. In our society, almost every man needs a will or an effective will-substitute, such as a revocable trust, to protect his family and preserve his property.

Some men may avoid making a will in order to bottle up the anger they feel toward their relatives. Others use a will to let such anger out. Because a will is a symbolic emotional expression, it can be a weapon, and some men have fired it with venom. Heinrich Heine, the German poet, left his entire estate to his wife on the condition that she remarry, because then, Heine wrote, there would be at least one man to regret his death. Another man's will said: "To my son I leave the pleasure of earning a living. For 28 years he thought the pleasure was mine, but he was mistaken . . ." The Fifth Earl of Pembroke gave "to the Lieutenant General Cromwell one of my words, the which he must want, seeing that he hath never kept any of his own." Perhaps the most vindictive will of all was written by a German who lived in Munich. It stipulated that a wake be held in an upper story of his residence. When his relatives gathered around the coffin, the floor collapsed, and most of the mourners were killed. It was later discovered that shortly before his death, the man had sawed through the supporting beams. Instead of taking his money with him, he took his heirs.

Will-making causes some men to feel a loss of power over their wealth and a lack of control over their families. Yet, if a man is well advised, a will can be a kind of last hurrah. Thomas Jefferson used his will to expand his creation, the University of Virginia. Other men's wills have constructively perpetuated a family business or converted such a business into a dynamic charitable entity. And a will can be used to regulate the personal conduct of relatives by the use of conditional bequests—bequests which result in disinheritance for failing to complete an education, for smoking, drinking or even marrying certain prohibited persons.

Fear of death, inability to quantify loving relationships in terms of one's property, and repression of anger over loss of power and control are but a few of the many reasons why men do not make wills. These and most others are weak excuses for inaction. The will-making experience can and should be a healthy and open confrontation with a man's true feelings about himself, his death, his property and the persons and causes he loves. After all, the testator will be gone forever when his will takes effect; he will no longer be paying taxes or involved in family fights. Accordingly, a man need not be a thanatologist to realize that he must get his psychological satisfaction from a life well lived and from an estate well planned to be a final, fitting expression of his philosophy of life. As Ishmael said in *Moby Dick* after signing his will, "I felt all the easier: a stone was rolled away from my heart. Besides, all the days I should now live would be as good as the days that Lazarus lived . . . I survived myself."

ABOUT THE CONTRIBUTORS

A. ALVAREZ is the author of *Offshore* and *The Biggest Game in Town.*

ISAAC ASIMOV, the science and science-fiction writer, is the author, at last count, of 351 books.

CHUCK BARRIS created a number of popular television shows and is the author of *Confessions of a Dangerous Mind* and *You and Me, Babe.*

DAVID BINDER is assistant news editor in the Washington bureau of *The New York Times.*

CLARK BLAISE teaches in the graduate writing program of Columbia University. His autobiography, *Resident Alien,* was published in 1986.

MICHAEL BLUMENTHAL teaches poetry at Harvard University. He is the author of *Days We Would Rather Know.*

JOHN BOWERS'S *In the Land of Nyx* is a collection of essays and articles.

KENNETH H. BROWN is a writer who tends bar in Greenwich Village.

NELSON BRYANT writes the "Outdoors" column for *The New York Times.*

WILLIAM F. BUCKLEY, JR., is the author of many books, among them *Airborne: A Sentimental Journey, Overdrive,* and *Right Reason.* He is the editor of the periodical *National Review.*

ROBERT FARRAR CAPON, who has been a parish priest and semi-

314 ABOUT THE CONTRIBUTORS

nary dean, is the author of *The Parables of the Kingdom, Between Noon and Three,* and other books.

LANCE COMPA is a lawyer in Washington, D.C.

JAMES C. G. CONNIFF is a Montclair, New Jersey, writer who reports frequently on medical subjects.

MALCOLM COWLEY, the literary critic and historian, has written many books, among them *The Flower and the Leaf, The View from Eighty,* and *Exile's Return.*

JOHN DARNTON is metropolitan editor of *The New York Times.* He was awarded the Pulitzer prize in 1982 for his coverage of Poland and is twice the winner of the George Polk Memorial Award for foreign reporting.

L. SPRAGUE DE CAMP is the author of science fiction, historical novels, and biographies.

HARVEY J. FIELDS is rabbi of the Wilshire Boulevard Temple in Los Angeles. He is at work on his first novel.

THOMAS FLANAGAN is the author of the prize-winning novel *The Year of the French.*

SAMUEL G. FREEDMAN is a reporter for *The New York Times.*

JIM FUSILLI is a corporate relations associate for Dow Jones and Company.

JOHN KENNETH GALBRAITH, the Paul M. Warburg Professor of Economics Emeritus at Harvard University, is the author of many books, among them *The Anatomy of Power* and *The Affluent Society.*

ANTHONY GIARDINA is the author of the novel *Men With Debts.* His second novel, *A Boy's Pretensions,* will be published in 1988.

HERBERT GOLD's novels include *A Girl of Forty* and *Mister White Eyes.*

MARK GOODSON is president of Goodson-Todman TV Productions.

MARTIN GOTTFRIED is the author of *In Person: The Great Entertainers* and *Jed Harris: The Curse of Genius.*

PAUL GOTTLIEB is publisher and editor-in-chief of the publishing company Harry N. Abrams.

WINSTON GROOM, a novelist who lives in New York City and

Point Clear, Alabama, is the author of *Only* and *Better Times Than These.*

ROGER HOFFMANN is at work on his first novel. He lives in Conway, Massachusetts.

FREDERICK KAUFMAN's first novel is *42 Days and Nights on the Iberian Peninsula with Anís Ladrón.*

MICHAEL KORDA is the author of the novels *Queenie* and *Worldly Goods.* Among his other books are *Male Chauvinism: How It Works* and *Power: How to Get It, How to Use It.*

MARK KRAMER is the author of *Invasive Procedures: A Year in the World of Two Surgeons.*

LEONARD KRIEGEL, author of the novel *Quitting Time,* is a professor of English and director of the Center for Worker Education at the City College of New York.

ERIC LAX is at work on the movie version of his book *Life and Death on 10 West,* to be filmed by Dustin Hoffman.

GENE LIGHT is president of his own design company and the former art director of Warner Books and *Life* magazine.

ALAN LIGHTMAN is a physicist at the Smithsonian Astrophysical Observatory and teaches astronomy and physics at Harvard University. His books include *Time Travel and Papa Joe's Pipe* and *A Modern Day Yankee in a Connecticut Court.*

ADAM LIPTAK, formerly on the staff of *The New York Times,* is a student at Yale Law School.

FRANK MACSHANE has written biographies of James Jones, Ford Madox Ford, John O'Hara and Raymond Chandler.

MIKE MALLOWE is a senior editor at *Philadelphia* magazine.

DAVID MAMET was awarded the Pulitzer prize for his play *Glengarry Glen Ross.*

BRIAN MANNING writes fiction and is at work on a play. He is a news assistant on the metropolitan desk of *The New York Times.*

MELVIN L. MARKS, a veteran of four major campaigns in World War II, heads a marketing consulting company in Chicago.

MICHAEL E. MCGILL is the author of *The McGill Report on Male Intimacy.* He is a professor at the School of Business at Southern Methodist University.

KEITH G. MCWALTER practices law in San Francisco. He is at work on his second novel and a collection of personal essays.

FREDERIC MORTON's new book is *The Crosstown Sabbath*. He is also the author of *The Forever Street* and *A Nervous Splendor: Vienna 1888–1889*.

GORDON MOTT, a freelance journalist, now lives in Paris.

TIM PAGE writes about music for *The New York Times* and is the host of a daily radio program on WNYC-FM in New York. He and his wife became the parents of a son in August 1986.

NOEL PERRIN is the author of several books on rural life. He teaches American literature at Dartmouth College.

RICHARD REEVES, a syndicated columnist, is the author of *Passage to Peshawar* and *American Journey*.

MARSHALL SCHUON, assistant editor of the national edition of *The New York Times*, also writes the "About Cars" feature in its Sunday sports section.

JEFF SHEAR is a freelance writer living in New York.

RICHARD F. SHEPARD is a reporter in the cultural news department of *The New York Times*.

DAVID SHERWOOD is an advertising copywriter.

CHARLES SIMMONS has written four novels: *Powdered Eggs, An Old-Fashioned Darling, Wrinkles*, and *The Belles Lettres Papers*.

TERENCE SMITH is the Washington correspondent for the "CBS Morning News."

BRENT STAPLES is first assistant metropolitan editor of *The New York Times*.

RAFAEL A. SUAREZ JR., a television reporter, lives in Chicago.

PHILIP TAUBMAN is a foreign correspondent in Moscow for *The New York Times*.

STEVE TESICH is the author of the novel *Summer Crossing* and of *Breaking Away* and other screenplays.

PAUL THEROUX's fiction includes *O-Zone, Half Moon Street* and *The Mosquito Coast*. Among his travel books are *The Kingdom by the Sea* and *Sunrise with Seamonsters*.

RODERICK THORP is the author of the novels *Rainbow Drive* and *The Detective*.

EDWARD TICK is a psychotherapist who practices in upstate New York.

JOHN TIRMAN, a writer and editor, lives in Cambridge, Massachusetts.

EDWARD TIVNAN has a wide range of credits in publishing and television and is the author of *The Lobby: Jewish Political Power and American Foreign Policy.*

MORLEY TORGOV, who practices law in Toronto, is the author of two novels, *The Abramsky Variations* and *The Outside Chance of Maximillian Glick.*

DAVID UPDIKE's stories have appeared in *The New Yorker.*

JOHN WALTERS, a retired newspaper and television reporter, is currently at work on the production of his play *Dearly Beloved,* and on his book of poems, *The Audible Eye.*

CAREY WINFREY is editorial director of CBS Magazines and a former television producer.

CHRISTOPHER S. WREN is assistant foreign editor of *The New York Times.*

WILLIAM D. ZABEL is a partner in the New York law firm of Schulte Roth & Zabel.

ABOUT THE EDITORS

EDWARD KLEIN holds a master's degree from the Columbia Graduate School of Journalism. He has been a reporter and editor for *The Japan Times* and a correspondent in Tokyo for United Press International. He joined *Newsweek* in 1965 as associate editor, became foreign editor in 1969, and was named assistant managing editor in 1975. He was editor of *The New York Times Magazine* from January 1977 to October 1987.

DON ERICKSON attended Yale and Oxford, where he was a Rhodes Scholar. He worked for many years as an editor at *Esquire* magazine and was that magazine's editor-in-chief in the mid-1970s. For Public Television, he started *The Dial*, a magazine for station members. He has been with *The New York Times Magazine* since 1983, and one of his assignments there is editing the "About Men" column.